The Workless State

Studies in Unemployment

edited by

BRIAN SHOWLER
and
ADRIAN SINFIELD

MARTIN ROBERTSON · OXFORD

For Lauri and Niki, Beth and Laura

*Brian Showler, who contributed so much to the planning, writing
and editing of this book, died on 11 September, 1980.
We mourn his loss as both friend and colleague.*

© Martin Robertson, 1981

All rights reserved. No part of this publication may be reproduced,
stored in a retrieval system, or transmitted in any form or by any
means, electronic, mechanical, photocopying, or otherwise, without
the prior written permission of the copyright holder.

First published in 1981 by Martin Robertson, Oxford.

British Library Cataloguing in Publication Data

The workless state.
   1. Labor supply — Great Britain
   I. Showler, Brian
   II. Sinfield, Adrian
   331.1'37941   HD5765.A6

ISBN 0–85520–327–7
ISBN 0–85520–340–4 Pbk

Printed and Bound in Great Britain by
Book Plan Limited, Worcester

Contents

1 Unemployment and the Unemployed in 1980   1
by Adrian Sinfield and Brian Showler

Introduction — the scale of rising unemployment — the causes
of increase unemployment — the evidence on unemployment — the
unequal burden of unemployment — the experience of unemployment — regional and area unemployment — income
support for the unemployed — poverty and unemployment —
the economic and social costs of unemployment.

2 Political Economy and Unemployment   27
by Brian Showler

Introduction — the natural order — the 'organisationists' —
the socialists — Keynes — full employment — the monetarists
and the 'natural' rate of unemployment — increased voluntary
unemployment? — increased friction and unemployability? —
the economic costs of unemployment — theory and policy.

3 Unemployment and Politics in Britain since 1945   59
by Alan Deacon

Introduction — the 1944 White Paper — the years of 'full employment' — first doubts: the late 1960s — the 'new' unemployables

Tables and Figures

The Contributors

ALAN DEACON is Lecturer in Social Policy at Leeds University. He is the author of *In Search of the Scrounger* (Bell, 1976) and has contributed articles on social security and the history of unemployment relief to: A. Briggs and J. Saville (eds) *Essays in Labour History Volume 3* (Croom Helm, 1977), *Policy and Politics*, *Political Quarterly*, and *Social and Economic Administration*. With Eric Briggs at the University of Southampton he is preparing a study of the means test in British social policy, which is to be published by Martin Robertson.

MICHAEL HILL, who has worked in the National Assistance Board and in an employment exchange, is Senior Lecturer in the School for Advanced Urban Studies at the University of Bristol. His previous publications include *Community Action and Race Relations* with Ruth Issacharoff (Oxford University Press, 1971), *The Sociology of Public Administration* (Weidenfeld and Nicholson, 1972), *Men Out of Work* with R. M. Harrison, A. V. Sargeant and V. Talbot (Cambridge University Press, 1973), *The State Administration and the Individual* (Martin Robertson and Fontana, 1976), *Social Work and Money* with Peter Laing (Allen and Unwin, 1979), and *Understanding Social Policy* (Martin Robertson, 1980).

BRIAN SHOWLER [d. 1980] was formerly Lecturer in the Department of Social Administration at the University of Hull. He was editor of the *International Journal of Social Economics* and his publications included *The Public Employment Service* (Longmans, 1976), *On to a Comprehensive Employment Service* (Fabian Society, 1973) and monographs and articles on unemployment and manpower policy. He was also Director of the Youth and Job Entry Project for the Department of Employment.

ADRIAN SINFIELD is Professor of Social Policy at the University of Edinburgh and has previously taught in the Department of Sociology at the University of Essex. His research includes primary studies of the unemployed in Britain and the United States. He has acted as consultant to the OECD (*The Long-term Unemployed*, 1968) and to the UN (*Industrial Social Welfare*, 1971). His other publications include *Which Way for Social Work?* (Fabian Society, 1969) and articles on the social division of welfare, the unemployed, and poverty and inequality.

CONSTANCE SORRENTINO is Labor Economist at the Bureau of Labor Statistics, US Department of Labor. She has also worked as consultant to the Manpower Directorate of the Organisation for Economic Co-operation and Development (OECD) in Paris. She is author of *International Comparisons of Unemployment* (US Department of Labor, 1978) and of articles in the field of international labour force statistics.

Foreword

Peter Townsend

This book is addressed to what is likely to be the central domestic issue of the 1980s — unemployment. Its authors are dedicated to illuminating our social and indeed international understanding of the phenomenon, and this is very welcome, because theoretically and politically the approach to the problem in Britain has become extraordinarily narrow. We have become victims of a monetarist perspective — assiduously fostered by a powerful combination of economists, politicians and multi-national companies — which is dry and mechanistic and sets little store by human suffering and social dislocation. Its power, as witnessed by events in countries as widely separated as Chile, Jamaica, Kenya and Britain, must not be underrated. A large number of people in positions of influence have come to believe that a high rate of unemployment does not involve much hardship, that the individual unemployed are in considerable measure responsible for their condition, that the privations of the unemployed will have to increase and the bargaining strengths of the representatives of labour materially reduced if the problem is to be reduced or contained, and that in the meantime a rising rate of unemployment is necessary or at least unavoidable. Each of these assumptions — which have to be set out with care — must be comprehensively challenged.

A great deal of evidence is marshalled in this book to provide just such a challenge and it deserves to be consulted eagerly in what are bound to be bitter years of intellectual conflict ahead. On the one hand, the analysis of historical and international as well as national trends in the unemployment rate, and the revealed inequalities, is authoritative and the results disturbing. On the other, the authors bring new ideas to bear on our understanding of unemployment and, by showing how poorly we have come to explain and treat the phenomenon, prepare the ground for a radically different approach.

The starting point for this analysis of unemployment in Britain must be the international setting. One significant early decision of Mrs. Thatcher's administration was to abolish exchange controls. At first this would seem to have been a strange denial of that administration's avowed purpose to encourage investment in British industries. But the decision was a perfectly logical and predictable one for a Conservative Government to take. It fits with the historical course of capitalism in the late twentieth century. Some might think it illustrates the natural allegiances of the already rich to class and property rather than to nationhood and community. The decision symbolised the change in the structure of the international economy. Economic conditions have been favouring both the merging of companies nationally — which has affected the hierarchy as well as type of employment — and the reorganisation of production internationally. Both have created more unemployment. As argued in *The New International Division of Labour* by Folker Fröbel, Jürgen Heinrichs and Otto Kreye, the traditional international division of labour is now being superseded. Industry is being relocated in poor countries where labour is cheap and where advantage can be taken of the translation of skilled manufacturing processes into straightforward operations which can be performed by workers with short spans of training. As early as 1975, for example, the workforce in foreign subsidaries of the Federal German manufacturing industry amounted to 20 per cent of the manufacturing workforce in Germany itself. Improvement in transport and communications, and the internationalisation of management and the professions are also playing their part in the redistribution of production. The industrialised countries are increasingly gripped by a crisis characterised by high rates of structural unemployment, a reduction of capital investment and paralysis of fiscal policy.

Let me spell out what this means. Many companies which are operating cross-nationally are not in difficulties. On the contrary, the annual reports of most large companies show that even in the years of the world recession they have been operating profitably. While investments, productive capacities and employment at home have been contracting those overseas have been expanding. Paradoxically this has been occurring at the expense of millions of people at both ends of the process. In industrial countries there has been flagging output, short-time working, mass redundancies and abrupt changes of jobs. Many workers have lost not only their jobs but their professions, trades or skills as well, and have been forced to sell their labour-power as unskilled or partly skilled workers for lower wages. Some young people have been forced into ignominious temporary forms of employment, subsidised or sponsored by the Government. The state has been obliged to increase expenditure on the support of the unemployed and their families and (through grants, loans and tax concessions) on support for newly established industry and for some existing private business. At the same time income has (in real terms) diminished because high unemployment has reduced the revenue from personal and even indirect taxation and because the precarious financial situation of some firms has made it difficult for the state to tax companies at high or even modest rates. Brian Showler estimates the cost of unemployment in Britain in 1978 at considerably more than £4,000 m, or just under 8 per cent of the Government's total budget. The steps that have been taken as a consequence to cut long-standing forms of public expenditure have tended to affect a number of poor minorities and not only the unemployed. Governments have acted in conformity with the social bias or discrimination built into the operation and management of the economic system. The costs of economic recession have not been shared widely by the population (as they might have been) but have been borne disproportionately by the working and non-working poor. (According to Clive Smee's research for the Economic Advisers Office of the DHSS the 'costs' have been concentrated on a narrower section of the population in Britain than in the United States and Canada.)

In developing countries, according to rough estimates by the ILO, there are even more unemployed and under-employed. The activities of multi-national companies and the policies of international monetarism have simultaneously increased the numbers unable to obtain subsistence in rural areas (including the landless) and the numbers fruitlessly seeking jobs in the so-called modern urban sector. In many countries urban slums are growing much faster than the capacity of those countries even to provide paid employment for the inhabitants of such slums. Their populations provide a source of the cheapest and most exploitable labour imaginable. But because industrialisation is ill-balanced and oriented to production for export it does not absorb a high proportion of the local labour-force. Industrialisation is fragmented. Very rarely can industry be said to be complete or securely established. Many industrial inputs are imported. Manufacturing processes are highly specialised. Finished or partially finished products are then exported. The connections with the local economy are relatively slender. Dependence on parent companies or countries elsewhere for imports of capital and other goods and for the maintenance of machinery and installations makes difficult any policies to combat unemployment, poverty and wage exploitation.

A fuller social and political understanding of unemployment (as developed especially by Adrian Sinfield and Alan Deacon) will help to provide better theory and therefore better policy solutions. This involves a number of elements nationally and internationally. Perhaps the element which is easiest to assimilate is the human impact of unemployment. In societies governed by the work ethic the psychological and social consequences of being denied an opportunity to fulfil a principal role assigned by virtue of membership of those societies are severe and have to be made known if measures are to be taken to prevent unemployment or diminish its severity. These consequences are documented carefully, and sensitively, in this book. Adrian Sinfield vividly conveys the misery and stress as well as poor living conditions imposed on individuals by unemployment. He and Brian Showler conclude 'that the weight of evidence demonstrates unequivocally that the causes of the incidence and severity of unemployment are external to the person out of work'. Alan Deacon traces the changes in attitudes to unemployment over a long period of politicians and public and documents the subservience of politicians to fashionable economic doctrine — 'all of which denied the ability of governments to determine the level of employment through demand management'. He concludes that in the late 1970s, as in the 1930s, 'unemployment is divisive', setting workers and not only Government against unemployed. With the rise in unemployment there are fewer jobs to be had; yet individuals are blamed all the more vociferously by the press and, partly in consequence, by the working poor, for not taking work that does not exist.

It will require courageous leadership — in the social sciences no less than in politics — to teach that the motivation to work is culturally induced and is not something narrowly dependent on the wage-rate and any alternative income offered by the State. People want to work because they are taught from childhood to fulfil themselves and earn their keep, and contribute to the community's needs; and the work they do is often necessary justification for their families and for themselves for their lives. That is why unemployment is such an appalling, and undeserved, indignity.

But the motivation to work is not the only feature of social life and organisation which is culturally induced. Principles or rules are adopted by all societies both to define the type and content of 'work' and the kind of people among the population who are eligible to undertake it. Unemployment is a consequence of definitions of employment, and until politicians and economists in particular grasp the fact that employment is fundamentally a *social* definition they will not sufficiently appreciate Britain's power to control and perhaps abolish unemployment. Society defines the period of compulsory schooling and the ages below which children are not permitted to be employed; whether and in what circumstances women can enter paid employment; and beyond what age people can be considered to be retired and become eligible for a substitute income on which to live. Decisions about who are to be considered as dependants of the wage-earner or the State are clearly open to constant review and amendment. We are readier to acknowledge that there are social determinants for these kind of decisions than to acknowledge that there are social determinants for the distribution of types of work and composition of the work-force. This is because the latter are decided predominantly by those in positions of power in the private market whose social assumptions and motivations are not much studied. Nonetheless, too little attention is devoted to the determinants of dependency in the population and — for young people in their teens, women, people with disabilities and people of pensionable age — correspondingly little attention devoted to the right to work.

The problem for the development of theory is not just how societies come to distinguish between the economically active and inactive but how the two categories come themselves to be differentiated according to social value. People in paid employment are a lot better off than people who are disabled, retired and unemployed, even allowing for household dependants. But among those in paid employment there is an elaborate hierarchy, with insecurity, bad conditions of work and risk of unemployment increasing towards the foot of that hierarchy, as Adrian Sinfield and Brian Showler show. The partly skilled and unskilled are far more likely to become unemployed than other employed people. Changes in the hierarchical form of employment, therefore, help us to understand both which jobs are liable to be lost and which people are liable to become unemployed. The acceptability to the population, as well as severity, of large-scale unemployment has a great deal to do with the form taken by the occupational class structure.

Questions about unemployment are ultimately concerned with

questions about the nature and value of employment. If we are concerned that people are debarred from work, as we should be, and therefore from adequate living standards, social status, dignity and self-respect, then we must also be concerned with dead-end, poorly paid, demeaning and socially valueless forms of employment. But how do these arise? In every country governments and public and private companies are taking decisions every day to open new plants and offices, establish subsidaries, reorganise workforces and introduce new machinery and work routines. Every day corresponding decisions are taken to close plants, wind up companies, make workers redundant and replace skilled jobs with less skilled jobs. There is a simultaneous process of job creation and job destruction. With some exceptions, for example, when announcements are made of large-scale redundancies in particular areas, the social consequences for the workforce, the local community and the nation as a whole attract little or no public scrutiny and are often given no thought at all. Occupational decisions are being taken fragmentarily and unreflectively and are dominated by the partial social assumptions of the tiny elites with market power. They make commercial judgements about what products or services people can be persuaded to buy rather than what products and services people would like to have or need. The creation and adaptation of the job structure and even the definition of work attract far too little of the attention of social scientists. That structure is taken largely for granted. Instead of asking what work deserves to be done, how it might be organised and how it should be distributed among the population, we concern ourselves almost entirely with the outcomes of the piecemeal policies of the market and the public sector. As a consequence employment policies are principally curative rather than preventive, peripheral rather than central. They are intended merely to smooth out frictions — to ease the return to work and provide temporary and wholly unsatisfactory substitutes, while preserving the historically crude function of unemployment as providing a reserve army of labour.

This book provides thoroughgoing criticism of these piecemeal policies and the lackadaisical compliance with market forces of successive conservative and labour administrations. It does not, of course, pretend to provide all the answers to the questions which are necessarily raised in pursuing the reasons for mass unemployment. It calls for a fuller social analysis of the evolution of both employment and unemployment and makes a powerful case against the bigotry and, more important, the fruitlessness and social damage of current monetarist principles. It calls too for a principled readoption of a policy of full employment, for which there was a political consensus for more than two decades after the war.

University of Essex
September 1980

Preface

Any attempt to present ideas and arguments to a wider audience usually owes its origin to a mixture of half-forgotten stimuli. On this occasion the underlying cause — the growing spectre of unemployment — has become even more obtrusive: all the more evident to analyse in some respects and all the more difficult to make sense of in others.

The immediate initiative for the book came from Edward Elgar at Martin Robertson who believed that people who had been discussing, writing and carrying out research into unemployment and the experiences of the unemployed for many years should be brought together to offer some public account of their own understanding of the issues and the problems. The various chapters emerged through successive draftings as the five contributors corresponded and met to discuss their individual analyses and the development of the book as a whole. In consequence, the editors owe a considerable debt of gratitude to the other contributors for their critical but constructive and sustained support and their close collaboration in the production of the volume.

We also wish to acknowledge the help and advice of many people and to thank especially Tony Atkinson, Neil Fraser, Geoffrey Fry, Jean Hartley, John Veit-Wilson and Alan Walker for their thoughtful and challenging discussion of various chapters. We are both particularly grateful to Dorothy Sinfield for her work as critic, progress-chaser and main compiler of the index. Responsibility for the views expressed and any shortcomings in analyses remain as always with the authors.

Brian Showler
Adrian Sinfield
May 1980

Abbreviations

AUEW	Amalgamated Union of Engineering Workers
BLS	Bureau of Labor Statistics, US Dept. of Labor
CSO	Central Statistical Office
CBI	Confederation of British Industry
CRE	Commission for Racial Equality
DE	Department of Employment
DEG	*Department of Employment Gazette (Employment Gazette* from 1980)
DHSS	Department of Health and Social Security
DRO	Disablement Resettlement Officer
EEC	European Economic Community
EG	*Employment Gazette*
EOC	Equal Opportunities Commission
GDP	Gross Domestic Product
GHS	General Household Survey
GNP	Gross National Product
ILO	International Labour Office
IMF	International Monetary Fund
MSC	Manpower Services Commission
NEDC	National Economic Development Council
NIESR	National Institute of Economic and Social Research
OECD	Organisation for Economic Co-operation and Development
OPCS	Office of Population Censuses and Surveys
PER	Professional and Executive Recruitment
PRO	Public Records Office
SBC	Supplementary Benefits Commission
STEP	Special Temporary Employment Programme
TUC	Trades Union Congress
TOPS	Training Opportunities Programme
URO	Unemployment Review Officer
WEP	Work Experience Programme
YOP	Youth Opportunities Programme

CHAPTER 1

Unemployment and the Unemployed in 1980

Adrian Sinfield and Brian Showler

INTRODUCTION

Even in the guarded language of the official commentary 'unemployment is on a strong upward trend' (*EG*, April 1980, p. 401). On 8 May 1980, 1,509,191 people were registered as unemployed in the United Kingdom, giving a rate of 6.2 per cent.[1] This was the highest total for the month of May since the war and the numbers are expected to continue rising into 1981 at least. Over the eight months from September 1979 unemployment increased by 18 per cent, after the usual adjustments for seasonal variations in the numbers out of work. To underline the deterioration in the economy, the total of vacancies (the job openings available and known to the government's employment service) has been dropping even more quickly since June 1979. The picture appears all the worse when it is compared with other market economies in North America and Western Europe. The United Kingdom has suffered the sharpest increase and 'in most other OECD countries unemployment has fallen recently' (*EG*, April 1980, p. 402).

Against the background of higher unemployment in Britain increasing even further, this book aims to provide an assessment of unemployment from five different perspectives. It analyses the theories by which unemployment is explained, the changing political response to the rising numbers out of work, the manpower and labour market policies that have developed in this context and the impact of unemployment on the unemployed themselves and the wider society. Finally, the British experience is compared with the trends in unemployment in other market economies. The objective of the writers is to contribute to discussion of these issues, encourage wider debate and stimulate further analyses.

The rest of this introductory chapter is devoted to outlining the current trends in unemployment and the characteristics of the unemployed to provide a backcloth against which the later, more analytical, chapters can be set. In chapter 2 Brian Showler examines the political economy of unemployment, tracing and evaluating the main developments in economic theories of unemployment, and providing an assessment of the economic costs of the current levels of joblessness. In chapter 3 Alan Deacon analyses the changes in the way that unemployment has been treated as an issue in British politics since 1945, examining in particular the reasons for the much greater acceptance of higher unemployment in recent years. In chapter 4 Michael Hill considers the development of manpower policy in Britain and its changing role and significance given the increasing numbers out of work. In chapter 5 Adrian Sinfield assesses the social dimensions of unemployment in the context of an unequal and classbound society and at differing levels of labour supply and demand.

These chapters focus on the British experience, and we are very conscious that much debate of both unemployment and policy in this country tends to occur as if the British experience were either typical or all that needs to be considered. In chapter 6 therefore Constance Sorrentino provides an analysis of unemployment in an international perspective, focusing particularly on the developments over the last decade. After adjusting for the differing statistical practices and the other factors that make comparison particularly hazardous, she discusses the various causes that might account for the differing patterns and trends in unemployment across Western industrial societies.

In the final chapter the two editors seek to pull together the range of themes that have emerged from the individual chapters and set out their personal view of the central issues and the possible policy options.

THE SCALE OF RISING UNEMPLOYMENT

With 1.5 million out of work in May 1980, a total of two million unemployed looks very much closer than it did in June 1979 when *The Observer's* main headline 'Two million jobless report hushed up' preceded claims that the Treasury's own detailed forecasts for employment and unemployment had not yet reached the Department of Employment. 'Ministers', it was declared, 'are bracing themselves for large-scale bankruptcies and even heavier unemployment than the forecasts show' and telling 'officials . . . to shy away from any mention' of the predictions (17 June 1979).

While the main economic forecasters generally agreed in predicting rising unemployment after the June 1979 Budget, the majority did not expect the recession to be as severe as the mid-1970s or inflation to rise as significantly (*Financial Times*, 3 September 1979). However, it became clear, even before the March 1980 Budget, that most short-term forecasts had underestimated the deterioration in the economy, and this lent greater credence to the much gloomier long-term prospects of, for example, the Henley Centre and the Charterhouse Group (*Financial Weekly*, 17 August 1979). The Cambridge Economic Policy Review (1980) amended its 1979 prediction of 2.7 million unemployed by 1985 to 3.5 million on then current economic policies without waiting for the 1980 Budget. By April 1980 even the Chancellor of the Exchequer was prepared to concede that the Treasury forecasts in the previous month's Budget were at best optimistic and unemployment could be 'somewhat higher' (*The Guardian*, 29 April 1980).

The full significance of the rise in unemployment becomes clearer when it is set in a longer term context. The twenty years when unemployment averaged only 1.8 per cent ended in 1966. By 1971 and 1972 the average annual rate reached 3 per cent for the first time in twenty-four years. After 1974 there was a further sharp increase till 1977, resulting in a nearly four-fold increase in the number out of work over ten years. Unemployment has been over 1 million since August 1975 and over 1.5 million for some months in 1977 and 1978, and again in 1980, when it is expected on current policies to continue climbing. This compares with an average total of some 400,000 people out of work for the first twenty years after the war.

The changes over the last seventeen years are well illustrated by Figure 1.1, although the use of a three-month moving average, seasonally adjusted, flattens the pattern a little. It shows clearly the way in which the number of jobs known to be available has failed to keep up with the rise in unemployment. At the last three peaks of unemployment the ratio of registered unemployed to notified vacancies was about 4 to 1 in 1963, 7 to 1 in 1972 and 8.5 to 1 in 1977. The ratio dropped with the improvement in the economy in 1978 but began to climb up again in the second half of 1979, reaching 7.2 to 1 by May 1980. The Department of Employment (DE) and Manpower Services Commission (MSC) estimate from one survey carried out in April–June 1977 that some 35 per cent of vacancies are notified (*DEG*, November 1978, pp. 1284–8). Allowing for these and the

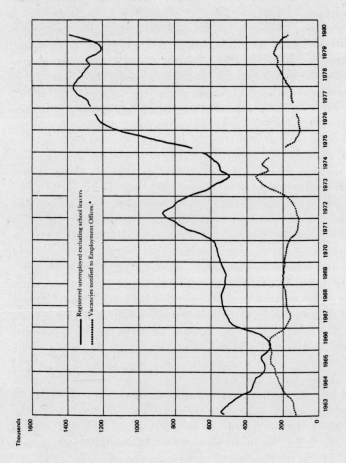

Figure 1:1 *Unemployed and Vacancies in Great Britain 1963–80* (three-month moving average, seasonally adjusted)
* Vacancies at Employment Offices are only a part, perhaps a third, of total vacancies.
Source: Department of Employment Press Notice, 20 May 1980.

non-registered unemployed, the numbers out of work has clearly exceeded the jobs available for the last six years at least; and even before then the closer balance between the totals did not of course mean that the jobs and the unemployed could be simply matched up.

Although economists of different theoretical persuasion argue about what, if anything, needs to be done about present levels of unemployment, there is general agreement not only about the direction of the trend over the next one or two years but also about the level to which unemployment might be brought down. Monetarists' 'natural' rates of unemployment and Keynesians' 'full' employment 'all lie substantially below' present levels and generally fall closer to 3 per cent unemployment (Dean, 1979, pp. 53–5).

THE CAUSES OF INCREASED UNEMPLOYMENT

Most 'advanced' industrial economies in Western Europe and North America have also suffered increased unemployment on a scale generally unprecedented since 1945, although the experience has not been uniform by any means (see chapter 6). Far from promising a return to earlier and fuller levels of employment, the 1980s presage a further decline. The position of Britain in a comparative perspective seems all the more serious, given a government that denies the desirability of bringing about fuller employment in the present economic situation, let alone its responsibility or ability to achieve this.

> A really satisfactory explanation [of the higher unemployment] across a wide range of countries with rather different economic strengths, still seems to be lacking [but] the most likely . . . seems to be one which relies on growing competitive strength in the industrialising countries . . . associated with the introduction of flexible exchange rates and a change in the terms of trade for raw material and food stuffs. [Hunter, 1980, pp. 44–5].

To this of course has to be added rising energy costs and inflation.

Within Britain the rising trend in unemployment through the 1970s was principally a consequence of an inadequate pressure of demand for labour. The level of GDP attained in early 1974 was not achieved again until 1978, and the recovery in GDP and manufacturing output lasted only up to the first quarter of 1979. It was reversed in the second quarter, leaving no net increase in GDP (excluding North Sea oil) since mid-1978. This rather flat net output performance in the last half of the 1970s was accompanied by a similarly flat level of employment. The employed working population rose rapidly between 1971 and 1974, reaching a peak of over 24.5 million, dropped back and then grew slowly again to mid-1979 when the total employed remained about 100,000 less than the 1974 peak; it is believed that employment has started to fall again, especially in the production industries (*EG*, March 1980, p. 288).

Against this tardy performance in output and the creation of employment a considerable increase in labour supply took place in the 1970s, leaving what has become known as a widening 'job gap' to be filled by the unemployed. Between 1971 and 1979 the total working population grew by some 1.25 million, although almost all of this increase had taken place by mid-1977. The net growth was entirely in female and part-time employment, with a fall of over 400,000 men in employment and in full-time jobs. Almost 1.1 million more women were employed in mid-1979 compared with mid-1971. Thus the net increase in those employed fell short of the increase in the working population, resulting in a rise of 293,000 in female unemployment and a rise of 265,000 in male unemployment between June 1971 and 1979.

Projecting the growth in the working population into the 1980s is of course fraught with difficulty (for one attempt, see *DEG*, June 1979, pp. 546–51). The number of school leavers entering the labour force and the increased proportion of young workers is likely to reach a peak in 1981. The rise in the economic activity rate for women has been underestimated in the past; but despite the deteriorating labour market there may well be another million women in the labour force by the end of the decade. So, even without any decline in the demand for labour, the job gap is likely to increase in the 1980s because of the growing labour supply: estimates suggest that at least 800 *new* jobs a day are required to hold declining demand and rising supply at present levels of balance.

The 'micro-chip' and 'deindustrialisation'

The gloom is deepened by what appears to be very much greater concern in Britain than in, for example, the United States about the employment-destructive effects of technological developments in microelectronics. A confidential report to the Department of Industry concluded that 'we are probably contemplating levels of unemployment of 10% to 15% of the workforce. . . roughly . . . the peak of the 1930s depression' (*Financial Times*, 13 November 1978), and there have been very much grimmer forecasts since then (for example, Jenkins and Sherman, 1979, and CIS, 1979; though see also CPRS, 1978, and Jones, 1980).

Where, how quickly and to what extent jobs will disappear, and what replacement there will be, is of course very uncertain. The likely effect of 'chips with everything' is greatly debated, but evidence that rising unemployment is being accompanied by higher productivity is at present missing, 'even in engineering where one might have expected large advances' as the result of the application of microelectronics (Dean, 1979, p. 51; see also Metcalf, 1980, p. 30). The danger may lie more in our failure to invest adequately in new developments, with the result that we lose more jobs because we become less competitive, than in a technological revolution that will cause the collapse of work (see Rothwell and Zegveld, 1980; Pavitt, 1980; and below, pp. 220–2).

'Deindustrialisation', with one million jobs disappearing in the manufacturing industries during the 1970s, has already created many social and economic problems that are perhaps most visibly revealed in the large number of redundancies. A quarter of a million payments were made from the Redundancy Fund in 1979 alone, with a third of these coming from mechanical engineering, the distributive trades and the construction industry, and many more from textiles, metal manufacturing, vehicles and electrical engineering. It is not known precisely how many more people lose their jobs at the time of a redundancy, as many leave early or do not qualify for a redundancy payment. Various estimates put the total affected by redundancy at two to three times the official number of payments (Fryer in Martin and Fryer, 1972, pp. 255–6; Mukherjee, 1973, ch. 2). Given the increase in redundancies already announced for early 1980, the total affected may well reach one million this year.

The process of 'deindustrialisation' is probably further encouraged by Britain's position within the EEC. Geographically, of course, the country is on the fringe of the Community and the Commission's own social report for 1979 pointed out that the United Kingdom regions worst hit by unemployment are 'in the north and west of the country, i.e., those furthest removed from the centre of the European Community' (EEC, 1980, p. 59). A large part of the country is defined as eligible for aid under the EEC's Regional Fund, but the broad policy stance of the Community in providing protection and subsidies for agriculture whilst encouraging internal free trade in manufactures has, when combined with the 'petro-currency' strength of sterling, led to an increase in the import penetration of EEC manufactured goods

into Britain and worsened the balance of payments. Salt is rubbed
into the wound in that Britain has become the largest net contributor
to the Community's budget. Metcalf argues that 'the very great
success of the British Temporary Employment Subsidy' in protecting
jobs in textiles, clothing and footwear, and 'exporting' the unemployment to the rest of Europe has 'caused the subsidy to be outlawed
by the EEC' (1980, p. 31). Thus any attempt to offset the adverse
effects on British trade and employment of EEC membership is
quickly opposed and reversed.

THE EVIDENCE ON UNEMPLOYMENT

Although these are supplemented by additional studies whenever
possible, the main statistics of unemployment for Britain used
throughout the book, unless clearly noted, are taken from the count of
people registered for employment and available for work at local
employment and careers offices on the day of the monthly count. Any
discussion of the unemployed is bound to be influenced by the
definitions and the methods of collecting data on unemployment,
employment and the labour force as a whole, and these issues are
discussed by Constance Sorrentino in chapter 6 (and for discussion of
debates over the numbers of unemployed in Britain, see chapter 3
below, pp. 72–5, and 77).

The DE data on the registered unemployed, the basic source for
this country, exclude students over the age of eighteen who are only
registered for vacation employment and other people who are not
working but are considered to have jobs, including workers on
holiday, on strike or 'temporarily stopped' but expected to return to
their jobs shortly. The value of the DE data is that they provide
regular and detailed information for relatively small areas and categories of the unemployed and they may be analysed over time, the
present series dating back to 1948 with very little change.

The basic shortcoming obviously is that these statistics are administrative returns: people who want work but do not register with the
official agency are excluded. Evidence of the scale of non-registration
has been provided in recent years by the annual General Household
Surveys (GHS). In 1979 an additional 25 per cent declared that they
were unemployed but had not registered, and in years of lower
unemployment such as 1973 and 1974 the non-registrants have comprised another 43 per cent. About half of those who have not

registered have been married women, but there are also a significant
number of men and non-married women. In 1979 these two groups
increased by 12 per cent and 34 per cent respectively when non-
registrants were included, while the numbers of married women out
of work rose by 92 per cent.

The proportion of married women who tell the GHS interviewer
that they are unemployed but do not register with the employment
service has been expected to drop for some years because of changes in
the national insurance system that involved the phasing-out of the
married woman's option to pay a reduced national insurance contribution. In consequence more women stand to gain from the full
contribution with its entitlement to unemployment benefit and can
obtain credited contributions while registering unemployed. This
may account for part of the drop in the proportion of this group not
registered from 69 per cent in 1976 to 52 per cent in 1979, when their
proportion of all non-registrants fell well below half for the first time.
The decline however may also mean that rising unemployment has
discouraged many more potential workers who have not re-entered
the labour force or left it altogether (*OPCS Monitor*, GHS 80/1, p. 7;
also *DEG*, December 1976, pp. 1331–6 on the non-registered
unemployed).

There is also evidence that sympathetic doctors may keep men or
women 'on the sick' whose poor health, disability and previous long
unemployment seem likely to condemn them to further unemployment at the lower rates of insurance or supplementary benefit
available to the long-term unemployed compared to the long-term
sick. This too will reduce the visible extent of unemployment, and
many of these may not appear in the General Household Surveys.

THE UNEQUAL BURDEN OF UNEMPLOYMENT

If the risk of unemployment were distributed evenly across the whole
labour force, we might all expect to be out of work for three weeks each
year. Alternatively, an equal share would mean each of us unemployed
once every six years — eight spells a lifetime for a man leaving school
at 16. Yet the available evidence indicates that a very large proportion
of the labour force rarely, if ever, experiences unemployment, while
recently 3 per cent have been bearing 70 per cent of the weeks of
unemployment in any one year (see for example, Metcalf, 1980, pp.
27 and 25).

Unemployment hits most harshly at the groups who are likely to be
among the poorest and least powerful in the labour force. Unskilled

manual and personal service workers experience most unemployment, and foremen, supervisors, professionals and managers the least. Two detailed surveys by the DE show the high incidence of unemployment among general labourers. This group, which forms about one-fortieth of men in work, accounted for one-half of the unemployed in June 1973. Even in June 1976, when unemployment had more than doubled and many other groups were suffering from loss of work, general labourers still made up two-fifths of the unemployed and well over half of those out of work for a year or more (Metcalf and Nickell, 1978, p. 320 and *DEG*, June 1977, p. 680).

The significance of the relationship between class and unemployment will be examined further below (pp. 126–9), but the unemployed are more likely to come from low paying and insecure jobs, from among the disabled and handicapped, the very young and the oldest in the labour force, from ethnic or racial minorities and generally from those with least skills and living in areas of highest unemployment. The unequal impact of the experience as well as the incidence of unemployment has been brought out clearly and vividly in individual case-studies and general statistical analyses (for the former, see Marsden and Duff, 1975, and North Tyneside CDP, 1978; for the latter, Daniel, 1974, and Daniel and Stilgoe, 1977; and for examples of both, Field, ed., 1977).

The very different chances for finding work for the unskilled are brought out by comparing the ratios of registered unemployed to notified vacancies. In December 1979 there were six people out of work for every job known, but for general labourers the ratio was 50 to 1. In the South East, where the overall ratio was less than 3 to 1, it was 18 to 1 for labourers. In the North and North West the general ratio was about 12 to 1 but over 100 to 1 for labourers. Northern Ireland had by far the worst ratio of unemployed to vacancies: the general rate was 52 to 1, higher than the ratio for labourers in the United Kingdom as a whole; while there were over 170 labourers for every vacancy (*EG*, March 1980, pp. 2647).

THE EXPERIENCE OF UNEMPLOYMENT

The regular monthly figures from the DE not only understate the total number out of work because they omit those who do not register with the state employment services; they also fail to tell us how many workers experience some unemployment in the course of any twelve-month period. This is an important indicator of the extent and concentration of unemployment in society and, after much pressure, some questions on this were eventually included in the General Household Survey (although they have now been dropped again). These tell us more about the *flow* of people becoming and ceasing to be unemployed over a period of time and not just the *stock* — those people out of work at any one time whether they have just become unemployed or have been out of work for a number of years.

In the 1977 and 1976 surveys some 10 per cent of men had experienced some time unemployed in the previous twelve months — at least twice as many as the percentage out of work in the week before the interview (GHS, 1977, p. 57; data not provided for women). In the United States where these data have been collected for many years, the proportion with some unemployment experience has been much nearer three times as large when the annual rate of unemployment has been at the same level. While there is still a very uneven distribution of unemployment across the American labour force, it is even more concentrated in Britain, particularly among the lower paid (Smee, 1980). Only one-third of those with any unemployment in the twelve months before interview in the 1977 survey had earned as much as £60 per week compared with three-fifths of those who escaped unemployment (GHS, 1977, p. 69; see also Townsend, 1979a, ch. 17).

Repeated unemployment

Given the high concentration of unemployment, many unemployed are likely to experience repeated unemployment within a short period of time. About one in seven unemployed were out of work more than once within twelve months according to the GHS for 1975–77. Single and younger workers are particularly prone to more than one spell, but the risk of becoming unemployed is also greater for anyone who has already been out of work once in the recent past. This partly reflects the fact that many firms, especially the smaller ones, still operate a 'last-in-first-out' procedure for any redundancies.

The scale of repeated unemployment is also brought out in the DE's own studies of the registered unemployed. In June 1976, with unemployment at 5.6 per cent, three out of ten men and one out of five women who had worked at all in the previous twelve months had also been out of work at least once before in that time. In the previous survey, in June 1973 with unemployment much lower at 2.4 per cent, the proportions were even higher: two out of five men and one out of three women (*DEG*, June 1977, p. 567 and March, p. 216). The recurrence of unemployment prevents the build-up of resources after a previous period out of work and makes such people particularly liable to poverty. As repeated unemployment is more common among those in some of the more poorly paid jobs, this is all the more likely to contribute to poverty.

Long-term unemployment

An extraordinary feature of the continuing rise in the numbers out of work in recent years has been the fact that the number of men becoming unemployed has not varied very much each year. The flow of registrations between 1967 and 1977, for example, averaged 2.9 million, with a peak of 3.1 million in 1975 and a low of 2.6 million in 1973. Yet over the ten years the stock of male unemployed — the numbers remaining out of work — rose by 136 per cent (Dean, 1979, p. 44). This has meant a marked increase in the length of time that men have remained out of work — the expected duration of completed spells of unemployment has doubled over the same period to seventeen weeks. Women have been even harder hit with both the numbers becoming unemployed and the length of time they remain out of work increasing much faster. The expected duration of a completed spell rose three-fold from four weeks to twelve weeks over the ten years (*DEG*, February 1973, p. 114 and September 1978, p. 1056).

These developments are particularly relevant to any assessment of the changing nature of unemployment because, however crude a measure it may be, length of time out of work is the best indicator of the likely impact of being out of work in the regularly published official data. Many people who become unemployed stop registering fairly quickly. In one detailed analysis of all spells of male unemployment ending between June 1971 and June 1972, 'over one quarter . . . lasted less than four days' and four-fifths less than 13 weeks; only one in twelve men were out of work for as long as six months (Stern, 1979, p. 69). But the picture has deteriorated since then, and it is important to recognise the close link between the overall level of unemployment and the length of time that individuals spend out of work. In January 1980 some 560,000 people had been out of work for at least six months, some 350,000 for at least a year — 40 per cent and 24 per cent of those registered as unemployed. Throughout the 1950s the long-term unemployed formed less than 25 per cent and the very long-term unemployed nearer 10 per cent of those out of work. In the middle of 1956, with unemployment at 1 per cent, the number of men and women registered unemployed for as long as a year was only 20,100; by the middle of 1979, with unemployment at 5.9 per cent, the number out of work that long had increased seventeen-fold to 340,500.

The year 1956 was one of very low unemployment even for the postwar years. More generally, the scale of prolonged unemployment has become so great that the number of men out of work for at least a year in January 1980 was virtually equal to the annual total out of work at all averaged over the twenty years to 1968. The 87,000 men out of work over *three* years not only exceeded the highest figure for men out of work over *one* year between 1948 and 1968 by over 7,000; it was more than double the average out of work over a year.

The significance of this is all the greater given the evidence that length of unemployment is itself a major cause of disadvantage in the labour market. Employers' discrimination against the long-term unemployed is reflected and in turn reinforced by the public employment service's failure to refer these unemployed for jobs. Past experience and evidence suggests that three months was the critical point at which length out of work reduced the chances of obtaining work: the continuation of high unemployment may well be bringing the critical duration down to two months, or even less, and it may be even shorter in areas of greater labour surplus.

The amount of long-term unemployment also deserves particular attention because current measures of income support are better geared to those only briefly out of work and fail to recognise that needs are likely to increase the longer unemployment continues. Poverty therefore is likely to be more common and much harsher among those long out of work, and this of course affects not only the unemployed but their families. To offer one illustration of the scale and seriousness of this, our own conservative estimate is that the total number of men unemployed for over a year and their immediate families probably exceeds the total population of Liverpool — nearly 600,000. Those out of work six months or more and their families may well exceed the one million population of Birmingham.

Female unemployment

Unemployment amongst women has become a major and increasing problem in Britain over the last decade. The extent of the growth of female unemployment is obscured by the way in which the regular statistics of unemployment are collected, and any economic, social and psychological impact is concealed because of the lack of research. The latest published figures for the United Kingdom show that 460,369 women were registered for work in May 1980. In 1979 almost half (48 per cent) of the married women found to be unemployed in the GHS and one-quarter of those not married had not registered for work with the government's employment service (GHS, 1978, Table 5.16). Adjustment for this would indicate that some 600,000 women at least were out of work.

Over the four years of rising unemployment up to the last peak in 1977, there was a more than five-fold rise in the number of women registered as unemployed — an increase twice as great as for men. Between that peak and the increase that began again in late 1979, male unemployment fell by 15 per cent whilst that of females dropped by only 3 per cent (based on seasonally adjusted data). This partly reflects the increasing labour force participation of married women and the changes in the national insurance system that lead more of them to register their unemployment (see pp. 5–6 and 9 above). But cutbacks in public expenditure have led to a reduction in many jobs, both full-time and part-time, in the social services in which women have been heavily concentrated. In addition, the decline in the clothing, footwear and textile industries, where there has traditionally been a very high proportion of women employed, means that the problem of female unemployment is likely to get worse even if the impact of microelectronics on clerical work is slower than some fear.

The increased duration of unemployment for women as well as the increased numbers becoming unemployed has already been emphasised; yet the social and economic significance of greater unemployment among women has received scant recognition, and there is still a remarkable tendency to treat women's earnings as 'pin money'. There seems little awareness that unequal pay and earnings-related benefits lead to smaller benefits for women; that married women's earnings are a crucial part of household income in very many poor families; that such earnings may reduce the dependence of women on a male wage earner; and that the increasing number of families headed by a woman makes these earnings all the more important (see for example Hamill, 1978, p. 13 and Townsend, 1979a, pp. 629–33 and ch. 22).

Unemployment and age

Younger workers, especially those under 18, are particularly likely to be unemployed and to experience subsequent periods out of work. Since 1977, while male unemployment has generally been about 7 per cent, the teenage rate has been into double figures, even discounting the high summer figures at the end of the school year when one in four or more have been registered unemployed (*DEG*, December 1979, p. 1258 and April 1980, p. 398). The greater contribution of the young worker to the flow into unemployment is shown by the fact that 44 per cent of males out of work for a week or less in January 1980 were under 25. By contrast only 14 per cent were 50 years old or over (*EG*, March 1980, pp. 318 and 234–6).

Older workers are vulnerable once they lose their jobs and so have a high rate of unemployment because of their difficulty in getting back to work. In consequence they form a larger proportion of the stock of unemployed at any one time and are particularly liable to prolonged unemployment. In January 1980 men aged 50 or over comprised 42 per cent of those out of work for six months or more while those under 25 made up only 18 per cent of the long-term unemployed.

Many more older people would swell the number of long-term unemployed if the discouraged workers who settle for early retirement, or the ill or disabled who remain registered sick longer, were included. Besides, the steady drop in the proportion of older people in the labour force under the combined pressure of institutionalised retirement schemes and high rates of unemployment has already led to a significant reduction in their demand for jobs (*EG*, April 1980, pp. 366–9). At the same time a major factor associated with poverty amongst old people is the length of time since they left the labour force. There seems little chance that any early retirement scheme would provide support that would prevent this process from continuing, and simply occurring earlier (a point overlooked in many discussions, see for example Hawkins, 1979, pp. 122–4).

Unemployment by race

This, of course, is a politically volatile issue where concerns about prejudice and discrimination become entangled with problems of poverty and racism. As in many other countries, racial minority groups are vulnerable to unemployment. Black and Asian workers, whether immigrant or born in this country, 'tend to be concentrated in unskilled and semi-skilled jobs for which it is difficult to recruit (or retain) other workers because of such features as the need to work awkward hours, an unpleasant working environment or relatively low earnings' (UMS, 1977, p. 1). Although there are enumeration problems that make it particularly difficult to obtain an accurate rate of unemployment for these and other racial minority groups, it is clear from the regular DE data that these workers are cyclically liable to unemployment. Over the 1973 trough in the numbers out of work to the 1977 peak, the increase in unemployment was almost twice as great as that for all workers. Their unemployment is characteristically concentrated in certain regions: in February 1980, for example, they accounted for 3.7 per cent of all unemployment, but for 9.2 per cent in the West Midlands, 7.6 per cent in the South East and 6.4 per cent in the East Midlands (*EG*, March 1980, p. 245). There is evidence of persistent discrimination in the recruitment of West Indians and Asians, and their higher levels of unemployment are only partially accounted for by their particular labour market and socio-economic characteristics, including occupational, industrial, regional and demographic factors. After reviewing the various sources of evidence, Showler (1980) concludes that minority worker unemployment rates exceeded the general rate in the late 1970s by at least 40 per cent. The difference was even greater for young and female workers from these groups.

Disability and ill-health

People in poor health or disabled are particularly vulnerable to unemployment: over a fifth of the men out of work in the 1972 General Household Survey 'became unemployed because of ill-health or an accident'. Many are vulnerable to repeated spells of both illness and unemployment and are likely to spend longer out of work than average (Metcalf and Nickell, 1978, pp. 312, 324 and 328). The only regular official figures are on workers registered as disabled (see chapter 4, pp. 98–100). Unemployment amongst this group was 10.8 per cent in January 1980 — or 12.4 per cent if those classified as needing sheltered employment were included (*EG*, March 1980, p. 283). In addition many more disabled are not on the official Disabled Persons Register, and they too are more vulnerable to unemployment — in the same month 73,000 not on the register against 52,000 registered (excluding those thought only suitable for sheltered employment). Others among the unemployed will not have had their disability recognised, let alone registered (Williams, 1967, p. 38).

Disabled workers find it particularly hard to get back to work once they have lost a job and form a disproportionately large number of the long-term unemployed. Those with disability or ill-health also appear to be more vulnerable to the recurrent spells of unemployment that slowly erode a family's resources and greatly increase their insecurity. Even among younger workers, disability markedly increases the risk of long-term unemployment: 46 per cent of those unemployed under 25 who were disabled had been out of work six months or more in July 1976 compared with 18 per cent of non-disabled. Among those unemployed under 18, more than one in eight disabled had been out of work for a year or more against only one in one hundred of the non-disabled (Walker and Lewis, 1977, p. 5).

One measure designed to help the disabled obtain and keep work is the quota system introduced in 1944 to require employers to take a certain percentage of registered disabled workers. This was fixed at 3 per cent in 1946 and has not been changed since: any employer falling below this quota cannot hire a non-disabled worker without a permit. Yet the proportion of firms failing to meet their quota has risen from 38 per cent in 1960 to 63 per cent in 1978; many employers must have been taking on new non-disabled staff without a permit, while a large number of block permits have been issued. Public employers such as local authorities and the nationalised industries have a generally worse record still. Although central government departments are technically not legally bound by the quota, they are said to have accepted it: nevertheless only two departments met the 3 per cent in June 1978. Given only nine prosecutions since 1947, 'the spearhead of the Government's policy on disabled employment has rusted through lack of use' (Jordan, 1979, pp. 28–31). The Manpower Services Commission has issued a discussion document on the future of the scheme (MSC, 1979b) but at present appears more likely to let it lapse altogether than to attempt to resharpen it; and cuts in the MSC budget from June 1979 have already brought some reduction in services for the disabled.

REGIONAL AND AREA UNEMPLOYMENT

The unequal geographical impact of unemployment has been so persistent for the last generation, and even longer for many areas, that

Table 1.1 *Male Unemployment Rates by Duration for each Region, January 1980 and 1970*

	1980 Per cent of employees unemployed				1970 Per cent of employees unemployed		
	All %	6 mths or more %	1 year or more %	2 years or more %	All %	6 mths or more %	1 year or more %
South East	4.8	1.8	1.1	0.5	2.5	0.5	0.3
East Anglia	5.5	1.9	1.3	0.7	3.2	0.8	0.5
East Midlands	6.0	2.6	1.7	0.9	3.3	1.1	0.7
West Midlands	6.5	3.0	1.8	1.0	2.8	0.8	0.4
Yorkshire and Humberside	6.9	2.9	1.9	1.1	4.2	1.7	1.2
South West	7.0	2.9	1.9	1.0	4.1	1.2	0.7
North West	9.0	4.3	2.8	1.6	3.8	1.1	0.6
Wales	9.0	4.0	2.9	1.4	5.3	1.9	1.2
Scotland	10.1	4.2	2.7	1.4	5.9	1.8	1.1
North	10.3	4.7	3.2	1.8	6.9	2.7	1.7
Great Britain	7.0	3.0	1.9	1.0	3.7	1.1	0.6
Numbers	970,361	409,281	264,204	142,329	523,519	149,699	89,138

Sources: 1980 — *EG*, March 1980, pp. 318 and 332
1970 — *Employment and Productivity Gazette*, February 1970, pp. 136–7.

Data by region for males out of work for two years or more not published in 1970, and duration data not available on the same basis for Northern Ireland.

this continuing imbalance has led to a greater burden of both the direct and indirect costs of unemployment on some communities. Northern Ireland has consistently had the highest rate of unemployment since the war and the North, Wales, Scotland and the North West have been amongst the next most badly hit for nearly every year in the last thirty. The pattern is brought out in Table 1.1, which ranks the regions by the jobless rate for males in January 1980 and shows the incidence by different durations of unemployment for then and January 1970, when the national rate was little more than half the 1980 level. (Comparable data are not available for Northern Ireland, and duration data for females are likely to have changed over the decade because of changes in the benefit system.)

There have been few changes in the ranking over the decade except that there has been a greater relative deterioration in the West Midlands and the North West. With the national total of the unemployed almost doubled in ten years, unemployment in the South East and East Anglia in 1980 has not yet reached the level of the North and Scotland in 1970. In 1980 the rate for those out of work over six months in the four worst-hit regions is almost as high as total unemployment in the South East.

Within regions, the impact may be concentrated on particular areas or communities. Even in the South East, the region with the lowest unemployment rate (3.8 per cent in March 1980), there was considerable variation — with Ramsgate, Newport (IoW), Chatham and Hastings at 6 per cent or above and St Albans and Hertford below 2 per cent. Within the larger cities of the regions with higher unemployment the contrasts may be sharper still. In Liverpool, for example, 40 per cent rates of unemployment in northern parts of the centre of the city are masked by a rate of 13 per cent for the city and 8 per cent for the whole North West region.

'Unemployment tends to be more intense' in the inner cities than in the wider conurbations, with a slightly higher rate of long-term unemployment as well. To an extent this reflects the higher proportion of unskilled and semi-skilled living in these areas, but even more important has been the general decline in local employment opportunities, and a 20–30 per cent fall in manufacturing in most inner areas between 1971 and 1976 (West and Martin, 1979, pp. 746–9 and 752).

But the impoverishing effect of unemployment on a community is not fully shown by the rate in any month or even year. It is the slow decay over time that leaves many long out of work, others prematurely retired from the labour force and many families faced with only one in two or three generations bringing home a wage. The poverty can generally be seen in both public and private services: poor schools and medical services with insufficient or less qualified staff, limited shopping facilities forcing the poor to pay more as the big super-markets believe that a branch would not pay its way.

Particular importance should be given to the high level of unem-ployment in cities and towns that have been hard-hit time and time again by unemployment and poverty (see for example Wilkinson, 1939, and Bulmer, 1978). The general run-down of the '*D*' villages in County Durham and the steady erosion of places such as Workington or Millom, the rural depopulation of parts of north-west Scotland or East Anglia and Lincolnshire also need to be highlighted. These costs are often less visible and dramatic than the sharp increase in unem-ployment — see, for example, the comparatively generous press coverage of Coventry in the mid-1970s. But it does mean that these areas lack not only jobs but a whole range of amenities that are taken for granted in more prosperous parts of the country.

The extent of unemployment over time may reveal a very different picture of the impact on the community from analysis of the current length out of work. An area such as North Shields on Tyneside in the mid-1960s had a rate of unemployment just below the regional average and an apparently small amount of prolonged unemploy-ment. Yet on average one quarter of the last five years had been spent 'signing on' by the unemployed interviewed when all the separate spells out of work had been added up. Over the next twelve years the numbers unemployed increased faster than the regional figure, and North Shields was experiencing unemployment in excess of 15 per cent in the mid-1970s when a second study was carried out. On the basis of the new sample, which included employed as well as unem-ployed, it was estimated that '*almost half* of the men of labour force age in the area were likely to have experienced unemployment to some degree in their recent past, *one in eight* were likely to have had patterns of frequent, predominant or continuous unemployment'. The effect of the depressed economy prior to the second study is shown by the fact that less than one in ten of the original sample of unemployed had been predominantly or continuously unemployed before they were interviewed in 1963–4 against more than one in three of the second sample in 1975–6. The labour market deterioriation also hit the original sample badly, or at least those two-thirds whose experience we were able to follow up till their re-interview, or their earlier retirement or death. Only fifteen out of sixty-eight had been able to avoid significant spells out of work and eighteen had been entirely or mainly unemployed for the whole time. In general, those who had been most marginal to the labour force continued to be so (North Tyneside CDP, 1978, pp. 42, 224 and 221).

INCOME SUPPORT FOR THE UNEMPLOYED

While the prolonged impact of poverty out of work has been hurting more and more people, the only evident public concern has been about the disincentive effect of generous benefits. Yet the last major changes left those long out of work with relatively less support. In the mid-1960s the introduction of the six-month earnings-related supplement, the Redundancy Payments Act, the Contract of Employment Act giving a right to notice, and the replacement of national assistance by supplementary benefits had the total effect of providing greater support for the short-term, but not the long-term, unemployed (see chapter 4, pp. 109–14). The denial of the long-term supplementary benefit rate (providing an additional £8.85 a week for a couple after November 1980) to those out of work over two years was followed by the introduction of a higher basic insurance benefit for those ill and off work for over six months, worth £8.20 a week more for a couple on invalidity benefit than unemployment benefit.

Benefits are highest for those most recently out of work with high earnings in the past. The basic insurance benefit from November 1980 is £20.65 for the unemployed person and £12.75 for any adult dependant. For the first six months this may be increased by up to a maximum of £17.67 a week by the earnings-related supplement. During this period too, any income tax rebate is likely to be paid: its amount is determined by the length of the tax year worked, the level of earnings and the size of any tax allowances and relief. The greatest beneficiary is the single person on high earnings becoming unemployed around Christmas. After six months, benefit drops to the flat rate insurance benefit, and resources may be increased by claiming rate and/or rent rebates or supplementary allowance: the latter will generally provide for rent and rates, but most resources including any earnings of the individual or spouse are taken much more into account in determining the amount of supplementary allowance than in the payment of insurance benefit.

Long-term unemployment over the last decade has increased: yet discrimination in the income support system has persisted and even increased against the long-term unemployed. The general failure of the original 'pillar of security' for the unemployed — national insurance unemployment benefit — has never been fully acknowledged. Even in periods of low unemployment, the proportion of unemployed receiving insurance benefit at any one time has never averaged two-thirds in any year and many times has been much closer to a half (annual average across the four quarterly counts since the first detailed collection of the data in 1960). The proportion who receive the insurance benefit for some period during their unemployment will of course be much higher, but there do not appear to be any data collected on this.

Since 1973, less than half the men registered unemployed have been drawing benefit at the detailed May analysis; and men are much more likely to qualify than women or young people. At the May 1979 count only two out of every five men and women registered unemployed were drawing this benefit, the first line of defence against earnings loss — and to the three in five without this, one might perhaps add another one in four out of work but not included in the official count of registered unemployed. The earnings-related supplement to insurance benefit that was intended to take the sting out of the first six months of unemployment only supported less than a sixth of all registered unemployed — less than half the proportion originally expected. And the full value of their contributions was not paid to one-fifth of those receiving the supplement because of the rule that prevents supplement and flat rate benefit together exceeding 85 per cent of weekly earnings in the previous tax year: with inflation many more are affected by this ceiling on payments (calculations based on unpublished data provided by the Department of Health and Social Security).

Meanwhile more and more unemployed have become totally dependent upon supplementary allowance, and others receive it in addition to their insurance benefit. The proportion has risen from less than three out of ten in 1966, the year that the allowance replaced national assistance, to one-half. In May 1979, 54 per cent of men registered unemployed received the allowance, a sixth of these as an addition to their insurance benefit.

The main reasons for the failure of national insurance for the unemployed have been the insufficient contribution record of many women and young people entering or re-entering the labour force, and for men the 'exhaustion' of their twelve-months benefit entitlement. At the May count over the last ten years the proportion of all males out of work who have exhausted their full insurance benefit has ranged from 23 per cent to 36 per cent. This means in high-unemployment regions that 40 per cent of all the unemployed men have used up their benefit, and in some areas this probably exceeds 50 per cent. It should be added that, because of a complex process linking separate spells out of work, many exhaust all insurance benefit and earnings-related supplement well within the twelve and six months respectively of the time they began their present period registered as unemployed.

In addition to these benefits, some unemployed receive redundancy payments, but these are a form of compensation for losing a specific job and not for being unemployed. Many redundant workers do not experience any unemployment and go straight to a new job, although they will have lost their seniority and often status and pay. The average payment in 1979 was £874, but the amount varies according to age, length of service and level of earnings, and many employers may make an additional payment. This, however, seems to bring little help to the unemployed: in 1973 only 7 per cent of the unemployed in a national survey had received any redundancy payment (Daniel, 1974), and it is possible that the proportion has declined because many losing their jobs will have already been out of work before and will not have served the two years necessary for any new entitlement under the state scheme.

POVERTY AND UNEMPLOYMENT

The main benefits available to the unemployed have been discussed in some detail because of the persisting prevalence of the belief that benefits are generous. The increased and continuing high level of unemployment has meant more and greater poverty for many out of work. In addition to the experience of welfare rights and social workers and the findings of individual studies undertaken outside government, there is now clear evidence from official reports. People out of work for three months or more are very much more likely to be in poverty than those in work. The Department of Health and Social Security (DHSS) estimated that 84 per cent had incomes that did not exceed the supplementary allowance scales by more than 10 per cent in 1976, compared with only 4 per cent of people in work (evidence cited in Townsend, 1979b, p. 546).

Government sources also show an increase in the numbers out of work who are living below the official 'poverty line' — the supplementary allowance level. Between 1974 and 1977, the latest published data, the number of people (those out of work and any dependants) below the poverty line rose more than three times (Field, 1979). Including those on supplementary benefit, the number of whom rose almost as fast, the numbers around or below this level were over one and a quarter million. Since the mid-1970s, as Beckerman has emphasised, the 'prolonged weak labour market has no doubt led to a considerable worsening of the living conditions of the poor and the near-poor' (1979, p. 6). This is all the more likely, given that the numbers out of work over a year have been growing more quickly than total unemployment, and the longer the time out of work the greater the risk of poverty. The MSC's in-depth interviews with people out of work for over a year in mid-1979 'revealed pervasive complaints of financial hardship. Most recipients found money extremely tight — enough for "existence rather than living" ' (Colledge and Bartholomew, 1980, full report, para. 7.6).

The poverty experienced by those supported by supplementary benefits emerges clearly from a special survey by the DHSS in October 1974, and the value of this benefit has not improved in relation to the rising cost of living since then. Very few of the unemployed interviewed had any savings or additional income. The largest families had the smallest resources and the greatest difficulty in making ends meet — and their problems were clearly exacerbated by length of unemployment (Clark, 1978). In comparison to other recipients of supplementary benefit,

> [the unemployed] are generally less likely than other claimants to have the full set of clothing listed in our B040 guidelines, less likely to own domestic equipment such as vacuum cleaners and refrigerators, more likely to live in overcrowded homes, more likely to have run up debts, and less likely to have savings. When debts accumulate, or savings are spent, the money is usually used to buy food and clothes and to pay the rent — the basic essentials for keeping the wolf from the door. [Donnison, 1977, p. 9].

The prolonged poverty of those vulnerable to unemployment is brought out in a national study of poverty in the United Kingdom. Those who had been out of work ten weeks or more in the previous year were two and half times more likely to be in poverty, or on the margins of it, than people who had no time out of work in the past year (Townsend, 1979a, Table 26.1). It was not simply that unemployment meant poverty for many, but there was often little escape because of recurrent illness and unemployment or a return to poor-paying and insecure jobs.

THE ECONOMIC AND SOCIAL COSTS OF UNEMPLOYMENT

A higher rate of unemployment leads to a general run-down of the economy and society, and is a burden not only on those currently experiencing it. Any comprehensive economic accounting has to take into account the loss of production, taxes and national insurance contributions and also the additional payments in redundancy payments, insurance and supplementary benefits and rebates and other means-tested services. The broad economic costs are examined in chapter 2 and the burden on the economy, and particularly on public expenditure, that results from higher unemployment is shown to be substantial (pp. 48–53).

There are also, of course, costs borne by people who are not currently unemployed. Overtime is cut back in some industries, and for a large number of workers it is the overtime element in their wages that enables them to achieve a decent income. Although overtime has not fallen as one might have expected, there have been substantial drops in some industries. There has, however, been a considerable increase in short-time working — probably a three-fold increase in the number of hours lost over the last ten years. Many of those who suffer such a reduction in their normal earnings, which causes them to dip into savings and generally reduce their resources, may later become unemployed themselves. There are also people who have dropped right out of the labour force because their chances of finding work have declined so much and others who are forced to work part-time who would prefer to have a full-time job. Among both groups are many mothers bringing up children by themselves and many married women whose full-time wage might have been enough to bring the family income above the poverty line.

In this chapter we have sought to present a brief account of trends in unemployment and the characteristics of the unemployed over the last decade. This is intended to provide a picture of unemployment that is current for the first half of 1980 as a backcloth for the study of the different issues discussed in the following five chapters. Chapter 7 offers our personal summary of these discussions.

Notes

1. Data on unemployment where no source is given are taken from the statistics published in the monthly Department of Employment *Employment Gazette* or in its predecessors, *Department of Employment Gazette*, *Employment and Productivity Gazette*, and *Ministry of Labour Gazette*.

CHAPTER 2

Political Economy and Unemployment

Brian Showler

INTRODUCTION

This chapter seeks to outline the development of economic theories of unemployment. The most cursory glance at the history of such theory cannot help but emphasise the significance of the particular social and political context within which economic theory has developed, and in turn the effect that theories of unemployment have had upon political and administrative attitudes and policies towards unemployment and the unemployed. The chapter begins by examining pre-Keynesian theories of unemployment, particularly the mainstream classical concept of a 'natural' state of full employment; the alternative theories of Marx and Hobson; and the 'organisationist' developments associated with, for example, Beveridge at the turn of the century. This is followed by an analysis of Keynesian theory and the revival of the 'naturalistic' concept of unemployment associated with monetarist theory. Critical attention is given to the view that the minimum attainable level of unemployment has risen, and estimates are made of the economic costs of high unemployment with particular reference to the public expenditure aspects. Finally, consideration is given to the various policy implications stemming from the different theoretical perspectives.

It is not intended to present a full history of economic theories of unemployment as these have been examined in some detail elsewhere (Harris, 1972, and Garraty, 1978), but some outline of the main development is necessary if current economic thinking on unemployment is to be considered in context.

THE NATURAL ORDER

To an extent the pre-Keynesian history of unemployment theory can be written with brevity. Until the 1880s the term 'unemployment' scarcely existed in the economic literature let alone any theories of it. The general assumption was that full employment was the natural state of affairs – a view that has had an exceptionally long history. The English Statute of Artificers, 1563, assumed that work was always available for those who would work. The mercantilists likewise made a similar assumption, concluding that unemployment was, therefore, wilful or voluntary (Blaug, 1968, p. 16). The power of 'nature' over economic events was developed further by William Petty in the seventeenth century. Petty emphasised that economic forces were determined by natural laws and by a natural harmony, and formulated as a consequence a basically laissez-faire ideology.

The eighteenth century saw the French physiocratic school developing the theme with the introduction into their systems approach (associated in particular with Quesnay's *Tableau Economique*) of Rivière's concept of the *ordre naturel*. Blaug argues that the physiocrats also first advanced the notion, later popularised or dogmatised by Say, that 'The creation of output automatically generates the income whose disbursement makes it possible to enter upon another cycle of production' (1968, p. 30).

Adam Smith reinforced the physiocratic natural order by introducing the invisible hand, based upon his deductive behaviour assumption of self-interest as the prime motivating force, and laissez-faire as the prime condition, for a self-regulating, wealth-creating equilibrium, which rested upon naturally determined levels of wages, interest and profits. Not surprisingly, Smith had little to say about unemployment, although certain doubts and contradictions were apparent in his analysis. He acknowledged certain marginal problems with cycles and seasons, and the difficulties presented by the existence of monopolies. A similar note of troublesome empiricism entered some of Malthus' writings. Observation of the trade depression following the Napoleonic wars led him to argue that there may have been an inadequate stimulus to reach full capacity, and that the assumed automatic and rapid adjustment of wage rates might be rather slow in practice. He failed, however, to make a concerted or consistent attack on the propositions of Say's Law, and Ricardo in a deductive defence of Say effectively silenced the Malthusian version of the under-consumptionist hypothesis.

Routh argues that during the nineteenth century 'Economics was ... consolidated into a set of dogmas' (1975, p. 105). The most significant of which, for our purposes, was of course Say's law of markets. The general proposition contained in Say's Law is familiar, owing to Keynes' choice of the Law as an archetype of the classical economic doctrine that he wished to confront, namely that 'supply creates its own demand'. Blaug, however, points out that Keynes' emphasis on Say's identity between supply and demand has tended to give an undue prominence to Say's Law in classical and neoclassical theory (1968, p. 154). It is clear that the classical economists were aware of trade depressions, but the fundamental point is that these were seen as temporary, and that there was an automatic tendency in a competitive economy towards a full-employment equilibrium. The mechanism for this self-regulating natural process of adjustment lay in the flexibility of prices, wages and interest rates. Any excess supply of goods, labour or money would be corrected by a corresponding fall in their market prices, thereby ensuring a return to an equality of demand and supply. Thus the classical case was not that periodic crises did not occur but that *general* over-production was an impossibility.

In terms of the dominant economic paradigm, the general assumptions of Say's law remained virtually unchanged until the challenge of Keynes and the gradual acceptance of Keynesian analysis. The development of neoclassical economics from the 1870s contributed little to the debate: 'The strength of neoclassical theory lay in micro-economic analysis, which was ill suited to the discussion of remedies for general unemployment' (Blaug, 1968, p. 662). Nevertheless, neoclassical microeconomics served to reinforce the naturalistic school of economic doctrine, with its emphasis on marginalist concepts, which 'are the little wheels that direct the urge to maximise, and drive the economy inexorably towards that equilibrium where scarce resources are so applied as to produce the most of the best' (Routh, 1975, p. 199). The other service performed by the neoclassical school was, of course, the overthrow of the labour theory of value and its replacement by the politically more convenient subjective marginalist theory of value. The labour theory of value was of use to the classical economists and to the emerging capitalist class in its confrontation with the landed interests, in that the theory stressed the significance of industrial labour rather than land as the source of value. But as Routh points out (1975, p. 200) it proved an embarrassment by the latter half of the nineteenth century with reformers such as Robert Owen and revolutionists such as Karl Marx annexing the labour theory of value to the socialist cause.

Thus neoclassical economists performed the double function of providing microeconomic foundations for the classical assumption of a natural long-run equilibrium state, and of removing the embarrassing labour theory of value. This helped to discredit the alternative theories of unemployment developed by Marx.

It is not surprising that neoclassical economies added little to the analysis of unemployment despite the fact that it was developed during a period of frequent economic crisis and when 'unemployment' began to be conceptualised and written about. Neoclassical economics, like classical economics, was largely deductive and based on a set of behavioural assumptions derived *a priori* rather than by empirical investigation. What is more surprising is that the development of empirical research into both unemployment and the unemployed around the turn of the century failed to make any original contribution to the economics of cyclical unemployment.

THE 'ORGANISATIONISTS'

Despite the promising title of Beveridge's book first published in 1908 *Unemployment: A Problem of Industry*, he accepted the general proposition of Say's Law: 'The demand will tend to grow up to the supply . . . This process of adjustment, moreover, is not and cannot be checked in the long run by deficiency in the demand for the products of labour' (Beveridge, 1912, p. 5). Yet he devoted a full chapter to charting cyclical fluctuations in unemployment and reviewing various possible theories. He argued that over-production in *some* industries was an observable phenomenon, and thought it possible that this might give rise to some simultaneous over-production, although the mechanism remained obscure; and in any case he was always careful to ensure that his analysis 'in no way offends economic doctrine as to the impossibility of general overproduction' (p. 60).

This then left Beveridge to analyse other types of unemployment that had been largely acknowledged by classical economists, namely voluntary unemployment, 'frictional' unemployment involving seasonal variations and occasional transformations of industrial structure, and recurrent casual unemployment resulting from 'reserves of labour', a form of friction that Beveridge regarded as a more important cause of unemployment than either structural or cyclical changes. This type of unemployment he ascribed to 'the dissipation of the demand for labour in each trade between many separate employers and centres of employment. Its result may be described as the normal glutting of the labour market. The counter-part of such glutting is the idleness at every moment of some or others of those engaged' (Beveridge, 1912, p. 13). This led Beveridge to advocate the organisation of the labour market principally through the establishment of the Labour Exchanges in 1909 (for an account of the Exchanges see Showler, 1976), and through the introduction of national unemployment insurance.

Whilst Beveridge considered that it was difficult to attach any scientific interpretation to the word 'unemployable', he did argue that 'The volume of unemployment is . . . appreciably increased by defects of character in part of the population' (1912, p. 137).

Beveridge's empirical work was concentrated upon aspects of the London labour market, as was Booth's work, which was even more censorious of the idle unemployed. Garraty argues that this led to an undue concentration on a narrow aspect of unemployment that had relatively little to do with mass cyclical unemployment (1978, p. 141). The labour market organisationists were given intellectual leadership by Beveridge and political expression by the Webbs through the 1909 Reports of the Royal Commission on the Poor Laws. But the solutions proposed tended to be highly coercive, involving the compulsory registration of unemployment, compulsory technical education for juveniles and retraining for older surplus workers, and penal labour colonies for the wilfully idle.

Thus the development of an empirical school failed to make any impact on the dominant naturalistic interpretation of the workings of the economic system, and indeed basically accepted such an interpretation as the starting point for their investigations, which consequently added little to the analysis of the nature and causes of cyclical unemployment. Nevertheless the establishment of the Exchanges helped reduce frictional unemployment, and national insurance helped relieve the effects of unemployment in some industries. But they were not particularly relevant policies in the context of a prolonged trade depression as the inter-war period clearly showed. It could be further argued that the concentration of attention upon relief and organisational measures deflected attention from the need to stabilise and increase labour demand; yet these policies were far more attractive to the prevailing liberal capitalist orthodoxy, and ones that is was hoped would buy off any pressure for more socialistic solutions (Harris, 1972, p. 365).

THE SOCIALISTS

Alternative theories of mass unemployment were, of course, developed by Marx and such writers as Hobson. For Marx, in total contrast to the classical and neoclassical assumption of a natural tendency to full employment, unemployment and crises were endemic in the structure of the capitalist mode of production. The process of capital accumulation requires recurrent crisis, and the Marxist analysis involves an interaction of structural and cyclical forces. The cycle of economic activity and unemployment is linked to the underlying structure and process of capital accumulation, and to what Marx saw as an exploitative capital–labour relationship. The process can be summarised as follows (see also Freedman, 1962, p. 148; and Blaug, 1968, p. 256): in an expansion the demand for 'variable capital' (labour) increases relative to 'constant capital' (e.g. machinery) thereby reducing the 'industrial reserve army of the unemployed'. This process increases the price of labour, thereby reducing the rate of profit from the accumulation of capital. This reduction in profitability slows down the rate of capital accumulation and, therefore, cuts aggregate demand, giving rise to an economic contraction, an increase in the reserve army of labour and a cut in wages. This restores profitability and enables capital accumulation to commence again. This process, combined with Marx's hypothesis of a long-run declining *rate* of profit, leads not only to recurrent crises but also to worsening crises, giving rise eventually to a collapse and overthrow of the capitalist mode of production.

Thus Marx's analysis did not indicate measures or policies to reduce or eliminate unemployment, as the problem was seen as a fundamental part of the total capitalist system of production: 'Marxian unemployment is a structural, not a cyclical, problem; and for that reason public investment or expansionary monetary policy, effective in curing keynesian unemployment, will merely produce inflation without leading to full employment' (Blaug, 1968, p. 16).

There were, however, other writers — principally J. A. Hobson (1896) — who were not as overawed with the mystique of Say's Law as Beveridge, nor as dismissive of solutions within capitalism as was Marx. Hobson argued that the cause of unemployment was underconsumption caused by income inequality. He did not attempt to overthrow the classical theory but argued that it was possible for an asymmetry to exist between the demand and supply for goods because all too often those with the power to spend preferred to save too much and invest it in already saturated areas of production. Hobson's analysis has, of course, some similarities with that of Keynes, in drawing attention to the possibility of 'over-saving' and, arguably, to a declining marginal efficiency of capital, although he did not fully explain the mechanisms involved. Deficiencies in his theoretical formulations, combined with his criticisms of the classical school, and his heretical views about saving, ensured that Hobson's insights into the social rather than the personal nature of unemployment were rejected and subsequently ignored by the established economists, as indeed was Hobson himself (Garraty, 1978, p. 127). Furthermore, his 'socialistic' proposals for a redistribution of income by taxing off excessive savings and transferring the money to those who would spend it were quite unacceptable in the political climate of the 1890s.

Thus the natural order survived intact into the 1930s. Only Pigou amongst leading establishment economists showed a particular interest in the theory of unemployment. He wrote a 'popular' volume on unemployment in 1913 and a more substantial theoretical work in 1933. In the former, whilst accepting that certain improvements in labour market organisation would do something to diminish the volume of unemployment, he argued that they were incapable of abolishing unemployment because 'some measure of unemployment will necessarily be present, so long as wage-rates are lacking in plasticity, and fail to move up and down . . . in conformity with the movements that take place . . . in the demand' (1913, p. 243). In the later volume Pigou reaffirms the classical doctrine that in perfectly free competition there will be a natural tendency to full employment, and that any unemployment was the result of 'frictional resistances [that] prevent the appropriate wage adjustments from being made instantaneously' (1933, p. 252). Cannan, in his presidential address to the Royal Economics Society in 1932, put the point bluntly: 'General unemployment appears when asking too much is a general phenomenon . . . [the world] should learn to submit to declines of money incomes without squealing' (1932, pp. 367 and 369). Robbins took an equally uncompromising stand. Whilst accepting that the Great Depression was of unparalleled severity, Robbins went on to argue that an even sharper 'purge' would have been preferable to the 'lingering disease' brought about by governments introducing tariffs and relief measures, thereby preventing natural competitive forces from shaking out 'bad business' and setting the stage once more for business recovery (1934, Ch. IV).

KEYNES

As Routh comments, 'By the spell of their own theory, economists were incapacitated from understanding what was going on, and it was going to take great magic to free them' (1975, p. 271). The magician, of course, was Keynes. Previous experience had shown that 'outsiders' such as social reformers, empiricists, socialists and Marxists stood little chance of shaking the foundations of the natural order. Only a liberal economist with impeccable credentials and an established reputation, working within the traditional methodology of the subject, stood any chance of reforming the accepted theory of unemployment.

Keynes was under no illusions as to the magnitude of his task, nor the profound challenge that his *General Theory* presented to the 'classical theory . . . which dominates the economic thought . . . of the governing and academic classes of this generation, as it has for a hundred years past' (1936, p. 3). Keynes accepted the presence of the classical economists' frictional and voluntary unemployment but opposed the view that these two categories exhausted the definition of unemployment: 'The classical postulates do not admit of the possibility of the third category, which I shall define . . . as "involuntary" unemployment' (p. 6).

The main emphasis of Keynesian analysis is on the determinates of aggregate demand, a subject, as we have seen, virtually ignored after the acceptance of Say's Law. Keynes' explanation of involuntary unemployment stems from his challenge to the classical theory that supply tends to create its own demand. His argument was that, as employment and aggregate real income increase, consumption also increases but not at the same rate as the increase in income. This he described as being caused by 'the psychology of the community' (p. 37). Given this assumed falling marginal propensity to consume, it follows, if employment is to be maintained, that there must be a sufficient amount of current investment demand to fill the gap. Keynes maintained that the level of current investment depended upon the inducement to invest, in turn determined by the relationship between the marginal efficiency of capital and rates of interest. The level of employment in equilibrium is, therefore, determined by the propensity to consume and the rate of new investment, but Keynes argued further that there is no reason, except in a special case, for this equilibrium to be equal to full employment.

The two main components of aggregate demand (i.e. in a closed, no government economy) were assumed to behave very differently. Whilst Keynes assumed a falling marginal propensity to consume in the long run, in the short run the level of consumption demand was relatively stable, whilst the level of investment demand was highly volatile. Its volatility stemmed from its determination not only by the rate of interest but also by entrepreneurial expectations about likely future levels of economic activity, which are obviously uncertain and probably unpredictable. A further reason why a full-employment equilibrium was unlikely in the Keynesian scheme lay in the point that, whilst the decision to invest needed to equal the decision to save (i.e. the residual from income and consumption decisions), the decision-makers in the two cases were mostly different groups and individuals, and the two sets of decisions were, therefore, independent of each other and could not be expected to match automatically. The Keynesian identity between aggregate savings and investment was, therefore, achieved by adjustments of employment and income through the multiplier process, giving rise to involuntary unemployment and deficient aggregate demand. This interpretation 'dethroned the rate of interest as the mechanism for reconciling savings and investment decisions' (Winch, 1972, p. 179). The failure of the rate of interest to achieve this reconciliation assumed in classical theory was, according to Keynes, the result of a possible liquidity trap where liquidity preferences could in a deep depression become highly interest-elastic, whilst the investors' demand for money is likely to be highly interest-inelastic. Thus monetary policy in such a depression is unlikely to bring about a recovery. Hence Keynes' preference for direct government intervention to increase the level of effective aggregate demand by stimulating both consumption and investment demand rather than by monetary policies.

The acceptance of Keynes' General Theory did not occur overnight, nor was it comprehensive. Winch (1972) examined this process of acceptance and shows that the early reaction to Keynes was mixed — a quite predictable reaction given the radical nature of both the theory and the policy implications. The dominance of the natural order thesis had encouraged a strong positivistic methodology within the economics discipline. Winch argues: 'It is not difficult to see how this belief in the organic nature of economic life . . . could form the basis for an elaborate defence of the status quo . . . one consequence is that the economist becomes an apologist for certain features of an unregulated, competitive form of capitalism' (p. 201). Not only that, but such influential economists from the London School of Economics as Robbins and Hayek virtually denied any role for economists to comment upon the ends or objectives of economic activity; only the means were an appropriate subject for analysis by economists.

Given this environment it is perhaps surprising that Keynes gained such acceptance as he did. There is no doubt that the severity of the Depression in the 1930s helped, with several empirical works charting the serious social and economic effects upon the unemployed, combined with a growing frustration within the economics profession with a set of theories that made no contribution to solving the most pressing economic and social issue of the day. This gradually led to the conversion of most of the economics profession and the absorption of Keynesian macroeconomics into the textbooks alongside neo-classical microeconomics.

The introduction of the theoretical possibility of involuntary unemployment caused by deficient aggregate demand did not result in any significant policy initiatives in the 1930s. It was difficult to convince governments and their economic advisors, in a context of low output, bankruptcies, falling state revenues and the growing cost of income maintenance and relief, that the state should spend massively and unbalance its budget. The Second World War effectively enforced this accommodation, removing unemployment and creating the conditions under which a displacement of established ideas and policy could take place.

FULL EMPLOYMENT

An important contribution to this end was made by Beveridge in 1944 with the publication of *Full Employment in a Free Society*. The book, like his earlier book of 1909, does not represent any new breakthrough in the theory of unemployment, but it provides a synthesis of Keynesian demand-deficient unemployment and Beveridge's earlier analysis of frictional/structural unemployment, a detailed empirical study of the characteristics of unemployment, and a fascinating analysis of the nature of full-employment policy.

The latter aspect, and in particular Beveridge's postscript, deserves re-examination in the light of the current debate, but for the present it will prove sufficient to note that, contrary to popular opinion, the 1944 White Paper on employment policy was a less than complete endorsement of Keynesian interventionism. Beveridge acknowledged that the White Paper was epoch-making in accepting the need for the expert study of general economic problems; in burying the prewar Treasury dogma that no permanent additional employment could be created by state fiscal policy; and in accepting as one of the primary aims and responsibilities of government 'the maintenance of a high and stable level of employment'. He was, however, highly critical of the practical measures proposed to achieve this aim: 'The policy of the White Paper is a public works policy, not a policy of full employment' (Beveridge, 1944, p. 262). He argued that the Paper contained no effective means of stabilising private investment and no measures to ensure the steady expansion of demand. Furthermore, he pointed out that the White Paper continued to accept aspects of orthodox monetary policy, principally concerning budgetary equilibrium, which was accorded equal priority with maintaining national income in the White Paper. Thus a full conversion to Keynesianism was not achieved in 1944; and arguably has not been achieved since.

Nevertheless it is undeniable that postwar governments have accepted a responsibility for the level of economic activity and employment and a degree of intervention that was unthinkable in the prewar context. It is also the case that Keynesian macroeconomic theory gained widespread acceptance within the economics profession and led to a considerable optimism about the ability of mixed capitalist economies to maintain full employment. Stewart, for example, claims 'the basic fact is that with the acceptance of the General Theory, the days of uncontrollable mass unemployment in advanced industrial countries are over. Other economic problems may threaten; this one, at least, has passed into history' (1967, p. 254).

This complacency was not, however, universal. Policy in both the USA and the UK during the 1950s failed to reconcile full employment with price stability, and cyclical unemployment was still in evidence, although the cycle was very mild and damped compared with prewar experience and the total level of unemployment, even in the recessionary troughs, was well below what the authors of the 1944 White Paper regarded as the likely achievable full-employment norm. Phillips (1958) gave academic respectability to the policy-makers' dilemma by showing that a trade-off had existed between unemployment and wage rates in the UK between 1861 and 1957. The rate of change in money wages tended to be high in conditions of low unemployment, and low or even negative when unemployment was high. Thus the Phillips Curve suggested that the maintenance of full employment would involve some inflation, and conversely that inflation was only likely to be reduced by an increase in unemployment.

The Phillips Curve did not represent any radical change in the theory of unemployment, nor did it necessarily conflict with Keynes' analysis of involuntary unemployment. What it did suggest was that other 'types' of unemployment may have been underestimated, particularly the degree of frictional and structural maladjustment. This hypothesis concerning the size of the frictional and structural element in unemployment has been a persistent feature of discussion concerning the level of full employment during the 1960s and 1970s, and will receive further consideration below. But what is apparent is that Phillips' analysis provided a backcloth against which some economists began to argue in favour of a higher general level of unemployment in order to provide 'a somewhat larger margin of productive potential' (Parish, 1970, p. 91) in order to bring down the rate of rise of prices. It would also appear that a similar upward creep was apparent in the policy-makers' perceptions of a tolerable level of unemployment. Blackaby (1976) shows that the rate of unemployment acting as a trigger for government reflationary action increased from 2.2 per cent in 1959, to 2.5 per cent in 1963, and to 3.9 per cent in 1972. Blackaby concludes that by the end of 1973 the predominant view amongst many leading commentators was that 'Two and a half per cent unemployment — which ten years ago was a certain trigger for reflationary action — be taken now as a trigger, if anything, for deflation. Once it was considered to be an indicator of deficient demand; now it is considered an indicator of excess demand' (p. 283).

It is not, of course, correct to lay the blame for this 'inflation' of the full-employment level of unemployment solely at the feet of Mr Phillips; it has been given further impetus by the resurgence of monetarist economic theory, which will be examined below. But before doing so it is necessary to examine the tendency in the 1960s to pay growing attention to frictional and structural factors.

This tendency was reinforced by the development of human capital theory, and arguably by dual labour market theory. Both theories emphasise differences in access to the labour market, by pointing to differences between individuals in their human capital endowment (e.g. educational and vocational qualifications and skills) or to the existence of primary and secondary labour markets 'trapping' some individuals and groups (lacking credentials or subject to race, sex or age discrimination) in low-paid insecure jobs, making them prone to long and/or repeated spells of unemployment.

These analyses of essentially frictional and structural factors have certain similarities with the work of Beveridge and others around the turn of the century. Not unnaturally they have also led to a similar emphasis in policy development, namely a concern with the organisation of the labour market. Thus during the 1960s most members of the OECD became involved in the development of 'active' manpower policies, involving *inter alia* the restructuring and expansion of employment and training services. This aspect of policy is not the central concern of this chapter and is fully analysed in chapter 4. It is, however, of significance to note that manpower policies were conceived on the assumption that macro-fiscal and monetary policies would continue to ensure full employment, and that their influence would be to help reduce frictional and structural mismatch within that context.

The last two sections have examined the emergence and establishment of the Keynesian theory of involuntary unemployment. But it has also been shown that this process was both incomplete (with, for example, the 1944 White Paper on employment — retaining elements of classical monetarist theory) and subject to attrition by the Phillips Curve and its influence upon perceived levels of tolerable unemployment. But by far the most serious and fundamental challenge to Keynesian unemployment theory has come from the counter-attack of the monetarist school.

THE MONETARIST AND THE NATURAL RATE OF UNEMPLOYMENT

Harry Johnson (1971) has argued that the speed at which the monetarist counter-revolution gained acceptance has similarities with the success of the Keynesian revolution. In particular, the most fruitful circumstance for any radical change in the accepted wisdom 'is the existence of an established orthodoxy which is clearly inconsistent with the most salient facts of reality' (p. 4). The failure of classical theory to explain or prescribe for mass unemployment was the principal launching pad for the Keynesian thesis. Likewise Johnson argues that the failure of the Keynesian orthodoxy to 'prescribe for what has come to be considered a major social problem — inflation' (p. 7) explains, *inter alia*, the propagation of monetarist theory and policy. Hirsch similarily argues that the abandonment of full employment, which experience had suggested to be a feasible policy option, 'required the public to be persuaded of greater evils. Inflation has been the central one' (1977, p. 278). Friedman, the originator and arch-disciple of monetarism, claims: 'The drastic change that has occurred in economic theory has not been the result of ideological warfare . . . It has responded almost entirely to the force of events' (1977, p. 31). The statement is, however, disingenuous given his clearly stated value preference for free market capitalism and laissez-faire, which so clearly influences his policy prescriptions. It also needs to be pointed out that these observations on the degree of acceptance of monetarism need to be 'qualified in the British context. Whilst policy-makers have given increasing attention to monetarist analysis, almost exclusively since the election of the 1979 Conservative government, the acceptance by the economics profession has been far from universal. Parkin, one of the leading exponents of the expectations-augmented Phillips Curve monetarist view, has acknowledged that the view was a minority one in Britain (Kranse and Salant, 1977, p. 475).

What, however, is the monetarist theory of unemployment? The basic starting point is the far from new argument that monetary causes are the most important source of fluctuations in national income and business activity (see Kaldor, 1970, p. 3). This causal link is deduced from empirical work, particularly in the USA, establishing a strong positive correlation between changes in the money supply and changes in business activity. The money supply has been shown to decline absolutely in major depressions in business activity, for example between 1929 and 1933, and its rate of increase to slow and drop below its long-run upward trend during minor recessions. The monetarist view of unemployment is that it results from government mismanagement of the money supply and the consequent fluctuations in business activity. Similarly, monetarists explain inflation by blaming it upon governments permitting excessive increases in the money supply.

It is not the correlation between money supply and business activity and inflation that is controversial, but the monetarist claim that there is a causal link. Keynesians, in contrast, emphasise the determinants of the level of investment, which they argue have relatively little to do with monetary factors, as the causal factor in levels of business activity. Indeed, many reverse the monetarist position by arguing that variations in the money supply are the consequence not the cause of differences in economic activity. Kaldor (1970, p. 16) argues that changes in the money supply are largely a reflection of changes in money incomes, which are in turn determined by the pressure of demand, the level of investment, exports, the influence of fiscal policy and the rate of wage inflation — itself partially influenced by the level of demand. Thus the extreme positions postulate on the one hand that only money matters in explaining economic fluctuations and on the other than money does not matter at all. It could, however, be argued that the vast majority of neo-Keynesians would accept that both monetary and non-monetary factors contribute to an under-standing of the behaviour of the economic system and that mismanaging the money supply is a potential source of economic fluctuation, but it is far from being the only or major determinant.

The fundamental distinction between the monetarist and Keynesian schools over the role of money in business fluctuation does not of itself offer a clear insight into its implications for the theory of unemploy-ment. In monetarist theory the level of unemployment is not clearly determined: 'there is a "natural rate of unemployment", which is consistent with the real forces and with accurate perceptions' (Friedman, 1977, p. 15). By 'real forces' Friedman means, for example, how effectively the labour market operates, the degree of competition or monopoly, the barriers or encouragement offered to take particular jobs, the extent of wage flexibility, and relative unem-ployment benefit levels. Thus there is no generally applicable natural rate, but a host of rates unique to each nation's situation. Friedman's 'accurate perceptions' relate to perceptions, expectations and processes of adjustment to any given level of inflation. This follows from the monetarist emphasis on the effects of unanticipated infla-tion. Fully anticipated inflation does not necessarily disrupt the 'real forces' at work in the labour market or affect the 'natural rate of unemployment'. It follows from this emphasis on the effects of unan-ticipated inflation that the stable trade-off between inflation and unemployment postulated in the Phillips Curve does not exist. If, for example, inflation proceeded at a fairly steady rate of 10 per cent p.a. and this was fully anticipated, and wage and price levels adjusted accordingly, there need be no change in the level of unemployment. In other words, in the long run, if this situation prevailed, the Phillips Curve could be vertical at a point corresponding to the natural rate of unemployment. If, however, the inflation rate was unsteady, increas-ing and not fully anticipated, wages and prices would be unlikely to adjust fully and freely in such an uncertain situation, and, therefore, the Phillips Curve could be either positively or negatively sloped, indicating the possibility of any level of unemployment for any given level of price or wage inflation.

This then brings us back to the monetarist interpretation of the causes of unstable or increasing levels of inflation, which as we have seen are blamed on government policy — 'in particular, policies of full employment and welfare state policies raising government spending' (Friedman, 1977, p. 25). Furthermore, government attempts at stabilisation by fiscal, monetary or incomes policies prevent free market forces from adjusting price and income levels to the new monetary reality. Thus, as Tobin points out, 'we have come full circle. Full employment is once again nothing but the equilibrium reached by labour markets unaided and undistorted by governmental fine tuning [and the] natural rate doctrine is the contemporary version of the classical position Keynes was opposing' (1972, p. 2).

There is, however, no necessary difference between the Keynesian full-employment position and the monetarist natural-rate position, only a difference in the interpretation of why the experienced rate of unemployment exceeds those positions and in the nature of the policies required to return to the full/natural rate of unemployment. But whilst the level of full employment and the natural rate of unemployment need not differ, most economists of a monetarist persuasion, and indeed some others, have argued that the natural or full-employment level of unemployment has risen over the last fifteen years or so. In other words, Friedman's 'real forces' in the labour market have changed, such that 'involuntary' unemployment is lower or even non-existent higher recorded levels of unemployment, and that voluntary and/or frictional/structural unemployment has risen. These two aspects will now be considered.

INCREASED VOLUNTARY UNEMPLOYMENT?

The argument that voluntary unemployment has risen has rested largely on the contention that unemployment benefits and redundancy compensation have increased in value relative to net employment income, and that this has had a significant disincentive effect, giving rise to more voluntary quits or to more, probably longer, voluntary unemployment amongst those dismissed.

Gujarati (1971), for example, sought to explain the shift that took place in the unemployment:vacancies ratio between 1966 and 1971 by claiming that the introduction of redundancy payments in 1965 and earnings-related unemployment benefits had changed job-search behaviour in such a way that the level of notified vacancies for any given level of registered unemployment would be higher. This view has been given further support by studies regressing male unemployment or unemployment duration on the benefit:income ratio. Maki and Spindler (1975) suggest that earnings-related benefit could account for an increase of about one-third in male unemployment between 1967 and 1972, although they acknowledge that male unemployment was still some 54 per cent higher after the effect of earnings-related supplements had been taken into account.

Their analysis has, however, come in for some substantial criticism. Firstly it is weakened by the use of notional rather than actual benefit levels, leading to a considerable overestimation of the benefit:income or replacement ratio for the vast majority of the unemployed. Atkinson and Flemming (1978) suggest that, because of the considerable differences in the financial circumstances of the unemployed, it is very difficult to develop any single indicator for the effects of changes in the replacement ratio. Nickell (1979) stresses that much of the statistical impact of Maki and Spindler's study is defused by the time-series trend, that is both the replacement ratio and unemployment have increased in the study period. He develops a cross-section analysis putting particular emphasis on the effects of benefit changes on the probability of leaving the unemployment register. This suggests that the introduction of the earnings-related supplement in 1966 may have added approximately 10 per cent to unemployment, although the effect is shown as being almost entirely confined to those unemployed for under twenty weeks. A Department of Employment report (DE, 1976) indicates that even this estimate would require an assumption that the earnings-related supplement had the effect of doubling the average unemployed man's duration of unemployment. There is little evidence that an effect of this order is realistic. Mackay and Reid (1972) estimated that for the average wage earner with two children the duration of unemployment might have been increased by up to one and a half weeks, representing an average increase in duration of less than 20 per cent. There is also some evidence that suggests that the supplement could have had a negative effect on unemployment. For example, Hill *et al.* found that there was a 'statistically significant tendency for those without an earnings-related supplement to remain unemployed the longest' (1973, p. 82). This is probably explained by the likelihood that those receiving the supplement were more stable, experienced and better qualified, and so were able to find alternative employment more quickly. Furthermore, the Nickell estimate takes no account of possible replacement effects —

those delaying re-entry into jobs may be replaced by other unemployed people, a probability that tends to increase as unemployment itself rises.

The evidence against the second major legislative change, namely the Redundancy Payment Act 1965, having an effect on search behaviour and unemployment duration is virtually conclusive. All the major case-studies of redundancy covering the relevant period (e.g. Parker *et al.*, 1971; Mackay and Reid, 1972; Daniel, 1972; and Hill *et al.*, 1973) failed to find any association between the size of redundancy compensation and the consequent duration of unemployment. Furthermore, Foster (1974) argues that to seek an explanation of the effect of redundancy payments on the supply side, i.e. in search behaviour, is misconceived. It is much more probable that the effect is on the demand side, with the payments influencing employer behaviour towards inducing redundancy amongst selected age groups, particularly the older worker least able to compete in a slack labour market.

The evidence concerning the effects of changes in the benefit:income ratio has so far related to its possible influence on the unemployment level between the late 1960s and early 1970s. If some increase in unemployment occurred in this period as a consequence of an increase in the replacement ratio, some reduction might be expected during the 1970s, as the ratio fell slightly. The National Institute of Economic and Social Research (NIESR, 1977), calculating the ratio of unemployment benefit entitlement (including the earnings-related supplement) to net disposable income for a married couple with two children on average male earnings, shows that this reached a peak of 71 per cent in 1968, slipped slightly to 70 per cent by 1970, but remained in the range of 65–67 per cent in all subsequent years to 1976. The ratio of supplementary benefit to net average income has shown only a marginal increase. A DHSS report (1978a) shows that the short-term scale rate plus average rent allowances as a percentage of average net male manual earnings was 48.5 per cent for a married couple in October 1967 and 50 per cent in November 1977. It is worth emphasising that both these calculations refer to net income, i.e. after account has been taken of the possible effects of any fall in the taxation threshold or increase in the rate of taxation, which are frequently advanced (see Brittan, 1975) as further factors reducing the incentive to work and inducing more and longer unemployment. More detailed comparisons by Atkinson and Flemming (1978) for different family compositions reinforce the NIESR findings and show that the replacement ratios, that is benefits as a percentage of net income, fell quite substantially between 1971 and 1977. They argue, however, that whilst this suggests the various analyses of the benefit-inducing effect may be an overstatement, this may be partially off-set by the disincentive effects arising from the peculiarities and discontinuities involved in the taxation system, which may lead some to delay in re-entry to the labour market.

Thus, accepting the terms of reference of those economists seeking to show that changes in social security provision have increased voluntary unemployment, the empirical evidence suggests that redundancy payments have had virtually no effect, and that unemployment, earnings-related and supplementary benefits may have had some marginal unemployment-inducing effects up to the early 1970s but that little additional inducement is likely to exist subsequently. Furthermore, such effects are likely to be concentrated amongst unskilled, low-paid workers with large families (Daniel and Stilgoe, 1977; DHSS, 1978a) — workers whose employment opportunities are most likely to have been limited by changes in the pressure and structure of labour demand.

One further aspect calls for comment, namely the assumption in the studies cited that workers behave as rational economic maximisers, responding and adapting their behaviour to changes in the relationship between work income and benefit income. Certainly the economic calculus is important, but account must also be taken of psychological and sociological forces influencing the perception of work as conferring status in our society. These aspects are more fully explored in chapter 5 but it is clear from the various sociological studies undertaken (Marsden and Duff, 1975; Harrison, 1976; North Tyneside CDP, 1978) that

> so strong are the pressures and informal sanctions supporting work in our society that some of the workless cling to the desire to work to a much greater degree than our society has a right to expect . . . For those we interviewed, talk about the 'opportunity' or 'leisure' afforded by unemployment seems decidedly premature'. [Marsden and Duff, 1975, p. 264]

INCREASED FRICTION AND
UNEMPLOYABILITY?

The second plank in the argument that the full-employment level of unemployment or the 'natural rate' is higher than in the early postwar period is that the level of frictional unemployment has risen and the structure of unemployment has changed, increasing the proportion of unemployables. Part of this argument has rested upon a concern with the accuracy of the unemployment statistics as a measure of the unused potential labour supply, and is most clearly associated with the work of Wood (1972, 1975) and Boulet and Bell (1973). Wood, for example, endeavours to exclude the short-term unemployment from the official statistics, and attempts to redefine them so that they can be 'described in some phrase which does not use the word unemployment', and suggests 're-deployment' or 'labour turnover' as alternatives (1972, p. 17). There is no doubt that there is a considerable amount of short-duration unemployment and turnover in the unemployment register. But as Hughes (1975) points out, it is mistaken to imply that all short-duration unemployment can be regarded as 'frictional', as the category will include many who will go on to be unemployed much longer, and equally mistaken to regard this group as voluntary quits seeking new jobs. Indeed, the higher the level of total unemployment the more likely it is that the ratio of quits to dismissals will fall. Wood also argues that such unemployment is beneficial and helpful to the process of economic change. This depends on how purposive the 're-deployment' that takes place is. There is no doubt that a substantial proportion involves unskilled workers moving from one relatively low-paid, low-productivity job to another, and suffering recurrent bouts of short-duration unemployment. There would appear to be no evidence to suggest that frictional unemployment (even when crudely defined in terms of short duration) increases relatively in periods of high unemployment. Hughes, using occupational unemployment and vacancy data, demonstrates that frictional unemployment was higher in 1965 in both absolute (82,600) and relative (37 per cent) terms than in 1971 when the respective data were 62,900 and 10 per cent (1975, p. 325).

The second main target group for exclusion from the official statistics is the so-called 'unemployables', either because they are unwilling to take jobs as a result of more generous benefit provision (an aspect already analysed above) or because they are personally deficient. The definition of personal deficiency in relation to employability is fraught with difficulty, but as Deacon shows in chapter 3 it is impossible to disentangle the category from the influence of the general pressure of labour demand. Nevertheless there is a serious and growing problem of long-term unemployment as a consequence of the persistence of high general levels of unemployment. Long-term unemployment tends to have a circular and cumulative effect. The longer an individual's unemployment the more likely it is that he or she will be screened out of consideration for jobs by employers; their experience and skills will be declining in value; and they are less likely to be referred to jobs by the employment service. The problem demands far more serious attention than it has so far received, but it is a consequence and not a cause of increased general unemployment.

Apart from attempts to use the unemployment statistics to show an increase in frictional unemployment and the analysis of the benefits: income ratio to show an increase in voluntary unemployment, there have been a number of other suggestions seeking to show that the full-employment level of unemployment has risen. These are mostly concerned with possible increases in labour market intervention and legislation impeding the free operation of the market. Some of the prime candidates for inclusion have been: (i) incomes policies reducing the flexibility of wage adjustments to market forces and compressing differentials, thereby deterring the acquisition and retention of skills; (ii) local authority housing policy reducing labour mobility by restriction and rigidities in the allocation of council housing; (iii) industrial relations legislation, particularly the Employment Protection Act, affecting employer decisions on recruitment and dismissal, although Daniel and Stilgoe's study (1978) has suggested that the effects are marginal; (iv) price controls restricting profitability and distorting relative prices, thereby reducing market signals and increasing any maldistribution of labour; (v) increased trade union membership and monopoly control tending to force up the minimum wage offer.

It is clearly impossible to quantify the effects of these diverse factors, although they would tend to indicate the likelihood of some increased friction or maldistribution in the labour market. It could, however, be argued with equal if not greater force that the effects of high and persistent levels of unemployment are far more deleterious to the efficient operation of the market. In these circumstances labour is likely to be more reluctant to be mobile both geographically and occupationally, is less likely to undergo retraining and vocational education, and is more likely to obstruct and restrict the introduction of labour-saving technological change, because of the uncertainty of re-employment. Furthermore, the major improvements in manpower policy, particularly improvements in the information, placings, guidance and counselling functions of the public employment service, the massive expansion in the scale and scope of government vocational retraining, and the improved availability of mobility and resettlement grants, will tend to off-set the adverse effects ascribed to other labour and industrial relations legislation mentioned above.

In an attempt to obtain some measure of the effect of all the various policies upon the full-employment level of unemployment, the NIESR (1977) endeavoured to estimate indicators of spare capacity and compare the prevailing unemployment level in years of roughly equal capacity utilisation. This applied in 1966 and 1973 and the respective unemployment rates were 1.2 per cent and 2.1 per cent. Part of the increase will be accounted for by increases in productivity, and the NIESR concludes that 'the evidence suggests that there has probably been a rather small increase in the full employment level of unemployment — an increase in the range of perhaps 100–200 thousand over the levels of the 1950s, and early 1960s'. This corresponds to a total unemployment level of about half a million or just over 2 per cent.

Thus, consideration of the 'real forces' determining the monetarist's natural rate of unemployment does not indicate any substantial increase in frictional/structural or voluntary unemployment. There is, therefore, little practical difference between the monetarist's natural rate and the Keynesian full-employment rate, and it is academic, in the worse sense of the word, to discuss whether the target should be 2 per cent or 3 per cent when the actual rate persists at around 6 per cent. The debate is a clear indication that definitions of full employment gain plasticity when the experienced level rises.

THE ECONOMIC COSTS OF UNEMPLOYMENT

Before examining the policy implications of the theories of unemployment outlined above, some attempt will be made to estimate the economic burden created by high levels of unemployment. Calculating the financial costs of unemployment is fraught with difficulty because the calculation necessarily involves a number of arbitary assumptions. Some estimates of the costs of unemployment to government (see for example Field, 1977, p. 84) have made assumptions about the 'average' characteristics of the unemployed, and calculated benefit payments assuming all the unemployed to be married with two children and receiving average adult male earnings. The fact that a disproportionate share of the increase in unemployment in the 1970s was borne by young people and women, and that the unskilled are over-represented amongst the unemployed, suggests that such estimates will overstate the public expenditure 'costs'. Field's study does not however, include an estimate for increased expenditure on employment training and special measures for the unemployed.

There are two major components in the costs of unemployment to the state: firstly the transfer payments and their attendant administrative costs, and secondly the loss of revenue or tax expenditures occasioned by the non-payment of employer and employee national insurance contributions and income taxes, and also reduced receipts from expenditure taxes.

Calculating the transfer costs involves fewer difficulties than the tax expenditure costs, and the main source for the calculation will be the National Income Blue Book (Central Statistical Office, 1979). Table 2.1 shows the total amount of national insurance and supplementary benefits paid to the unemployed, an estimate for the administrative costs involved, the amount of net government contribution to redundancy payments, and the cost of employment service provision for 1973 (unemployment rate 2.7 per cent) and 1978 (unemployment rate of 6.1 per cent).

Where assumptions have been made concerning the allocation of a proportion of a total budget to the unemployed, these have been as conservative as possible. For example, given the very rapid increase in the numbers and proportion of unemployed dependent wholly or partially on supplementary benefit between 1973 and 1978, it is unrealistic to assume that the percentage of total benefits attributable to the unemployed remained the same in 1978 as in 1975. Thus the £650m for supplementary benefit is almost certainly an underestimate. Inclusion of employment service expenditure in its entirety is of course open to criticism, but there is little doubt that a very high proportion of the increased expenditure is directly attributable to the increase in unemployment and to attempts through, for example, the Youth Opportunities Programme and the Temporary Employment Subsidy to reduce the numbers of registered unemployed. The table shows a four-fold increase in total transfer payments to the unemployed and related expenditure in the five-year period at current prices, representing an increase from 3.1 per cent of total public

Table 2.1 *Government Transfer Payments to the Unemployed and Related Costs in 1973 and 1978*

	1973 £m	1978 £m
Benefits:		
National insurance unemployment benefit	160	667
Supplementary benefit[a]	218	650
Administrative costs:[b]		
National insurance unemployment benefit	32	76
Supplementary benefit	37	130
Redundancy payments[c]	52	182
Employment services:		
Current expenditure	107	536
Subsidies	8	262
Grants	90	295
TOTAL	704	2,798
Total as percentage of total central government current account expenditure:	3.1%	5.2%

[a]31 per cent of total supplementary benefits payments, i.e. the percentage attributable to the unemployed in December 1975 (see DHSS, 1978a, *A Statistical Note*).
[b]Estimated as 20 per cent of total national insurance administrative costs, and 34 per cent of supplementary benefit administrative costs (DHSS, 1978a, *A Statistical Note*).
[c]Calculated assuming that the government paid out net an equivalent amount to employer contributions to the Redundancy Fund.
Source: Central Statistical Office (1979).

current expenditure in 1973 to 5.2 per cent in 1978. It should be noted that this is likely to be the minimum impact figure. There are other areas of transfer payments, subsidies and benefits in kind that have not been included in the calculation. There is little doubt that high unemployment leads to a reduction in the economic activity rate of post-retirement-age workers (see Showler, 1974). Thus some part of retirement pensions (the largest single item of national insurance payments) should be added to the estimated total cost. Similarly, further additions are needed from the local authority budgets to cover the increased number of free school meals and rent and rate rebates occasioned by the rise in unemployment.

Calculation of the 'tax expenditures' side of the cost to government of unemployment is more complex and requires a number of assumptions about probable earnings levels and income tax and national insurance contributions in order to determine the revenue loss involved in unemployment. An upper limit for 1978 can perhaps be estimated by assuming that if the average 6.1 per cent of employees registered as unemployed in 1978 were employed, they would contribute in equal proportion to government revenue as all other employees in the year. The total amount of income tax on wages and salaries and national insurance contributions made by civilian employers (including the surcharge) and employees in 1978 was £26,227m. Were all the unemployed employed on the same basis, income tax and contributions collected would be £1,600m higher.

This may, as suggested, be regarded as an upper limit, because it assumes the unemployed to be likely to receive average earnings levels and to be subject to average tax and contribution deductions. To assume average earnings levels is unrealistic given the higher proportion of unskilled and younger workers amongst the unemployed. To provide an alternative estimate, it has been assumed that the seasonally adjusted total unemployed (excluding school leavers) in June 1978, that is, 942,300 males and 362,400 females, would have earned the cut-off average gross weekly earnings level for the lower quartile (i.e. £66.1 per week for males, and £42.6 per week for females) as revealed by the New Earnings Survey for April 1978. This yields a total additional gross income for the year of £4,035m. Had this been subject to the average level of income tax deduction and national insurance contribution (18.4 per cent and 10.6 per cent respectively), the revenue loss amounts to £1,170m. It could be objected that applying average income tax deductions is likely to overestimate the revenue loss, as earnings levels are low. It could, however, be argued

that the deductions are realistic given the high proportion of young
and unskilled, which would tend to depress tax thresholds (e.g. few
allowances for dependants, mortgages and insurances), and given
that national insurance contributions are likely to be higher than
average for the group given the contribution ceiling and the greater
likelihood of contracting out for the higher paid, thereby off-setting
any possible lower average income tax level.

These two estimates of possible income tax and contribution losses
do not exhaust the 'tax expenditure' costs of unemployment. Neither,
for example, includes any estimate for tax refunds that will have been
made to any of those registered as unemployed who had been in
employment and had paid income tax during the relevant period.
Furthermore, they do not include any estimate for losses of consumption taxes (e.g. VAT, customs and excise, and motor vehicle duties)
occasioned by the difference between net benefit income and likely net
earnings. Using the gross earnings figure calculated above and de-
ducting both the direct transfer payments to the unemployed revealed
in the table and the tax and national insurance contributions made,
suggests a net additional disposable income figure of £1,074m. All the
various consumption taxes in 1978 represented 14.7 per cent of total
consumers' expenditure, which would suggest further consumption
tax losses of unemployment of about £160m.

Taking the lower estimate for tax and contribution losses, and
adding this to total transfer and related payments and to the estimate
for consumption tax losses, gives a total of £4,128m loss in public
expenditure in 1978 due to unemployment, representing 7.6 per cent
of the government's total budget. It is not, of course, suggested that
the whole of this figure could be saved directly by a return to full
employment, as clearly some unemployment would remain. The
foregoing discussion has, however, suggested that the level of unemployment prevailing in 1978 could be more than halved, yielding
public expenditure savings of at least £2,000m. Higher levels of
employment would also increase activity rates as well as reducing
registered unemployment, thereby yielding savings in transfer payments (e.g. pensions) and higher tax and national insurance
contributions not included in the above calculations. In addition,
some of the costs of unemployment borne by employers, through for
example contributions to the Redundancy Fund not included in the
above calculations, would be saved.

Apart from the direct and indirect effects upon public expenditure,
there is, of course, the loss of Gross National Product resulting from

running the economy at below full employment. Several studies estimated this loss to have amounted to between 7 per cent and 8 per cent of GDP by 1976 (NIESR, 1977; MSC, 1979a; Field, 1977). Timbrell (1980) calculates the annual loss by the late 1970s to be some £4,000m. These figures suggest that the cumulative loss of national output would have exceeded £20,000m by the end of the decade. Had that output been available, the tax revenue generated would be greater than that projected for the mid-1980s from North Sea Oil, and would not be subject to the same impermanence.

In addition to the fiscal and product costs, there are perhaps less tangible losses in labour market efficiency, some of which have been outlined in the preceding section. As Blackaby (1976) points out, a high demand for labour tends to stimulate investment in labour-saving technology, and usually has the added attraction of reducing menial, dangerous and unpleasant work. Similarly, full employment puts pressure on employers to redesign work in such a way as to reduce its more unpleasant aspects. The fear of job insecurity and unemployment reinforces restrictive practices and increases workers' resistance to changes in methods of production, thereby undermining attempts to improve productivity. The existence of spare capacity in industry compounds the problem by forcing firms to recover their overhead costs from below-capacity output and sales.

The main justification for the need to run the economy with higher unemployment has, of course, been the need to contain inflation. But high unemployment and the virtual absence of economic growth since 1973 may themselves be a source of inflationary pressure. As Hirsch shows, the process of economic growth helps to avoid the economic and political difficulties involved in a direct redistribution of a static economic cake (1979, ch. 12). Lack of economic growth and high unemployment exacerbates the distributional struggle and is likely to lead to 'excessive' money wage demands. Furthermore, as Lekachman points out, guaranteed full employment is likely to reduce the economic and social consequences of the distributional struggle by reducing income inequality (1976, p. 76). The biggest income gains would be made by the young, black and female, amongst whom unemployment is most severe and wage rates lowest.

The above discussion is a far from exhaustive account of the economic costs of unemployment, but it has endeavoured to highlight the adverse effects upon public expenditure, production, labour market efficiency and inflation.

THEORY AND POLICY

Finally, it is necessary to consider the policy options presented by the various theoretical perspectives for a return to full employment. The monetarist perspective in practice presents very few options, as the whole basis of the theory is one of non-intervention and support for 'free' market forces to determine the outcome. Thus, using fiscal policy to fine tune aggregate demand levels is ruled out: 'The key to the doomsday machine is that Keynesian stimulation does increase output and employment in the short run, but only prices in the longer run' (Brittan, 1978, p. 181). Similarly, the post-Keynesian advocacy of incomes policy is also dismissed by monetarists as unworkable or useless: 'an incomes policy will always founder on the rock of relatives and differentials, and there is no such thing as a fair or scientific assessment of relativities' (Brittan, 1978, p. 176). Direct government control of prices is also ruled out because price controls are seen as interfering with the allocative efficiency of the market by dampening and confusing market signals dependent upon relative profitability. Some monetarists, including Friedman, also argue that monetary policy, because of its potency in their model, needs to be exercised with restraint. Nevertheless, the main policy proposal of the monetarist school is for a reduction in public expenditure, in particular where this is financed by a large borrowing requirement.

The last Labour government did make a substantial cut in public expenditure between 1975/6 and 1977/8 from £72,621m to £67,911m (at 1979 survey prices). Transfer payments, however, increased; therefore the burden of adjustment fell upon state expenditure on goods and services. The results of this deflation were a fall in output and a doubling in the level of unemployment. Thus Roll's conclusion is supported:

> There was never any doubt . . . that a strong dose of monetary restraint can . . . stop an inflation. But it does so only precisely because it reduces economic activity and creates unemployment. It is thus not a means of removing the choice between the two evils (of unemployment and inflation) but only another and, in my opinion, a particularly violent method for alternating between them. [Roll, 1978, p. 42]

Monetarists do not deny that cutting public expenditure in present circumstances will create more unemployment. This they see as the necessary price for longer-term monetary stability enabling the achievement of the 'natural' rate of unemployment. But how long this process will take and how much 'transitional' unemployment would be created is not specified.

There are both empirical and theoretical reasons for suggesting that this may involve a long period and a substantial rise in unemployment. The main explanation advanced by the monetarist school for the existence of unemployment above the natural rate rests on the assumption that markets for labour and goods will clear, provided that actual wages and prices correspond to the expectations of workers and producers. Unemployment above the natural rate is therefore the consequence of excessive real-wage expectations by the unemployed and the holding back of labour seeking a higher wage than is offered. As Akerlof (1979) points out, this requires unemployment to be generally of short duration, but 'if unemployment spells are quite long, the New Classical Macroeconomics seems implausible in explaining changes in aggregate unemployment'. Akerlof goes on to demonstrate that USA unemployment duration data when analysed in terms of average completed spells of unemployment show considerable long-term unemployment. British unemployment by duration data (which deal with interrupted spells) reveal substantial long-term unemployment, which would be even greater if Akerlof's completed spell definition were adopted. Thus the monetarist assumption that labour markets will clear if expectations could be forced to accord with 'reality' is untenable.

Not only are monetarist assumptions about the nature of labour markets mistaken, but assumptions about the relationship between price and wage inflation and excess money supply are equally open to empirical refutation. Tarling and Wilkinson show clearly that 'in the UK, the money supply and inflation were not correlated except in the early 1970s, and then only as the result of an entirely fortuitous coincidence of separate events' (1973, p. 56). For monetarist policy prescriptions to work requires the assumption that money wages are determined simply by market forces. The evidence against such a simplistic view is overwhelming and is adequately summarised by Phelps–Brown (1977) and Cripps (1977). It has already been shown in the previous section that rising unemployment (the inevitable consequence of monetary deflation) imposes heavy public expenditure overheads, further squeezing the real income of wage earners and likely to increase the pressure for pay rises to compensate. Thus as Cripps points out, the monetarists' 'cure' 'may well perpetuate high unemployment and make inflation worse, not better' (1972, p. 111).

Some, but by no means all, monetarists would accept that inflation has been exacerbated by the power of trade unions giving rise to greater monopolistic practices on the supply side of the labour market. The arguably more impressive growth of industrial concentration, multinationalisation and monopolisation of the demand side of the labour market receives no acknowledgement from the monetarist school. Holland argues:

> It is not union growth so much as a growth in the power of monopoly–multinational capital which has accompanied the trend to uncontrolled inflation . . . in the 1960s and early 1970s . . . The main reason for the crisis has been not so much the mis-application of Keynesian techniques of demand management as their erosion by a new mode of production [1975, pp. 14 and 134]

There is no doubt that there has been a rapid process of industrial concentration over the last twenty years or so, resulting in about one-half of all manufacturing production being directly controlled by some 100 mainly multinational companies. These companies, therefore, have unprecedented decision-making power over one-half of the economy in terms of output, employment, investment, prices and international trade. Holland argues that these 'mezo'-corporations have escaped control by national governments as a result of their ability to avoid taxation and understate profitability, principally through the process of transfer pricing (1978, p. 142). Sherman (1976) presents impressive evidence of the association between the emergence of inflation in recession and the growth of monopoly power in the USA. He demonstrates that the monopolistic sector of the economy is able to maintain or even increase profitability during recessions through its control over prices, forcing all the adjustment upon the declining competitive sector and upon the labour force, through increased unemployment and reductions in real wages.

This alternative radical analysis provides some indication why Keynesian demand management policies seem to meet with less success. The analysis also suggests that the reality of the monetarists' 'free market forces' is very different from what they assume it to be, and cannot be relied upon to provide an equilibrium 'natural' rate of unemployment, price stability and economic growth, or re-establish the paramountcy of consumer sovereignty. However, it must be recognised that the process of industrial concentration has been a continuous one on the postwar period, and proceeded throughout the 1950s and 1960s when there was little evidence of stagflation.

There is no doubt, however, that changes in the social and institutional framework of the economy in recent decades have made the achievement of full employment more difficult. The above analysis has sought to show that simplistic monetarist non-intervention is a wholly unrealistic strategy in the face of such changes. It is also apparent that to suggest an equally simplistic Keynesian reflation by fiscal policy is unlikely to provide a long-term solution alone. The constraints are formidable. It may well be thwarted by monopolistic and multinational organisations and by Britain's high marginal propensity to import, leading to further balance of payments difficulties or to the use of North Sea Oil revenues to pay for consumer imports rather than for any rejuvenation of domestic industry and employment.

The international trade constraint has of course been the central theme of the alternative strategy put forward by the 'Cambridge School'. As the highly unsympathetic Mr Eltis puts it, 'the Keynesians have lost their multiplier' (Harris, 1979, p. 125). Were a Keynesian expansion through fiscal policy to be pursued, the very high marginal propensity to import, related specifically to a high marginal income elasticity of demand for imported manufactured goods, would mean that the bulk of any expansion in manufacturing production would occur abroad, thereby severely limiting the multiplier effect of the fiscal expansion in Britain. The 'Cambridge' view is as follows:

> For the U.K. ... neither incomes policy nor fiscal and monetary restriction nor devaluation will provide a remedy for problems of slow growth, unemployment and inflation which are becoming more and more severe. Incomes policy may help a little: financial restriction or devaluation will positively make matters worse. General import controls and reflation to expand internal demand are now an urgent necessity. [Cambridge Economic Policy Review, 1979, p. 2]

There is little doubt that British manufacturing industry has been losing its relative share of both overseas and domestic markets (see Moore and Rhodes, 1976) and the spectre of 'de-industrialisation' has been raised. There is equally little doubt that there would be difficulty in reversing that relative decline even if a Keynesian expansion were to be engineered. In such circumstances import controls combined with a policy of fiscal expansion appear hopeful. The practicality of such an option, however, seems unlikely in the face of increased international economic and political interdependence and during a period when international recession is almost universally predicted

with all the overtones of the inter-war 'beggar-my-neighbour' protec-
tionist policies that import controls could trigger.

In conclusion, whilst the monetarist theory of unemployment is far
from universally accepted by economists, it has made major inroads
into what had been the postwar Keynesian consensus and has been
particularly influential on policy since in the mid-1970s. Its basic
analysis and prescriptions are little different from the pre-Keynesian
'naturalistic' theory of unemployment. The re-emergence and increasing acceptance of monetarist theory provide some justification
for Routh's sceptical comments on the general history of economic
ideology: 'it is misleading to think of a flow of economic ideas.
Basically the ideas have remained where they were and economists
have flowed' (1975, p. 19).

Maintaining full employment or low unemployment became mani-
festly more difficult during the 1970s with slower economic growth,
increased inflation and a severe deterioration in the terms of trade and
the balance of payments. Neither Keynes or Beveridge underestimated the difficulties involved in removing involuntary unemployment from a basically capitalist economy — with problems of
monopolisation in capital and product markets, unionisation in the
labour market, and open to a substantial volume of international
trade. It seems all too obvious that attempting macroeconomic
management by fiscal policy alone is insufficient. It ought to be
equally obvious that attempting to manage the economy by monetary
policy alone is similarly doomed to failure.

CHAPTER 3

Unemployment and Politics in Britain Since 1945

Alan Deacon

INTRODUCTION

The Government accept as one of their primary aims and responsibilities the maintenance of a high and stable level of employment after the war.

Thus began the White Paper on *Employment Policy* published by the Coalition Government in June 1944 (Ministry of Reconstruction, 1944). *The Economist* commented: 'The revolution of thought involved in this new policy is far larger than dwellers in the present day can easily realise unless they are skilful at recapturing their own past moods' (3 June 1944). A similar revolution of thought could well be said to have taken place in recent years. It is easily forgotten, for example, that for much of the 1950s the number of people who remained out of work for over a year was less than than a tenth of the current figure, or that until the mid-1960s it was generally believed that any government that failed to keep unemployment below half a million would face almost certain defeat at the polls.

The purpose of this chapter is to examine the significance of unemployment as an issue in postwar British politics. It does so for two reasons: firstly, because the changes that have occurred in attitudes towards unemployment are important and need to be documented and explained, and, secondly, because the documentation itself is relevant to the current debate. There is nothing new, for example, in arguments that a substantial proportion of the unemployed are unemployable, or that unemployment benefits are over-generous and vulnerable to abuse, and such issues cannot be understood or discussed without reference to the past. Similarly, the implications of high employment for labour discipline and wage bargaining have been debated for decades and it is instructive to compare the conclusions reached at different times and in different circumstances.

The first task, however, is to clarify whose opinions and attitudes are being discussed. It is unlikely, for example, that the perceptions of unemployment held by politicians are influenced by the same factors as those held by the general public or the unemployed themselves; nor do their attitudes necessarily change at the same time or in the same way. There are a number of possible classifications, but for the present purpose it is most helpful to distinguish between three groups. The first comprises those directly responsible for the formulation of government policy — the ministers and senior officials of the relevant departments. Secondly, there are the informed commentators in the press, parliament and the major pressure and interest groups. The most obvious interest groups are the CBI and the TUC, though the importance of their views depends upon which party is in power and the length of time they have been in office (Keegan and Pennant-Rea, 1979, pp. 121–4). Less publicised, but central to the concerns of this chapter, are what Pringle calls the 'opinion forming circles'. These consist of economists from a number of different institutions who maintain 'a rich variety of formal and informal links' with the policy-makers and who 'concern themselves with evaluating current policy'. He argues that these groups perform a 'filtering function . . . inter-mediating the results of research in so far as they may be relevant to policy and keeping an eye on what is thought to be within the range of political acceptability'. In this way, they exercise a crucial influence upon the politician's perception of what is 'practical' and what is 'impractical', 'politically possible' and 'politically impossible' (1977, p. 61). The membership of such circles is not static, and it will be seen later that changes in the relative prestige of particular individuals and bodies have been enormously significant in recent years.

Finally, there is the general public, a not inconsiderable proportion of which is now unemployed. It is, of course, extremely difficult to assess attitudes on such an issue as unemployment. An obvious problem is the extent to which the press shapes, or merely reflects, public opinion. Moreover, popular opinion is not homogeneous. Banting argues, for example, that politicians distinguish clearly between 'elite and mass opinion' (1979, p. 80), while Addison warns that the latter may be somewhat nebulous: 'Judgements about the movement of popular opinion have always to be tempered by the knowledge that many people never change their opinions, while some never have any to change' (1977, p. 15). Nevertheless, there are several indicators of popular sentiments to which the policy-makers respond — most notably poll data, press comment and the number and tone of the letters they receive.

It should be emphasised perhaps that this chapter does not seek to provide a detailed picture of the processes by which a particular set of policies has been adopted or rejected.[1] Rather, the intention is to examine the ways in which the issue of unemployment has been defined and discussed and the factors that have influenced the priority accorded to it. Above all, it tries to explain why high unemployment seemed to have become tolerable, even acceptable, to many politicians, economists and voters by the late 1970s.

THE 1944 WHITE PAPER

The obvious starting point is the 1944 White Paper on *Employment Policy*. This, as noted earlier, formally acknowledged the government's responsibility for the maintenance of high employment. As such it marked a decisive break with the defeatism of the inter-war years, and it both expressed and reflected a genuine conviction that the end of war need not signal a return to the dole queues of the 1930s. Even so, the White Paper was something of a paradox — enormously significant in political terms, yet relatively conservative on economic policy. It was far from being an official endorsement of Keynesian interventionism, and the proposals of the White Paper are often compared unfavourably with the more radical ideas put forward by Beveridge in *Full Employment in a Free Society* (1944).

The conservatism of the White Paper is usually explained as a result of the need to reconcile the views of those economists in the Economic Section of the War Cabinet who were eager to adopt Keynesian techniques and those officials and politicians who remained more than a little sceptical. Addison, for example, describes the outcome as a 'masterpiece of compromise' between the two (1977, p. 243). Two points need to be extracted from what was a long and complex debate. First, even those who were most suspicious of the new techniques accepted that something along those lines would have to be attempted after the war. Second, not even the most enthusiastic Keynesian believed that unemployment could be reduced to the levels that were actually achieved in the 1950s.

Unemployment fell to around 100,000 during the war, and by 1944 there were few in Whitehall who did not fear the consequences of a return to mass unemployment after the Armistice. In January, Churchill was warned by his advisor Lord Cherwell that 'the British people will not tolerate a return to the old figures. They will demand that the Government produce a programme for achieving comparable results in peace' (PRO, 1). The urgency of the problem was underlined by the reports of both Mass Observation and government intelligence, and it seemed to many that the issue transcended party politics and even threatened the survival of democracy itself. Hitherto, unemployment had been abolished in only two circumstances: political dictatorship or war. Neither constituted a satisfactory model. In Britain in 1944, five million people were either in the armed forces or were working in munitions. More generally, the war had required the introduction of rationing, compulsory saving and an unprecedented degree of central control over the movement of labour and materials (Gowing, 1972). Thus unemployment had been conquered only in societies in which there were extensive state controls and a drastic reduction in personal freedoms. But could it be removed without such controls? As Meade noted in an early memorandum, the question was whether high employment could be sustained in a 'free society' in which people were free to choose what proportion of their income they saved, the items on which they spent it or the places and occupations in which they worked (PRO, 2). Moreover, if unemployment could not be reduced, would such freedoms survive? In October 1943 *The Economist* was convinced that 'If liberal democracy is not compatible with full employment, then it is liberal democracy that will go' (3 October 1943), while five months later *The Times* considered that the success of employment policy could well determine the 'fate of democratic institutions' (16 February 1944).

These fears explain why a Coalition formed for the prosecution of the war decided to produce a White Paper on such a long-term question, though its publication was hastened by the intense hostility that Beveridge aroused amongst many people in Whitehall, and their determination to pre-empt his forthcoming book (Robbins, 1971, p. 190; PRO, 3).

Another influence upon attitudes towards unemployment at this time was the way in which the experience of war had undermined the belief that a substantial proportion of those out of work were either unemployed or simply malingering. This belief had been widely held between the wars, and as late as 1938 *The Times* had demanded that attendance at training or industrial centres be made compulsory for 'chronic or constantly unemployed young men'. In a 'considerable number', it claimed, 'there is a slackness of moral fibre and of will as

well as of muscle. . . . There is no genuine desire for employment and
no willingness to undergo either instruction or training' (22 February
1938). In its *Report for 1938* the Unemployment Assistance Board
estimated that around 25–30 per cent of its applicants under 30 had
become resigned to their fate and had stopped looking for work
(UAB, 1939, p. 49). However, the Board was relatively liberal in its
attitudes. It recognised that 'apathy and listlessness are bred in men
by long periods of unemployment' and proposed that a clause be
inserted in contracts for public or defence works to the effect that a
number of jobs had to be reserved for the long-term unemployed
(p. 51). In consequence, it was entitled to see the wartime rate of
unemployment as a vindication of its stand, and its *Report for 1944*
made the point with some relish: 'In the towns of Rugby and Reading
there were no applicants in receipt of unemployment assistance by
September 1944, in the city of Leicester there were 6, in the city of
Birmingham there were 8, in the city of Bristol about 30; and in the
whole London Civil Defence Region . . . about 500' (AB, 1945, p. 15).

The sense of national purpose and social cohesion created by the
war led many to adopt a relatively generous view of human nature.
Beveridge, for example, concluded that 'the first condition of human
happiness' was 'the opportunity of useful service' (1944, p. 122).

It cannot be overemphasised, however, that the phrase 'a high and
stable level of employment' had a very different meaning in the early
1940s from that which it acquired in later years. In 1942, for example,
Beveridge's report on *Social Insurance and Allied Services* was based upon
the well-publicised assumption that mass unemployment could be
abolished (1942, p. 164). Beveridge meant by this that unemployment could be kept to an average of 8½ per cent, and even this
relatively modest target was too optimistic for the committee of
officials set up to examine the Report:

> It is impossible not to feel warm sympathy with the standpoint from
> which such opinions are expressed, and not to share the hopes under-
> lying Sir William Beveridge's assumption as to post-war employment.
> But recollections as to the actual course of events after the last war must
> obtrude themselves [PRO, 4].

In the event, the figure of 8½ per cent was taken as the basis of the
National Insurance Act of 1946, and it also appeared in an appendix
to the 1944 White Paper. However, it was never adopted as an official
target. Indeed, the idea of a target figure was specifically rejected by
the Steering Committee on Post-War Employment, a group of civil

servants and economists whose report formed the basis of the White
Paper. At their second meeting they agreed that they should do no
more than 'examine probable conditions and available remedies' and
try to assess 'within the broadest limits' what those measures might
achieve (PRO, 5). This approach led to some comic stonewalling
when the White Paper was debated in the Commons in June 1944.
Pressed to define what the government would regard as a reasonable
level of unemployment, Sir John Anderson, the Lord President, told
the House: 'There are figures in the Report, and there were figures, if I
may venture to refer to them, in the Beveridge Report. It will be found
also that when the Government's proposals for dealing with social
insurance are submitted, there will be figures there' (*Hansard* vol. 401,
col. 405).

This caution should be seen in context. In 1935 it had been expected that unemployment would average 15½–16 per cent between
1936 and 1945, and reach a peak of 20 per cent in 1940 (Howson and
Winch, 1977, p. 136). Moreover, the state of the economy was
scarcely encouraging. During the war Britain had accumulated massive debts, run down her export trades and sold off many of the
overseas investments that had been an important source of invisible
earnings in the inter-war years. As a result she was bound to face a
huge balance of payments deficit once the war was over (Dow, 1970,
p. 14).

Nonetheless, much of the caution expressed by economists about
postwar employment stemmed from their analysis of the problem,
and it is striking to note how far the ideas and emphases that have
become popular in recent years were discussed at this time. Meade,
for example, stressed that 'effective mobility of labour' was essential,
since without it an increase in demand would involve a 'greater and
greater danger of inflation'. An expansion of demand would also do
nothing to reduce frictional seasonal or — in the short run —
structural unemployment (PRO, 2). The views of Keynes himself
have been the subject of a protracted — and heated — debate, but it is
clear that he did not envisage unemployment falling below 6 per cent
(Hutchinson, 1977; Kahn, 1976). The only exception was Beveridge,
who by 1944 had come to believe that it could be cut to an 'irreducible
minimum' of 3 per cent, a belief greeted with some scorn in Whitehall
(Harris, 1977, pp. 335–40; PRO, 6).

One aspect of the problem worried everyone: what would be the
impact upon wage bargaining and factory discipline of a higher
demand for labour? As E. H. Carr wrote in *The New Society*, the worker

was unlikely 'to abandon the time-honoured view of his relations with the employer as a hard-fought bargain at the moment when the bargaining conditions have turned so dramatically in his favour. If he is now reproached with behaving selfishly, he can reply that that is how he has been taught to behave' (1951, p. 50). The need for moderation in wage claims was stressed in the White Paper (p. 18) and in virtually every discussion of the subject. There seemed no alternative, however, but to rely on the common sense of the trade union leaders and the patriotism and responsibility of the individual worker. Here again, the experience of war was seen as a cause for optimism (Beveridge, 1944, pp. 200, 250).

These hopes and fears related to the longer term. Few doubted that there would be a boom after the war as industry reverted to peacetime working and struggled to meet the pent-up demand for consumer goods. This is what happened and the postwar Labour government was confronted with an acute shortage of labour, especially in the export industries. It made repeated appeals to married women to rejoin the workforce (*Economic Survey*, 1947, p. 27), while a number of more drastic solutions were canvassed. In January 1947, *The Times* called for the 'selective immigration of up to 500,000 foreign workers during the next few years', while Professor Robbins challenged the miners to admit 100,000 to the pits (17 January 1947). In September, the Cabinet even considered banning the football pools so that the women they employed could be diverted into 'more useful employment' (PRO, 7).

Most remarkable of all, however, was the attempt to clamp down on the so-called work dodgers towards the end of 1947. In August, the government had been forced to announce the reintroduction of a number of labour controls. Henceforth all vacancies were to be filled through the Exchanges and anyone registering as unemployed could be directed into essential work (Ministry of Labour, 1948, pp. 32–6). Popular resentment at the controls was increased by the belief that there existed large numbers of people who performed no useful service but were exempt from compulsion, and the TUC insisted that the government ensure 'equality of sacrifice' by setting to work those who were 'making no contribution to the national well-being' (PRO, 8). As a result, Attlee told the Commons on 6 August that the government would 'take all action open to us against these "spivs" — as I think they are called — or other drones' (*Hansard*, vol. 441, col. 1508). Though often referred to in the same breath, the 'spivs' and the 'drones' were quite distinct. The spivs were black marketeers, while a drone was anyone of working age who was not gainfully employed. The latter were primarily middle or upper class. In the words of one rather sceptical official, they were 'either the "born tireds" or "the Duke's daughter" who is alleged to ride hounds [sic] every day and dance throughout every night' (PRO, 9). It was these 'idle rich' who aroused the anger of the labour movement, especially as their numbers were constantly exaggerated because of defects in the manpower statistics. In September, for example, the Minister of Labour, George Isaacs, told the TUC that 'some of these gentry' could be likened to eels and butterflies: 'Eels are slippery, and butterflies are hard to catch and not much use when you have caught them' (TUC, 1948, p. 355). The government's proposals were given front-page coverage in the press. The *Daily Mail*, for example, told its readers that the Ministry of Labour had 'a plan to comb out all Britain's "spivs" ', adding that 'Scotland Yard will be asked to help to round up the work dodgers'. It claimed that the Ministry expected to add 'at least 1,500,000 people to Britain's labour force by these means' (7 August 1947).

The reality was less dramatic — and less effective. By the Registration for Employment Order of November 1947, persons employed as street traders or in such establishments as amusement arcades or night clubs were required to register at the Exchanges and to accept more useful work if it was offered to them. A similar obligation was laid upon the 'drones'. The order aroused tremendous opposition. It was denounced as an infringement of personal liberty and as an unnecessary witch-hunt that would penalize the innocent. For the Liberals, Frank Byers claimed that since Attlee's 'unfortunate speech . . . stigma is bound to attach to the people who register', while Quintin Hogg — a future Conservative Lord Chancellor — said that the Order would be ignored by 'anybody who has the spirit of a free Englishman' (*Hansard*, vol. 445, cols. 487, 501). In fact, the order had little impact and only a handful of people were placed in essential work (Deacon, 1980). Nonetheless, allegations of work dodging were to recur in later years, though the roles of accuser and defender were to be played by different people.

THE YEARS OF 'FULL EMPLOYMENT'

Apart from the 'freak' winter of 1946/7, unemployment rarely exceeded 2 per cent during the lifetime of the Attlee government. It is not clear when ministers ceased to regard such levels as part of a temporary boom and began to believe that they could be sustained in normal conditions. In March 1951, however, the Economic and Social Council of the United Nations asked member countries to establish a 'full employment standard'. Gaitskell, Britain's Chancellor of the Exchequer, adopted a rate of 3 per cent, though he stressed that this figure was on the high side to allow for changes in external factors outside the government's control. It did not mean that they would 'allow unemployment to reach 3 per cent before taking vigorous counter action' (*Hansard*, vol. 485, col. 319).

Not surprisingly, Labour made much of its success, and Nicholas (1951) records that a 'dominant theme' of the elections of 1950 and 1951 was the Conservative Party's attempt to persuade the voters that it would not allow a return to the 1930s. This promise was kept after their victory in 1951. The new Chancellor was 'Rab' Butler, who had done much as head of the Conservative Research Department to adapt Conservative thinking and policies to the postwar political climate (Butler, 1971, pp. 126–53). As Chancellor his policies were so similar to those of Gaitskell that *The Economist* created the famous composite character of 'Mr Butskell' (13 February 1954), and the term 'Butskellism' came to refer to the apparent consensus on economic policy that characterised the 1950s and early 1960s.

A central feature of this consensus was the priority accorded to full employment, and in this respect Butskellism appeared to be remarkably successful. Between 1948 and 1966 unemployment averaged 1.7 per cent, and for much of the period the number of long-term unemployed was negligible. It is doubtful if this was solely, or even primarily, due to the policies pursued (Mathews, 1968). Nonetheless, the politicians and economists not unnaturally claimed the credit and thereby created the impression that such rates could be maintained indefinitely. Certainly, the 'opinion forming circles' were dominated by the neo-Keynesian belief that full employment and economic growth could be maintained through the exercise of demand management, and this policy was adopted by successive governments (Hutchison, 1977, p. 27). Occasionally a Chancellor would appear to give greater priority to price stability or to the external value of the pound, the best-known example being Peter Thorneycroft in 1958 (Brittan, 1971, pp. 211–18). Such episodes, however, were infrequent and short-lived. As Dow records, 'Conservative governments, no less clearly than Labour governments before them, in fact put full employment first as the main object of policy' (1970, p. 70).

The emphasis given to full employment stemmed in part from the commitment of the politicians involved. This was especially true of Harold Macmillan, who succeeded Butler as Chancellor of the Exchequer in 1955 and was subsequently Prime Minister from 1957 to 1963. His experience as MP for Stockton-on-Tees in the 1930s made a deep impression on Macmillan, and he retained an 'instinctive and violent' dislike of the idea of using unemployment as a weapon against inflation. Indeed, officials in Whitehall were said to count the number of times he mentioned Stockton in any one week (Blackaby, 1978, p. 25; Brittan, 1971, p. 203).

There is no doubt, however, as to the importance of unemployment to the electorate. As *The Economist* wrote in 1952: 'There is no other issue of public policy, except only that of war and peace, that is charged with half the emotional content that the inter-war years injected into employment policy' (29 March 1952). Unemployment retained its significance well into the 1960s. Goodhart and Bhansali examined the findings of Gallup and National Opinion Polls and found that the number unemployed was by far the most important influence upon the recorded popularity of the governing party. Indeed they observed that 'the apparent impact of changes in unemployment upon political popularity seems too large to be plausible' (1970, p. 63). Butler and Stokes also found a 'marked relationship' between unemployment and the government's lead in the polls, and concluded that 'unemployment probably provided the leading test of a Government's handling of the economy' from 1945 to the mid-1960s (1974, p. 391).

This was certainly the view of contemporary politicians. On the rare occasions when unemployment did rise much above 2 per cent the result was always a furore and an expansionary budget. As Brittan has noted, between 1951 and 1970 'Chancellors behaved like simple Pavlovian dogs responding to two main stimuli: one was "a run on the reserves" and the other was "500,000 unemployed" — a figure which was later increased to above 600,000' (1971, p. 455). A good example of the importance attached to the unemployment statistics was the general belief that the sharp rise in the number out of work during the winter 1958/9 would lead to a Labour victory in the forthcoming general election (*The Economist*, 18 October 1958; 24 January 1959). In fact, the total rose from 400,000 in July 1958 to over 600,000 in February 1959, a rate of 2.8 per cent. In March, Labour attempted to increase the government's embarrassment by tabling a censure motion in the Commons. During the debate, however, Iain Macleod, the Minister of Labour, announced that the figures for

March would show a drop of 58,000. As *The Times* reported, 'The effect on the Government's ranks was electric. Their jubilation knew no bounds . . . [they] . . . cheered and went on cheering in crescendo' (19 March 1959). A few weeks later Heathcoat Amory brought in what Brittan has called 'the most generous budget ever introduced in normal peace-time conditions', and unemployment had returned to 400,000 when the Conservatives won the election in October (1971, p. 224).

The fact that there were so few long-term unemployed meant that there was little talk of unemployables. In 1956 the National Assistance Board interviewed the 32,175 men and women under 60 who were claiming on the grounds of unemployment. The proportion whose attitude towards work was considered to be 'not keen' or 'workshy' was 35 per cent, and three-quarters of these were recognised to be handicapped in some way (NAB, 1957). Similar results were obtained from a smaller survey in Scotland two years later (NAB, 1959).

It is not surprising, therefore, that little attention was paid to allegations of malingering or scrounging. Similarly, there was virtually no pressure to reduce benefits for the unemployed. From 1958 onwards *The Economist* was arguing that benefits should be graduated according to previous earnings (20 December 1958), and in 1963 it proposed that the basic national insurance benefits be doubled. This would be an 'entirely sensible thing to do' since it would 'pump new purchasing power . . . to precisely the right people, in precisely the right places . . . at precisely the right time' (12 January 1963).

In summary it can be seen that by the early 1950s the three groups mentioned in the introduction had come to share three assumptions, and that these assumptions dominated discussion of unemployment in subsequent years. Firstly, that it was possible for governments to keep unemployment below Beveridge's 'irreducible minimum' of 3 per cent without seriously prejudicing their other economic objectives. Secondly, that since it was possible to maintain this level of employment any government that failed to do so would be rejected by the electorate. Thirdly, that only a tiny proportion of the unemployed were unemployable and that the number who preferred living on benefit to working was equally small. To these should be added a fourth assumption, which was voiced less often but which had been implicit in every discussion of unemployment since the 1930s. This was the assumption that it involved substantial hardship for those affected, not only because it caused a drop in income but because of the stigma experienced by someone without work. The existence of these assumptions has been documented, albeit briefly. The remainder of the chapter examines what happened to them.

FIRST DOUBTS: THE LATE 1960s

The idea of a turning point is always dubious and it is impossible to point to a single date on which attitudes began to change. Moreover, once that change had begun it is by no means certain that it was a continuous, uninterrupted process.

Even so, the deflationary measures introduced by the Labour government in July 1966 were of special significance. As early as 1961 a growing concern at the structural weakness of the economy had led to a revival of interest in economic planning and the establishment of such bodies as the National Economic Development Council (NEDC) (Fry, 1975, p. 11). In 1964 Labour had entered office committed to the view that a more comprehensive use of such planning was necessary for the restructuring of industry and the achievement of a faster rate of growth. In consequence, the 1966 deflation not only led to an increase in unemployment from 1.1 per cent in July to 2.3 per cent in November, but marked the abandonment of a strategy that had been held to be essential if full employment was to be preserved in the future. Indeed, Crossman suggests that the Chancellor, James Callaghan, had come to accept the 'Paish thesis' and believed that an unemployment rate of 2–2½ per cent would curb inflation and avoid the need for devaluation (1976, p. 123). The pound was finally devalued in November 1967, but unemployment remained above 2 per cent as Callaghan's successor, Roy Jenkins, imposed a further squeeze on the economy in order 'to make devaluation work' and divert resources into exports (Blackaby, 1978, pp. 43–51).

The rise in unemployment did not escape criticism. Before 1967, it was attacked as wasteful and unnecessary by a number of pro-devaluation economists, including Samuel Brittan and Peter Jay. After devaluation, the criticism came mainly from the left and focussed upon the priority given to the balance of payments. In July 1968, for example, Alastair MacIntyre claimed that Labour's acceptance of half a million unemployed represented 'the strange death of social democratic England' (*The Listener*, 4 July 1968). However, the opposition was muted for a number of reasons. Perhaps the most important was the fact that the new unemployment was not called unemployment. It was widely believed in the mid-1960s that a pre-condition of a faster rate of growth was a 'shake-out' of labour from the service industries into manufacturing. This was to be achieved through the introduction of a Selective Employment Tax, and redundancy payments and earnings-related benefits were also brought in to lessen the burden of unemployment upon the worker. The process was described by the then Prime Minister, Harold Wilson, as one of 'redeployment'. He told the Labour Party Conference in October 1966 that 'industrial change without labour redeployment is a meaningless concept', and that the government was introducing 'the social conditions in which redeployment could be made tolerable'. Even the July measures were described as a 'once and for all opportunity to break out of the miserable cycle we inherited', which 'by creating the opportunity for a new breakthrough in export production . . . holds out the surest guarantee we have of full employment for a generation' (Labour Party, 1967, pp. 164, 167). This argument proved to be remarkably effective and, in Brittan's words, 'the vast majority of articulate public opinion discussed the measures in this newly invented language' (1971, p. 33).

A second, closely related reason was that unemployment had been displaced by the balance of payments as the central measure of the government's performance. Butler and Stokes argue that 'Mr. Wilson virtually invited the country to judge his government by whether it could overcome Britain's trade deficit. The Conservatives, believing that Labour could not do so, to a remarkable extent agreed upon this test' (1974, p. 399). Finally, popular attitudes may well have been influenced by the stories of scrounging that received considerable publicity in the summer of 1968. These concerned the abuse of benefits by young people congregating at seaside resorts, and led to the introduction of new restrictions on the benefits paid to unskilled single men (Meacher, 1974).

Nonetheless, the changes that occurred in the late 1960s were minor compared with those that came later. Writing in 1971, for example, Brittan said that the alternative to devaluation in 1967 was unemployment at 4 per cent: 'Apart from its human consequences, a setback of this kind would have had a catastrophic effect on profits and investment' (p. 372). As late as March 1974, Blackaby told a conference that there was a 'risk that politicians will discover that they can run the country with 1 million unemployed without committing electoral suicide' (1976, p. 303). The last remark is perhaps the most striking indication of the extent to which perceptions of unem-

ployment have been transformed in recent years, and the speed with
which that transformation has taken place.

THE 'NEW' UNEMPLOYABLES

In *The Growth Merchants* Pringle argues that the groups of top officials,
economists and journalists who comprise the economic establishment
resist new ideas until the arguments for their adoption seem overwhelming. Then the conversion is rapid: 'once fashion changes,
everybody discovers that this is what they really thought all along'
(1977, p. 66). This was certainly the pattern in the case of unemployment, and it is essential, therefore, to examine the impact upon
both the 'experts' and the politicians of the new theories of unemployment discussed in chapter 2 by Brian Showler.

It is important not to over-generalise. Substantial differences
remain within both of the major parties, and between the Labour
Party and the TUC. Equally, people may arrive at similar conclusions for very different reasons. Nonetheless, it remains true that a
major reason why unemployment was not a more important issue in
the 1979 election was the simple fact that the leading politicians on
both sides had lost faith in their ability to provide full employment
and consequently chose to campaign on other things. This loss of faith
owed much to the influence of the monetarists who, as Brittan
explains, challenge the idea that governments have the power to fix
the level of unemployment by monetary and fiscal policy: 'The most
fundamental of the monetarist contentions is that governments do not
have such powers. The minimum sustainable level of unemployment
is, on the contrary, determined by the functioning of the labour
market' (1975, p. 15).

It is helpful at this stage to distinguish two strands of the argument.
Firstly, it is contended that the nature of unemployment has changed
and that the official statistics exaggerate the degree of slack in the
economy. Secondly, it is argued that the unemployment that does
exist cannot be removed by the demand management policies adopted
in previous years.

The belief that the unemployment statistics have become less
accurate as an indication of the state of the labour market is shared by
many non-monetarists. For example, Laslett has recently calculated
that in 1973 an unemployment rate of 2–3 per cent would have
corresponded to full employment as it was understood before 1966,

and that the figure had risen to 2.99 per cent in 1977 (Scott and Laslett, 1978, p. 134). Nonetheless, the argument is primarily associated with monetarist writers, and one aspect of their case is of great relevance to this chapter: the remarkable revival of the notion of the 'unemployables'.

The recent debate was initiated by John Wood in his 1972 monograph, *How Much Unemployment?* Wood believed that the concept of a hard core of unemployed was 'an unhappy one for the economist', but estimated that it numbered around 200,000. These were not necessarily unemployable — that would have meant negative unemployment for much of the postwar period — but were 'in varying degrees less employable than normal workers'. In short, the hard core had 'soft edges' (pp. 31, 36). Wood's suggestion that those unfit for normal work should be placed on a separate register was rejected as impracticable by an Inter-Departmental Working Party set up by the then Prime Minister, Edward Heath (DE, 1972, p. 18). In 1975, however, Wood published a second, more polemical study, *How Little Unemployment?* By this time the number of difficult cases had increased and the soft edges had hardened dramatically: 'There can be absolutely no advantage in parading as "unemployed" between 200,000 and 250,000 who are in varying degrees unemployable, and who can *never* be brought into permanent employment by any rate of monetary expansion' (p. 35).

This assertion was based primarily upon a study of the characteristics of the unemployed conducted by the Department of Employment in June 1973 (DE, 1974). A sample of 1 in 30 of those on the unemployment register was drawn and their case papers were examined by the department's officers.[2] Around 30 per cent of the sample were considered to be 'somewhat unenthusiastic for work'. This was a similar proportion to that found in 1938 and 1956, when the numbers out of work were very different. Not surprisingly, those with a poor attitude towards work were those who had been out of work for a long time and had only a poor chance of securing a job in the near future. The problem, as the department recognised, was that there was no way of telling from the survey whether the association was because long spells of unemployment sapped enthusiasm or because the length of unemployment was determined by the respondent's attitude (p. 213). However, the department did stress the subjective nature of the assessments, and pointed out that a follow-up survey in January 1974 had revealed that over a third of those described as having a poor attitude towards work had in fact secured employment in the intervening six months (p. 215). A further enquiry was carried out in June 1976. At that time 24 per cent of men and 13 per cent of women were assessed as being 'somewhat unenthusiastic for work' (DE, 1977a, p. 559). In this case, however, the follow-up study discovered that the subsequent employment record of these respondents was only marginally different from that of people described as being 'keen or relatively enthusiastic for work' (DE, 1977b, p. 967).

It is true that a survey conducted by Political and Economic Planning (PEP) in 1976 found that at least 9 per cent of the unemployed judged themselves to be too old or too unfit to cope with a job (Daniel and Stilgoe, 1977, pp. 10 and 14). It also found, however, that the morale of such people increased remarkably once they had reached 'the magical age for formal retirement' (p. 62). This would support the contention that their classification of themselves was often a rationalisation, a response to the stigma of unemployment. More recently, a study conducted for the Manpower Services Commission (based on 'depth interviews' with fifty long-term unemployed people) suggested that

> there comes a point when people can no longer sustain their motivation in the face of continued rejection, heightened awareness of their own shortcomings, disillusionment with the job finding services, belief that all available options have been covered and a knowledge that jobs are scarce anyway. [Colledge and Bartholomew, 1980, p. 10]

This conclusion would not have seemed surprising thirty years ago. In 1943, Ernest Bevin told the Cabinet,

> Protracted unemployment itself is a major cause of demoralisation and is perhaps the least understood. A man who remains compulsorily unemployed for many months gradually adjusts himself to a lower level of mental and physical activity. He does so in self-protection and often he develops a protective ailment: he loses heart, and the better man he is the more he deteriorates, for the chief sufferers in this respect are those to whom it is morally intolerable to be one of the unwanted. [PRO, 10]

It should be emphasised that not all of those who subscribe to the existence of large numbers of unemployables share either the extremism of Wood's position or the immoderation of his tone (Brittan, 1975, pp. 78–9). Nonetheless, it is contended here that both the historical and contemporary evidence demonstrate that 'unemployability' is a function of the tightness of the labour market. It is quite wrong, therefore, to present the findings of the department's enquiries as evidence that the nature of unemployment has changed, though this does not mean that none of the criticisms that have been made of the statistics is valid.

There are, of course, a number of other reasons that are put forward to explain why the unemployment rates of the 1950s and 1960s can no longer be achieved. These are discussed — and sometimes challenged — elsewhere in this book. They do not, however, account for all, or even most, of the unemployment experienced in recent years, and it is here that the second strand of the argument has been influential. Demand management no longer seems to work.

THE CONSERVATIVES AND THE GREAT DEBACLE

In the case of the Conservative Party, the events of 1972–74 were of critical importance. The dramatic failure of economic policy in these years had a profound impact upon many of the party's leaders and led to a sharp change in their attitude towards economic management in general and unemployment in particular.

There are a number of studies of the period, and only a bare outline of events can be given here (Harris and Sewill, 1975; Pringle, 1977; Blackaby, 1978). In March 1972 the Conservative Chancellor, Anthony Barber, made substantial cuts in personal taxation as part of a programme of demand expansion that was intended to achieve a growth in output of 5 per cent p.a. It is generally agreed that this relatively ambitious target was a response to the rise in unemployment, which had reached the emotive figure of one million during the winter. Indeed, Keegan and Pennant-Rea refer to the 'wholesale panic in the ranks of the Government' at this prospect (1979, p. 199). It is possible that when it took office in June 1970 the government had anticipated that some rise in unemployment would have a beneficial effect in damping down wage claims. In 1972, however, a million unemployed was seen as both electorally disastrous and an obstacle to securing trade union acceptance of changes in industrial relations (Cosgrave, 1978, p. 91). In any case, the expansion was warmly applauded by many of the experts, including the National Institute of Economic and Social Research (NIESR), which had long been regarded as the most influential and prestigious advocate of demand management. The NIESR similarly welcomed the decision to move to a floating rate of exchange in the following June and the introduction of an incomes policy in November.

At first the policy appeared to be succeeding. By the first quarter of 1973 output was rising at over 8 per cent p.a. and the expectations this aroused have been mercilessly chronicled by Pringle (1977, pp. 40–55). In March, *The Economist* declared that Britain was 'no longer on the brink of an economic miracle but right in the middle of one', while in May the NIESR saw 'no reason why the present boom should either bust or have to be busted so long as the additional instruments of incomes policy and the floating exchange rate are retained'. In September, *The Economist* declared that Britain was now 'two thirds of the way' towards her 'economic miracle', but the government was becoming apprehensive as the balance of payments plunged into deficit and shortages of labour and materials began to develop. In consequence it had already begun to restrict demand before the onset of the oil crisis in October marked the beginning of a series of disasters for the Conservatives that culminated in their defeat in the general election of February 1974. In November, their incomes policy came under direct challenge from the miners whose overtime ban led to the proclamation of a three-day week on 13 December. Four days later the Chancellor was forced to outline what his Special Assistant later called 'one of the most deflationary budgets ever introduced' (Harris and Sewill, 1975, p. 46). On 4 February 1974 it was announced that the miners had voted 4 to 1 in favour of a total strike. It was the final blow. Three days later Edward Heath called the election for 28 February. It returned a Labour government, albeit one without an overall majority.

The 'dash for growth' ended in a mounting trade deficit, rising inflation, industrial conflict and defeat at the polls. This debacle was due to a combination of factors, and their relative importance has been — and remains — the subject of heated debate. The important point here is that the position of the monetarists was enhanced; it was they who had urged caution in 1972 and it was their predictions that seemed to have been borne out. As Britain's rate of inflation accelerated during 1974, the star of the 'sound money' men rose accordingly (Brittan, 1977, pp. 34–40; Keegan and Pennant-Rea, 1979, pp. 131–2). By the same token, the prestige of the NIESR was dented, particularly in the eyes of the Conservatives.[3] More specifically, the fact that the rate of unemployment did not fall below 2.6 per cent during the boom appeared to vindicate the critics of the official statistics. It was later argued that the labour shortages of 1973 were due to the rate at which demand increased, rather than its overall level (Blackaby,

1976, p. 285), but the fact remains that the NIESR and others seriously overestimated the slack in the economy.

There were very few Conservative rebels in 1972 or 1973 (Norton, 1978), but the reaction to Heath's defeat was swift. By far the best-known, and most important, example was Sir Keith Joseph's conversion to monetarism in the summer of 1974. Having failed to win support in the Shadow Cabinet in July, he made his famous speech in Preston on 5 September. This was a succinct resumé of the monetarist analysis and a frank 'confession' of past mistakes: 'We were dominated by the fear of unemployment. It was this which made us turn back against our own better judgement and try to spend our way out of unemployment, while relying on incomes policy to damp down the inflationary effects' (*Times*, 6 September 1974). Their greatest error was to believe that the million unemployed in 1972 were the 'gaunt, tight-lipped men in caps and mufflers' of the 1930s. They were not. Over 30 per cent were unemployable or voluntarily unemployed and another tenth, he claimed, were working and signing on or practising some other form of fraud. Over and above these groups, there were those who were simply changing jobs, or were receiving an occupational pension and had to register as unemployed in order to qualify for a state pension at 65. Only when all these people were excluded could the extent of real unemployment be estimated. This unemployment was concentrated in a few parts of the country and amongst certain categories of workers. This meant, Sir Keith continued, that it could not be removed by a general reflation. Indeed, successive governments had created 'desperate inflation by too often expanding demand above supply as a single cure for a whole variety of forms of unemployment'. Instead, the approach should be to fix demand at a level consistent with stable prices and to work to reduce unemployment by measures to encourage labour mobility, expand training and improve the incentive to work.

Coming on the eve of a second general election, the speech did not endear Sir Keith to his colleagues, and at the time the only leading Conservative to support him was Margaret Thatcher (Butler and Kavanagh, 1975, p. 94). It is not surprising, therefore, that his views became far more influential after her election as Leader in February 1975. In any case he was only the most prominent of a clutch of former ministers who took it in turns to disavow the policies of the Heath government. By the time of the 1979 election the new approach was firmly entrenched, and the Conservative Manifesto contained a range of proposals designed to lessen union power, restore work incentives and encourage mobility. It did not promise full employment. To do so would have run counter to its whole philosophy. Sir Keith had told the Bow Group in August 1978, 'Full employment is not in the gift of governments. It should not be promised and it cannot be provided' (1978, p. 20). Thus the Conservatives took office committed to the view that the central overriding objective of economic policy should be a reduction in the rate of inflation. Introducing his Budget on 26 March 1980, the Chancellor, Sir Geoffrey Howe, declared that it was an 'illusion to suppose that we have any real choice between defeating inflation and some other course . . . Nothing, in the long run, could contribute more to the disintegration of society, the destruction of any sense of national unity, than continuing inflation' (*Financial Times*, 27 March 1980). In response to criticism that its policies would lead to a rise in unemployment, the government could point to the fact that the number out of work had more than doubled under Labour.

LABOUR AND THE GREAT INFLATION

Parties are not monolithic, and it would be facile to suggest that 'monetarism' now enjoyed total support amongst Conservatives, though the dissidents remained quiet during the first months of the new government. In the Labour Party, dissension is seldom a quiet affair, and here the position is complicated by a number of factors. Firstly, both the TUC and a significant number of Labour MPs were formally committed to the adoption of the so-called 'alternative strategy', which involved physical controls on imports and a far greater degree of state intervention in industry. Secondly, the Labour government introduced a range of job creation schemes and employment subsidies. The effectiveness of these is considered in chapter 4, but in political terms they served to demonstrate to the back benches and the Party Conference that 'something was being done about unemployment'.

Perhaps the greatest complication, however, is that only rarely did the Labour government explicitly acknowledge that its stance had changed. Indeed, several of its leaders continued to denounce unemployment as passionately as before. Michael Foot, for example, told the Party Conference in 1975 that it could only be conquered by the 'supreme quality in politics, the red flame of socialist courage' (Labour Party, 1976, p. 166). The speech was greeted with prolonged cheering, though in reality the government had already abandoned its commitment to full employment.

To a large extent, that commitment had been abandoned because the problem of unemployment had been swamped by that of inflation. In the summer of 1975, unemployment again rose to a million, but this time the rate of inflation was over 25 per cent. According to the economic nostrums of previous decades this could not happen, but it had. Moreover, the spectre of hyper-inflation began to be discussed in the same terms as unemployment had been in 1944.

In November 1974, Wilfred Beckerman had written that full employment could no longer be the main objective: 'the threat of runaway inflation is now too great, and with it the threat to demo-cratic government in this country' (*New Statesman*, 1 November 1974). However, the most forthright exponent of what came to be called the 'democratic doom' thesis was Peter Jay, then economics editor of *The Times*. In July 1974 he had predicted that democracy would come to an end in Britain by '1980, give or take a couple of years' (*Times*, 1 July 1974). A year later he saw 'no reason to change' his mind (*Times*, 18 June 1975), and in December 1975 his Wincott Memorial Lecture set out the case in full (Jay, 1976). The essence of the argument was that since trade unions were able to demand a monopoly price for labour, they reduced the demand for labour and thus created unemployment. Political pressures then forced the government to expand demand to 'mop up' that unemployment. This generated inflation, which fuelled further wage demands, which in turn led to more unemployment and ultimately a fresh expansion of demand. Each cycle was characterised by a higher and higher rate of inflation. Incomes policy could offer only temporary relief, and the only solution was for governments to abandon the objective of full employment, which Jay believed to be politically impossible. Parkin similarly expected that the pressure to reduce unemployment would become irresistible and that 1977 would see 'inflation rates into the 20s and 30s rather than the mere teens' (Parkin, 1975).

The relevance of all this is that it created a climate in which reflation was unthinkable and in which unemployment came to be seen as a lesser evil. The most gloomy forecasts were soon confounded by the fall in the rate of inflation that followed the introduction of an incomes policy in mid-1975. Nonetheless, the view that unemploy-ment was increasingly due to workers pricing themselves out of jobs was no longer confined to market economists. James Callaghan, newly installed as Prime Minister, told the Labour Party Conference in October 1976 that the 'cosy world . . . where full employment could be guaranteed by a stroke of the Chancellor's pen' was gone. Unem-

ployment was 'caused by paying ourselves more than the value of
what we produce'. It was generally believed that the speech was
drafted by his son-in-law, Peter Jay. Certainly, there is a familiar ring
about the assertion that the option of spending 'your way out of a
recession . . . no longer exists, and that insofar as it ever did exist it
only worked on each occasion since the war by injecting a bigger dose
of inflation into the economy' (Labour Party, 1976, p. 188).

It has already been noted that the authors of the 1944 White Paper
had laid great emphasis upon the need for wage restraint. By the late
1970s the wheel had turned full circle as a number of Keynesian
economists had come to give much of the credit for the success of the
1950s to trade union leaders who had remembered the unemployment of the inter-war years and moderated their demands accordingly.
The implication of this argument was that a return to full employment would have to await a major change in union attitudes, a reform
of the machinery for wage determination, or both (Scott and Laslett,
1978). The possibility of either was considered remote, and the emergence of this thesis reinforced the fatalism with which unemployment
was viewed.

There remains the question of why the government did not adopt
the 'alternative strategy' espoused by some of its supporters. One
reason was that such measures were precluded by the IMF loan that
was negotiated at the end of 1976. It is unlikely, however, that the
IMF loan was more than a convenient excuse for ministers opposed to
the strategy in any case. Certainly it had few, if any, supporters
amongst the 'opinion forming circles'. Perhaps the most intriguing
question is why the TUC did not exert more pressure over the issue.
Lewis Minkin's work has illustrated the complexity of intra-party
politics and the difficulty for outsiders of estimating the significance of
particular resolutions or decisions. As he says, it is all 'a question of
priorities and push' (1979, p. 229). Nonetheless, it seems likely that
many members of the TUC either did not believe in the strategy —
and had had it forced upon them by their own conferences — or did
not feel sufficiently sure of their ground to challenge the relevant
ministers.

The stance adopted by the TUC is extremely important because,
with the Conservative opposition advocating the policies discussed
earlier, it meant that the Labour government was under no great
pressure to seek further remedies for unemployment. Another,
perhaps crucial, factor was that the issue no longer seemed to excite
much interest amongst the electorate.

UNEMPLOYMENT AND THE PUBLIC

Public attitudes towards unemployment appear to have changed dramatically in recent years. Any government facing the electorate in the 1950s against the background of a million unemployed would have expected to suffer a massive defeat. As late as 1972 the Conservatives panicked at the prospect. Yet the issue could hardly be said to have dominated the campaign in 1979, even though the number out of work was over a million and a quarter, and had exceeded one and a half million during the lifetime of the government.

There are two relatively straightforward explanations for this that should be considered first. One is that attitudes have not changed, but that in 1979 the electorate was not offered a choice. It was the parties who determined the issues and they chose to give greater prominence to such questions as inflation, union power and law and order. It is true that the results of the election did seem to indicate that unemployment remained an important issue in the less prosperous parts of the country. Nonetheless, the proposition that concern with unemployment is as high as before is contradicted by a wealth of evidence, some of which is discussed below.

The second 'obvious' explanation is that unemployment is no longer the same thing as it was ten or twenty years ago. The social security provision is now so generous, the 'hidden economy' so extensive and the tax burden on the lower paid so onerous that much unemployment is now voluntary. Hence it is naive to expect it to arouse discontent.

At first sight there would appear to be considerable evidence to support this claim. The real value of benefits has increased substantially over the past thirty years, and they have also risen relative to net earnings. There are a number of difficulties about making comparisons over such a long period, but in 1948 the national assistance paid to man with two young children represented less than half of the net earnings of the average male manual worker. In 1977 the supplementary benefit he received was equivalent to over 66 per cent. In the case of a man with four children the proportions were 47 per cent and 75 per cent respectively.[4] These figures relate to average earnings and the difference between benefits and the incomes of the lowest paid will be smaller. Thus, the Supplementary Benefits Commission (SBC) told the Royal Commission on the Distribution of Income and Wealth that whilst the number of cases in which benefit equalled or exceeded earnings was small, there were 'many more cases in which an unemployed man returning to work could well be demoralised by the narrowness of the gap' between the two (SBC, 1977). Further evidence is provided by the 1979 MSC study. Almost a quarter of those interviewed regarded pay 'as the dominant constraint on the job flexibility'. Many of these people felt that the amounts they were likely to earn were 'inadequate compensation for the rigours of a job and the expenses incurred by travel and extra food' (Colledge and Bartholomew, 1980, p. 9). Moreover, the popular belief that increasing numbers of the unemployed are abusing the benefit system is strengthened by the rise in the number of prosecution for fraud from 15,400 in 1975 to 19,000 in 1976 and to 26,000 in the year ended February 1978 (DHSS, 1978b, p. 19). Evidence on the hidden economy is necessarily vague, but some assessments of its size have been dramatic. In April 1979, for example, Sir William Pile, Chairman of the British Revenue Board, estimated that it amounted to £11,000 m, or 7½ per cent of GDP (*Financial Times*, 9 April 1979). More recently, the Central Statistical Office put the figure at £5,000 m (CSO, 1980).

These figures must be treated with caution. Whilst the hidden economy clearly exists, tax evasion by those in work is far more important than abuse of benefits by the unemployed. Similarly, it is not clear whether the increase in the number of prosecutions — which relates to all claimants and not just the unemployed — is due to a growth in fraud or improved detection. In 1977 the Labour government introduced a number of additional measures to detect abuse, including a 50 per cent increase in the local manpower committed to this task. At the end of the year, the minister responsible, Stanley Orme, said that it was this 'more vigorous approach' that accounted for the bulk of the rise in prosecutions (Deacon, 1978, pp. 129 and 133). Furthermore, the figures should be seen in context. In its evidence to the Public Accounts Committee, the Department of Health and Social Security said that detected frauds amounted to £2.6 m, or 1p in every £32 paid out. It added that there was 'no reason to suppose' that undetected frauds were more than 'two or three times' greater (PAC, 1976–7, Q2626). It is true that when the Conservative Minister for Social Security, Reg Prentice, announced a new anti-scrounger campaign in February 1980 he anticipated savings of up to £50 m a year (*Guardian*, 15 February 1980). At the time, however, the official responsible for the estimate described it as a 'speculative figure'.[5] Finally, it should be remembered that the value of the supplementary benefits left unclaimed by unemployed people was £90m in 1977 (SBC, 1979, p. 103).

Similar qualifications must be made to the alleged erosion of work incentives. The increase in short-term benefits accounts for little of the growth in unemployment (chapter 2, p. 42). The rise in the value of supplementary benefits paid to the long-term or recurrent unemployed may have caused some of them to relax their efforts to find work. However, this 'better off' problem would only apply to men with several children; hence it would be expected to alter the distribution of unemployment rather than increase its actual amount. Daniel and Stilgoe (1977) did find evidence of such a 'benefit effect', but added that it represented a 'cruel poverty trap' since unemployment still created intense misery and was 'most miserable for married men with dependent children' (p. 46). This is confirmed by a number of studies that have documented the poverty and deprivation of the long-term unemployed (chapter 5, pp. 157–160).

Thus the increase in benefits does mean that the living standards of the unemployed are higher than they were in the 1950s and 1960s. Equally, the introduction of redundancy payments has lessened the impact of unemployment in some cases (Fryer, 1980). Nonetheless the evidence does not support the claim that the nature of unemployment has changed so dramatically as to make its neglect unsurprising.

In fact, the indifference displayed towards unemployment has a number of causes. To some extent it stems from a popularisation of the factors already discussed. Undoubtedly, the rapid increase in the rate of inflation in 1975 frightened many people and diverted their attention from unemployment.[6] In addition, unemployment was presented more and more as an international problem, the solution to which was beyond the capacity of a single government. Runciman has argued persuasively that the reason why unemployment did not generate more discontent in the 1920s was that it 'seemed the consequence, not of a detectable blunder but rather of an incurable disease. Its victims did not appear to be the victims of remediable injustice so much as an Act of God' (1966, p. 61). Much the same could be said of the mid-1970s, and the mood of resignation could only be deepened by the coverage given to predictions that the introduction of microelectronics — 'chips' — would lead to massive job losses in the not too distant future.

The impression that unemployment was beyond the control, and hence not the fault, of the government was reinforced by its association with strikes and irresponsible wage demands. A good example of this was the closure of the car factory at Speke on

Merseyside (Beynon, 1978). This aroused little opposition, largely, it is suggested. because the plant had acquired an unenviable reputation for strikes. absenteeism and poor quality work. An even clearer example is the coverage given to the announcement of 25,000 redundancies at BL Cars in September 1979. The *Daily Telegraph* expressed little sympathy with 'Over-manned strike-racked plants' and argued that the whole company should be placed 'into receivership' (11 September 1979). The *Daily Mail* similarly referred to 'the lame mammoth . . . kept alive by wishy-washy patriotic sentiment and massive and continuing doses of taxpayers' money' (11 September 1979).

Another factor of immense significance was the furore over 'scrounging' that erupted in the summer of 1976 and lasted into the spring of the following year. Stories of widespread and gross abuses of benefits received extensive coverage in the press and had an enormous impact (Golding and Middleton, 1978). As Hugo Young wrote in the *Sunday Times*, it gave unemployment a 'new political colour. It may be a vote-loser not merely because it is a symptom of economic stagnation . . . but also for the opposite reason: because the man in the factory . . . sees himself as more of a victim than the man in the dole-queue' (29 October 1977).

The causes of 'scroungerphobia' are complex and have been discussed elsewhere (Deacon, 1978). Nonetheless, two points are clear: first, that there exists a deep-rooted hostility towards the unemployed, second, that hostility has become more intense at certain times and has then been reflected and further inflamed in the press. This hostility cannot be explained without reference to societal values, and especially to the importance of work as a source of social status. Neither the spiv in the 1940s nor the tax dodger in the 1970s aroused anything like the same indignation as the drone or the scrounger. It is equally obvious that the press plays an important role, a point made with some force by Reg Prentice in April 1971. He told the Commons:

> The myth about widespread abuse is perpetrated by some of the most reactionary newspapers in the country and is used by the Tories for party reasons. Apart from the damage done in general, awful damage is done to individual people in need, because these myths help to create among some people . . . the sense that there is something shameful about applying for benefits to which they are entitled. [*Hansard*, vol. 816, col. 89/90]

Perhaps the most striking point, however, is that public concern at abuse seems to increase in periods of high or rising unemployment. This was true of the 1920s (Deacon, 1976), the late 1960s and 1976/7. In other words, people on benefit are most likely to be condemned as scroungers at the time when it is most difficult for them to get a job. This paradox is often explained by the fact that during such periods the population as a whole experiences a fall in its standard of living. Thus Donnison (1976) argued that the 'panicky cruelty' of 1976/7 stemmed from a loss of confidence in economic growth:

> Once you convince people that their living standards will not rise . . . they are compelled to realize that any help given to poorer people must be paid for by real reductions in their living standards. When in addition you allow tax thresholds to fall . . . to a point at which even the poorest workers are paying income tax, it is not surprising that the springs of compassion dry up pretty fast. [1976]

It was the fall in the tax threshold, coupled with the effects of pay restraint, that really fuelled the scrounging controversy of 1976. Its effects were aptly described by Jon Akass in the *Sun* (17 November 1976) as a 'new national irritability'. The same irritability, in fact, that was generated by Roy Jenkins' 'two years hard slog' or the restrictions and frustrations of austerity. The drone, the layabout on the beach and the scrounger all served as a focus for discontent and a scapegoat for wider ills. Similar episodes are likely to occur in the future. Certainly the basic antagonisms and misconceptions are still there. In 1978, for example, a survey carried out for the Institute for Economic Affairs found that people believed that unemployment benefits accounted for a greater proportion of government expenditure than health, education or pensions.[7] The crucial point for this chapter, however, is that in 1976 the post-bags of MPs were filled with letters complaining, not about the high level of unemployment, but about the incomes and activities of the unemployed.

CONCLUSION

It was stated at the outset that the perceptions of unemployment held by different groups may be influenced by different factors and change at different times. This is what has happened in the years since the war.

The politicians and the 'opinion formers' moved swiftly from the caution and hesitations of the 1940s to the swaggering confidence of the 'full' employment era and then just as rapidly to the fatalism of the mid-1970s. That fatalism stemmed from the impact of a range of theories, all of which denied the ability of governments to determine the level of employment through demand management and which appeared to have been vindicated by the collapse of the Barber boom of 1972/3. These theories had much in common with the fears and beliefs that were current in the 1940s. Indeed, this chapter provides ample illustration of the accuracy of Routh's picture of economists 'flowing' between economic ideas (chapter 2, p. 31).

In the 1940s, however, politicians were under immense political pressure to seek new solutions. They were not under such pressure in the late 1970s. To some extent this reflects the interrelationship of the perceptions held by the different groups. The fact that no one seemed able to reduce unemployment generated a pervasive fatalism amongst the public that curtailed protest and created a political climate in which experiment was inhibited and commitment eroded. The apparent acceptability of high unemployment to the electorate had other causes too: benefits were more generous, memories of the 1930s were fading and the popular press continued its enthusiastic pursuit of scroungers.

At the time of writing (March 1980) there seems little reason to expect that a rise in unemployment in the early 1980s will provoke a significantly greater response. The 1980 Budget reduced the real value of national insurance benefits for the unemployed, but none of the other factors are likely to change or to recede in the near future. It is possible that the collapse of a particularly 'deserving' firm — or industry — might induce a mood of protectionism amongst the press and public and thereby lead to a shift in government policy. Equally, the government may come to regard the social tensions generated by unemployment as a serious threat to the preservation of law and order. Nonetheless, there would appear to be little prospect of either of these things happening in the foreseeable future. It will be difficult for the present leadership of the Parliamentary Labour Party to mount a credible campaign against unemployment, given its record in office (Coates, K., 1979; Coates, D., 1980). Nor would such a campaign necessarily command widespread popular support. The experience of the late 1970s has confirmed the lesson of the 1930s: unemployment is divisive. It is, in the phrase made famous by Beveridge, 'the misery that generates hate'.[8] People preoccupied with the preservation of their own jobs have less time and less concern for those without work. This trend can only be reinforced by the growing concentration of unemployment in particular regions, industries and types of worker. All of these things are helping and will continue to help British society to adjust to high unemployment. At the beginning of the 1980s the question most often asked was not, what happened to full employment? It was, why did anyone believe that it would be sustained? This is, perhaps, the most tragic feature of current British politics.

Notes

1. Keegan and Pennant-Rea (1979) provide a fascinating account of the workings of the 'economic policy machine'. Their analysis is broadly compatible with that of Pringle (1977) whose more polemical study was concerned with events between 1971 and 1974. The extensive literature on policy formation in general is summarised and discussed in P. Hall *et al.* (1975).

2. The department's use of the word 'survey' to describe this exercise is misleading. The claimants were not interviewed by the officers making the assessments, though men aged 55–64 were contacted to see if they were receiving a pension from their employer (DE, 1974, p. 211). The same procedure was followed during the 1976 enquiry. (DE, 1977a, p. 560).

3. In February 1980 the Conservative government reduced its grant to the NIESR by a half in real terms, a decision interpreted by the *Financial Times* as a 'ministerially approved sign of the erosion of [the Institute's] former pre-eminence' (25 February 1980). Another consequence of the 1973 debacle was the rise in the prestige of a small group of analysts in the City who had consistently opposed Barber's monetary policy. Henceforth they began to have an enormous influence over financial market opinion on such questions as the level of government spending and its implications for interest rates, and thereby over government policy. In 1977 the Labour Chancellor Denis Healey was said to have remarked that a 'few young men in stockbrokers' offices are now virtually in charge of economic policy' (Keegan and Pennant-Rea, 1979, pp. 131–2). The important point, of course, is that these 'young men' had no faith in demand management.

4. SBC (1978) p. 21. In its *Report for 1978* the SBC has changed the basis of its estimates, though the value of benefits relative to earnings did drop between November 1977 and November 1978 (1979, p. 28).

5. BBC Radio 4 (13 March 1980). The figure of £50 million appears to

have been based upon an estimate of the amount saved by each officer in earlier years. The new campaign involved the recruitment of an additional 1000 officers, bringing the number employed on this work to 5400.

6. Mosley (1978) argues that the opinion poll data for 1953–75 show a trend for inflation to become more important at a time when prices are rising, and for unemployment to become more important when that is increasing. He also suggests, however, that there is a long-term tendency for inflation to become more important.

7. A sample of nearly 2000 men and women were asked to estimate how much was spent on each of seven items of government expenditure out of every £100 spent on all seven. The average guess was £20 on unemployment benefits, compared with £17 on education, £16 on health, and £11 on pensions. The actual proportions for these four are 2 per cent; 24 per cent; 17 per cent and 22 per cent respectively (Harris and Seldon, 1979, pp. 123–6).

8. The phrase comes from Charlotte Brontë's novel *Shirley*. It was spotted by Beveridge's wife and appears on the title page of *Full Employment in a Free Society* (1944).

CHAPTER 4

Unemployment and Government Manpower Policy

Michael Hill

INTRODUCTION

The way we evaluate public manpower policies depends upon the way in which we view unemployment. In chapter 2 Showler explored the development of economic theories of unemployment. He outlined the way in which classical economic theory adopted a 'natural' view of unemployment that attributed it to an imbalance between supply and demand, which should not occur, except in the short run, if economic forces are allowed to operate in an unfettered way. Clearly if this is the case then the role of government is only to ensure that these forces do operate. Such 'manpower' policy as it develops should have as its sole function the checking of any attempts to restrict the adjustment of labour supply to demand. The curbing of trade union activity, through for example the Combination Acts of the early nineteenth century, might, in this light, be interpreted as manpower policy. In the same light, the role of the Poor Law, particularly as envisaged by the 1843 Act, was to ensure, through the 'workhouse test' and the principle of less eligibility, that the supply of labour was maintained however low the price level at which demand and supply were balanced. In Marxian terminology, the concern was to maintain a reserve army of labour.

Here, then, is one conception of the role of 'manpower policy', a minimalist one in which government merely has a role to ensure that 'irrational' men do not interfere with the working of the 'rational' economy. It is outlined here as a bench mark for the consideration of other policies, but also as a view of the role of policy that still influences the way in which unemployed people are treated in capitalist societies.

Towards the end of the nineteenth century the adherents of the 'classical' theory began to acknowledge that it was perhaps necessary for government to play a role in assisting the 'natural' market system to operate more smoothly. In particular, the problems of adjustments, in the short run, began to be regarded as sufficiently serious to justify interventions. One such problem concerned the linking of 'sellers' of labour with the 'buyers'. To this end systems of Labour Exchanges were created. In 1909 the British government decided to improve upon the early initiatives of voluntary organisations and local government and set a national network of Exchanges. Thus evolved an approach to manpower policy motivated largely by economic considerations.

Such an approach was clearly open to further elaboration as faith in the working of the market waned. Nineteenth-century theory had seen labour as an essentially flexible factor of production — one unit of labour was regarded as readily interchangeable with another. As, in the twentieth century, economic theory began to come to terms with the complexity of markets and the complications associated with large units of capital, so it began to recognise that labour was a complex phenomenon too. Attention began to be given to the problems of securing, training and maintaining a stock of 'human capital'. In other words, still firmly in the impersonal traditions of economics a recognition developed of the importance of attention to the preservation of labour as a resource. This implied that manpower policy should be concerned with training, occupational guidance and assistance with occupational mobility. In this tradition, however, it is still debatable whether these issues should be tackled by independent entrepreneurs developing their own manpower policies or whether governments have a role to play in relation to 'human capital'.

The final ingredient in the developing of the 'economic' case for manpower policy came with the influence of Keynesian theory, and with the recognition of the fact that the impact of trade unions upon money wage levels was something with which economic thinking had to come to terms. In short, it was recognised that there were sources of inflationary pressure in the economy that governments might seek to control, and that 'active' approaches to the deployment of manpower might play a part in this activity.

These, then, are some of the economic considerations for the evaluation of the role of manpower policy in relation to unemployment. It may be seen in terms of its contribution to the maintenance of the 'natural' balance between supply and demand. Even for those who have little faith in the feasibility of the original 'classical' ideal, it may still be judged in terms of its contribution to flexibility in the system: the removal of manpower 'bottlenecks', the prevention of 'over-heating' in a fully employed economy, and the long-run maintenance of an effective labour force.

But the evolution of political views on unemployment in the twentieth century has not merely involved a concern to stabilise the capitalist economic system. Manpower policy may also be evaluated in terms of the contribution it makes to the maintenance of full employment, with that regarded as a desirable political end without reference to economic considerations. The concern about unemployment has been an important element in the socialist critique of capitalist economics. In the 'command' economies of the Eastern bloc it is claimed that full employment has been made a paramount goal. This entails other economic complications that are not our concern here. It also seems to imply limitations upon the freedom of action of the suppliers of labour as much as upon those who 'buy' it. The political challenge to democratic socialists has been how to achieve the goal of full employment whilst maintaining a measure of flexibility for both buyers and sellers of labour. This has involved trying to embed the active manpower policies dictated by economic considerations in an economy in which labour demand is kept high and accompanied by a social security system that, by protecting the workless, preserves a measure of freedom for the, hopefully temporary, casualties of the economic system.

Manpower policy need not, however, be examined in terms of its contribution either to economic efficiency or to full employment. It may be evaluated in terms of its contribution to the relief of the suffering experienced by the casualties of the economic system, and to the reduction of the disadvantages of those casualties. Its role may not merely be to ensure that unemployment is not experienced disproportionately by a limited number of individuals, but also to help those who tend to secure the worst jobs to advance up the economic ladder. Such social goals may be seen as contributions to economic efficiency and/or the achievement of full employment, but they may also be treated as ends in themselves. One of the major debating points about contemporary manpower policy concerns the extent to which goals of this kind can be achieved even in the absence of full employment.

This introductory section has, therefore, suggested a number of considerations for the evaluation of manpower policy. They include, in particular, its contribution to economic efficiency, the part it may play in the achievement or maintenance of full employment, and its role in alleviating social and economic inequalities.

THE DEVELOPMENT OF BRITISH MANPOWER POLICIES

The following discussion, which focusses upon contemporary British manpower policy, relates to these considerations. It will be suggested that in the past few years Britain has begun, in common with the United States and most European countries, to adopt a wide range of 'active manpower policies'. Reference has already been made to the setting up of a system of Employment Exchanges in 1911. Once this had been created, some of the social problems of destitution associated with unemployment could be tackled through an insurance scheme to protect workers in trades where work was generally available but was from time to time disrupted by economic fluctuations. The Exchanges were required to run, and therefore police, the unemployment insurance scheme set up in 1911 (see Harris, 1972 and 1977).

Between 1911 and the Second World War continuing evidence that the economy could not readily absorb all who wanted work kept the issue of unemployment on the political agenda. There were strong pressures that forced the erratic development of income maintenance measures for the unemployed (see Gilbert, 1970; Deacon, 1976). But manpower policies changed very little in Britain. A few very limited job-creation and training schemes were developed, but economic orthodoxy was against the heavy public expenditure on the creation of work that, by the middle of the 1930s, began to characterise the policy response in the United States. Only as preparation for war began to alleviate unemployment did official thinking begin to come to terms with its structural character. This change of approach is primarily associated with the Keynesian revolution in economic thinking that linked unemployment with under-consumption and urged governments to spend, and if necessary to unbalance budgets, to get out of a recession. The primarily policy response required was in this case a macroeconomic one, rather than a form of manpower policy *per se*. However, at the same time, the special problems of certain regions, particularly those where employment had depended upon declining heavy industries, also began to be recognised (see Booth, 1978). Hence during the Second World War a British strategy for full employment was developed that involved a combination of Keynesian economic management with special measures to stimulate investment in declining regions.

In the late 1940s and early 1950s, Britain was enabled to dismantle the direct controls over industry and the use of labour that had been adopted during the Second World War without succumbing to high unemployment. How much this was due to successful Keynesian policies, and how much to the Cold War and the continuing involvement of the United States in European economic affairs, is a question beyond the brief of this chapter. It did, however, enable British governments to continue to adopt a comparatively passive stance on manpower policies. Efforts were made to stimulate employment in the deprived regions, to develop New Towns as centres of industry in place of the congested urban areas, and to curb investment in areas where labour was scarce. Individual enterprises, including public employers like the health service and London Transport, actively sought to attract labour not only from the more depressed regions but also from overseas. But the public employment service itself played a minor part in employment policy. The Labour Exchanges continued to be closely identified, as they had been in the inter-war period, with the administration of benefits for the unemployed.

In the late 1950s concern developed about the imperfections of Keynesian economic policies. They tended to be inflationary, though mildly so by the standards of the 1970s. In Britain, rising inflation at the high point of the trade cycle brought with it balance of payments problems. Government checks to prevent these getting out of hand were seen as inhibiting smooth and effective economic growth. Economy management was characterised by a 'stop–go' pattern, in which there were problems about the amount and timing of the measures used alternately to check and stimulate the economy (see Brittan, 1971). Policies were sought that would help to smooth out the trade cycle and its effects. One such group of policies were manpower policies. The tendency of the economy to 'overheat' and for inflation to accelerate was partly attributed to skilled manpower shortages. It was argued that 'active manpower policy' could involve the use of 'contra-cyclical' policies. A valuable form of public spending to get the economy out of the trough in the trade cycle could be measures to train the unemployed and boost public employment. This would then increase the supply of trained manpower and improve the public services infrastructure to ensure really effective growth once industry revived. The United States, forced by much more uneven economic prosperity, led the way in efforts like this. In Europe, the OECD played an important role in the dissemination of these new ideas, and Sweden was prominent amongst the innovating countries (See Bakke, 1969; OECD, 1964 and 1970; Mukherjee, 1972).

British policies were slow to change. Fiscal policies remained the key regulators in the 1960s, with the efforts to shift the balance between the regions enhanced in various ways through taxation and subsidies. An important ingredient of Swedish active manpower policy was assistance to people to leave the depressed northern counties. Britain continued to prefer to seek to encourage jobs to move to people. Some efforts were made in Britain to stimulate training in this period, with the development of a grant and levy system that aimed to secure public investment in training where firms were unwilling to train for their own needs. But the basic structure of the manpower policy system remained unchanged.

Then, on coming to power in 1970, the Conservatives decided to restructure the public employment service as part of their efforts to make public administration more dynamic. A consultative document *People and Jobs* (DE, 1971) declared that the employment service needed to be modernised. The Employment Exchanges were too identified with a limited service to the unemployed. A new active service needed to be created that would seek to have a real impact upon the working of the labour market. The responsibility for man-power policy was given, in 1973, to the specially created Manpower Services Commission (MSC), containing representatives of both sides of industry. The implementation of policy was taken out of the hands of the Department of Employment and given to two agencies, the Employment Services Agency and the Training Services Agency, which were to be separate accounting bodies, required to operate, as far as possible, on similar lines to private enterprise. While these new organisations were, by and large, staffed by civil servants from the Department of Employment, the government initiated an effective reappraisal of its role in manpower policy, and created a system that was to be very much more open to the development of new initiatives. The structure created in 1973 was modified a little in 1978, with the creation of a new administrative structure within the MSC, consisting of three divisions: Employment Services, Training Services and Special Programmes.

While the institutional reorganisation of 1973, and the trans-formation of both the employment and the training functions that followed it, seemed to represent the British conversion to 'active manpower policy', by the 1970s the economic context had begun to change quite radically. In 1971/2 there was a trough in the trade cycle much more severe than any since the 1930s, and the 'peak' that followed it, in 1973/4, involved a relatively inadequate recovery in the level of unemployment. Then in 1975 unemployment rose well above the low levels of 1971/2, without there being the strong check to the rate of inflation that had always previously been expected in such a situation. The government became involved in fighting unemployment and inflation simultaneously. Inflation was checked from the high levels of 1975/6, but unemployment continued to rise until 1978. Now, in 1980, both unemployment and inflation are rising again. The measures the government is using against the latter are expected to worsen unemployment. In other words, the British manpower policy initiatives of the 1970s occurred against the background of rising unemployment and inflation. Any comparison with the Swedish contra-cyclical active manpower policy of the 1960s — attempting to iron out the modest ups and downs of the trade cycle in a context of nearly full employment — is inappropriate. On the other hand, the American experience of superimposing social goals upon comparatively modest economic goals, particularly in the efforts associated with the 'poverty programme', remains very relevant.

A brief reference must be made to the main ingredients in the economic context because of their implications for new developments in manpower, policies (for a more detailed discussion, see chapter 2). The two phenomena of a less controllable trade cycle and the ending of the simple 'trade-off' between inflation and unemployment have not been experienced by Britain alone. International economic developments associated with changing world trade and the increasing power of the oil-producing nations are clearly of relevance. Internally, in Britain and elsewhere, the development of sophisticated institutionalised wage bargaining has also played its part in altering the relationship between unemployment and inflation. Another widely shared feature is the decline in the capacity of industry to absorb workers: new investments are increasingly capital intensive. Service industries, including the public sector, have been the main growth areas of employment. They are highly sensitive to deflationary measures, particularly when those measures are motivated by a concern to curb activities that make no contribution to exports. Finally, on top of this catalogue of economic problems, unemployment has been exacerbated by an increase in the potential size of the labour force. Two phenomena are of note here: the bulge of

young people reaching working age (with no corresponding bulge of
people retiring) and the increased desire to married women to secure
employment. In short, three groups of factors contribute to the
current problem of unemployment — associated with difficulties in
the management of the economy, the changing character of industry,
and the nature of labour market participation (Leicester, 1978;
Lindley *et al.*, 1978; *DEG*, May 1978). The following discussion of
British manpower policies needs to be considered in the context of
these factors.

The Job-Centres

At the heart of the work of the employment services are the 'Job-
Centres', which seek to link potential employees with employers.
These are the modern heirs of the older Employment Exchanges,
which are gradually being phased out. The service is committed to
moving away from what it sees as 'the dole queue image' (DE, 1971).
Job-Centres are located in commercial and shopping centres with
'shop fronts' containing displays of job information. There is an
emphasis upon self-service, in which individuals select suitable jobs
from open display. All they have to do then is to ask a member of the
Job-Centre staff to give them further details and put them in touch
with the employer. The member of staff may ascertain that the job
seeker is qualified for the job in which he is interested but is not
expected to operate a pre-selection filter. There is also what has been
described as a second-tier service of employment advisers available to
people who want some advice in addition to access to the self-service
system (Lewis, 1978). These advisers will interview people who register at a Job-Centre because they are unemployed, and will re-
interview them if they remain unemployed for some time. By this
means the Job-Centres are able to continue to monitor the operation
of the unemployment benefit scheme, and to initiate the process by
which sanctions are applied against unemployed people who are
deemed to be 'voluntarily unemployed'.

The aim of the new system of Job-Centres is to compete effectively
with the private employment agencies (which charge employers fees),
which have expanded considerably in recent years. When the system
was set up, concern was expressed about the low proportion of
vacancies, particularly vacancies for the more skilled jobs, notified to

the public employment services. The MSC states that:

> The concept of the Job-Centre was developed with a view to meeting the needs of the labour market and to putting right the main deficiencies of the public employment service as they were then perceived to be. The aim was to bring together all the local services of the Employment Service in a way which was administratively practical, operationally efficient and publicly visible and convenient.
>
> Through the Job-Centre premises programme it was planned to remedy the deficiencies of the local office network, which had been established with the administration of unemployment benefit very much in mind. The local offices in the network were neither designed nor sited to encourage job seekers not claiming unemployment benefit to make use of them, and many were housed in buildings that were old, and below present-day standards. [MSC, 1978a, p. 7]

This is from an evaluation of the progress of the Job-Centre programme, published in March 1978. At that time, 418 Job-Centres were operational, handling about a third of all the vacancies notified to the employment service. In addition, improvements had been made to a considerable proportion of the old Employment Exchanges. In 1977, in a situation of high unemployment that was likely to make it very difficult for any agency to secure the notification of vacancies, it was estimated that the employment service was being given details of about 30 per cent of all vacancies. But 'in Job-Centre areas 33 per cent of vacancies had been notified compared with about 25 per cent elsewhere' (MSC, 1978a, p. 11). The evaluation also suggested that Job-Centres were more efficient at filling vacancies.

The Job-Centre programme has been perhaps the primary innovation in the public employment service. Alongside it the special services to professional and executive employees have been developed into a separate system — Professional and Executive Recruitment — charging fees to prospective employers and offering a range of specialised advisory and pre-selection services. The intention was to make this part of the system self-supporting; but this has been difficult to realise. Again, clearly, it has had to start its life in a very difficult job market. It is not helped by the fact that the public service does its own recruiting, and employers of several other professional groups make no use of its services. The Public Accounts Committee has questioned 'the wisdom of spending public money to compete in this area with commercial firms who appear to be providing an adequate service' (House of Commons, 1978, para. 78).

Services for the disabled

One important employment service, developed long before the modernisation of the main service, is that for disabled people. This was initiated early in the Second World War but received its main impetus from the Disabled Persons (Employment) Act of 1944. There is a semi-specialised cadre of employment service staff, the Disablement Resettlement Officers (DROs), working from Job-Centres, employment offices and some hospitals. DROs are informed of all new vacancies notified and may keep a job back from the normal display system if they know of a disabled person for whom it is suitable.

A rehabilitation service helps to prepare people after illness, injury or unemployment to re-enter the labour market. Short courses are run during which such individuals have their work potential assessed and efforts are made to enhance their motivation and self-confidence. Some of the seriously disabled may be provided with sheltered employment. There are about 13,000 such places, about 8000 of which are in a state-managed and subsidised company (Remploy), while the remainder are in subsidised voluntary organisations and in workshops run by local authorities. There are also two occupations 'reserved' for the disabled — lift attendants and car park attendants. However, automation has made heavy inroads into the opportunities they provide.

A recent development has been subsidies to facilitate the employment of disabled people — to pay journey-to-work costs, to enable the adaption of equipment and premises, to help with the development of self-employment, and to 'introduce' disabled people to employers reluctant to take them on. These developments are small in scale, and, in particular, the experimental job introduction allowance paid to employers willing to take on disabled people for a trial period of six weeks has been used most sparingly. Considerable use is also made of the training facilities, discussed later in this chapter, to help the disabled.

However, the main device to assist with the employment problems of the disabled is the 'quota system'. Since 1946, firms with over 20 employees have been required to ensure that 3 per cent of their workforce are 'registered disabled' people. The DROs, who are available to help all disabled people whether registered or not, maintain this Register and are expected to enforce the quota. There has been a general preference for seeking compliance with the quota rule by voluntary means. It is markedly under-enforced and there is a high unemployment rate amongst registered disabled people. MSC reluctance to enforce the quota is clearly linked with reservations about the employability of some of the people the DRO service is expected to help. The position is clearly complicated by the wide and loose definition of disability used. It is feared that if measures other than persuasion were used to enforce the quota employers would merely cease to use the employment service. Then, while legislation could be enacted to force them to take on disabled people it is quite likely that many employers could discover unregistered disabled people within their existing workforces with disabilities sufficient to justify registration. When the quota scheme was set up, a high proportion of the disabled had clearly visible physical conditions; today an increasing number of those who seek the help of the DROs have 'spinal conditions, mental handicaps, organic nervous conditions and various age-related impairments (arthritis, rheumatism, heart disease)' (MSC, 1978b, p. 17).

Disabled people are often reluctant to be formally 'registered', seeing this as stigmatising and thus perhaps damaging to their job prospects. The official definition of a disabled person in the 1944 Act is 'a person who, on account of injury, disease or congenital deformity is substantially handicapped in obtaining or keeping employment . . .'. This implies a definition resting upon two notions — of being disabled and of having employment problems. The relationship between the two is unclear, particularly when the more controversial disabilities are involved, and especially when the illness is psychological. Accordingly one alternative way of developing the DRO service would be to give it a general responsibility for the 'hard to place'. This would imply, however, a clear departure from the organisation of the service to operate the quota system. Instead, the MSC is experimenting with special advice and counselling services for the non-disabled 'hard to place'. It stated, in autumn 1977:

> . . . for an experimental period of one year, some 50 extra staff will be introduced, mostly specially trained employment advisers, who will work in areas with a substantial number of people with special employment needs. Just under half of the additional staff will work in inner city areas. Many of the disadvantaged jobseekers to be dealt with by the new service will be younger men and women, those over 50 and members of ethnic minorities who have been long unemployed. Other jobseekers with special employment needs such as ex-prisoners and single parents of families will also be covered. [MSC, 1977a, p. 32]

These are not propitious times for such an experiment and the
evaluation of its results has been inconclusive. Meanwhile a thorough
re-examination of the services for the disabled has been initiated.
Early in 1979 the MSC published a 'discussion document' on the
quota scheme, examining its shortcomings and setting out some of the
ways in which it might be changed or replaced. Amongst the alternatives set out are:

> Modification of the quota system, such as the revision of the existing
> figure, and its variation for certain types of work;
> Reform of the system by widening the range of people protected by it or
> by particular focusing upon hirings over a year instead of the compo-
> sition of the whole work force;
> Altering the sanctions enforcing the system, by requiring below quota
> firms to notify vacancies or imposing a levy upon them;
> Replacing or supplementing the quota system with anti-discriminatory
> legislation, statutory obligations upon employers to make special
> provisions for disabled workers, or special rights for the disabled;
> The abolition of special statutory provisions. [MSC, 1979b]

The document expounds some of the disadvantages attached to some
of these ideas, particularly those relating to the ambiguities inherent
in definitions of the disabled for formal enforcement purposes. But the
function of the document is to solicit comments and no options are
acknowledged to be closed.

Services for young people

Before 1974 the provision of employment services to those under 18
was the responsibility of a separate youth employment service. The
split between the youth service and the adult service was widely
criticised. The government considered the option of abolishing the
former, but in the end decided that the youth service, renamed the
careers service, should continue to operate as a source of vocational
and employment assistance within the schools and should be available to help school leavers if they preferred to keep in touch with it for
a time. At about the same time, the limitation of the service to help for
the under-18s was abandoned. The new system requires close liaison
between the local staff of the MSC and the careers service, run by the
local education authorities. Careers officers have been closely involved in the planning of new policies for unemployed teenagers,

which have begun to loom very large in the provision for young
people. (They will be discussed separately below.)

Training

The main training venture of the MSC is the Training Opportunities
Scheme (TOPS), which provides a wide range of training courses to
help individuals into areas of employment for which their earlier
education and training has not equipped them. In 1976 nearly 90,000
people completed these courses and a target of 100,000 places for 1980
has been set. (MSC, 1977a). The considerable expansion of industrial
training (only about 18,000 trainees went through the system in 1971)
has depended upon the provision of large numbers of places in
colleges of further education. This growth of training has not occurred
as a deliberate response to unemployment; indeed the expansion plan
was made before the recent rapid rise in worklessness. However,
politicians have been prepared to refer to this growth alongside their
other 'responses' to unemployment. The MSC appears to remain
unwilling to see training in these terms, sticking instead to the
commitment to it as 'for the needs of industry'. In its 1977 *Review and
Plan*, it reflects on the dilemma:

> If TOPS training remains popular and continues to meet labour
> market needs there would seem good reason to maintain the present
> programme, especially as there is considerable unsatisfied demand for
> some of the courses provided. But should adult training be expanded at
> times of high unemployment so that more of the unemployed are given
> a chance to find new employment in a different trade? Or is it wasteful
> and inefficient to undertake the heavy investment cost of expanding
> training facilities, or even to maintain the numbers in TOPS at a high
> level, when many workers with various types of skill are already unem-
> ployed and TOPS trainees may find difficulty in getting work? [MSC,
> 1977a, p. 34]

The MSC also helps individual enterprises and the statutory
Industrial Training Boards to develop relevant training schemes.
The latter are supported by a system of levies upon firms. They do not
cover all industries, and their impact is most significant upon the
manufacturing, construction and distribution industries. Within the
industries covered, firms may claim exemption from the levy if they
can show that they are training adequately for their own needs. On
the other hand, the firms that pay the levy may receive some of it back
in grants towards training schemes or in other help towards meeting
training needs.

Despite the extensive growth in the amount of government-financed training directed towards meeting the 'needs of industry', considerable concern continues to be expressed about skill shortages in British industry (NEDC & MSC, 1977; CBI, 1979). It is particularly poignant that employers should be complaining bitterly about this problem not, as has occurred in the past, at the peak of a boom but rather when unemployment is remarkably high (Cowper, 1978). It seems to be the case that, as government training has increased, training by employers has declined, and that comparatively little of the public effort has been directed towards the needs of the manufacturing sector. It is perhaps not irrelevant here that, overall, this is the employment sector that has been declining (see Leicester, 1978; Lindley *et al.*, 1978; *DEG*, 1977). Considerable numbers of skilled workers have left this sector for other employment in the face of low rewards and insecurity caused by firms being unable or unwilling to invest in the future.

The situation is complicated by the long periods of training required for some of the most skilled jobs, and the continued importance of the apprenticeship system. Hence 'dilutees', equipped for skilled jobs by means of special training schemes, are often resisted by trade unions and distrusted by employers. There is still a great deal of inflexibility in the British industrial training system.

Some of the examples of labour shortages that have been identified seem, however, to involve work for which long or expensive training is not essential. Shortages of staff on London Transport have been a favourite example of this problem for the economic commentators. To explain shortages of this kind it is necessary to consider a number of complicated interacting factors such as inadequate wage levels, unsatisfactory conditions of work and inflexible recruitment practices alongside failures in the training system. Problems of this kind draw attention to the way in which labour markets are highly localised and segmented. For instance, there are journey-to-work problems in many areas, or there may be quite unnecessary restrictions in the minds of both employers and employees about work capabilities and suitabilities.

Manpower policy and regional policy

The coexistence of extensive unemployment and large numbers of unfilled vacancies is, as was acknowledged above, significantly associated with the problems of regional or local imbalance in economic development. By the end of the 1930s a search had begun for measures to deal with the decline of work opportunities in the regions of Britain where major sources of employment, particularly in the heavy industries, were in decline. In this account of public manpower policy, attention has been primarily focussed upon the major initiatives associated with the Department of Employment and its related agencies, but a brief acknowledgement of the impact of regional policy is necessary. (McKay and Cox (1979) provide a more detailed account of policy developments of this kind.)

Back in 1940 the Barlow Report called for coordinated economic and planning policies to regenerate the depressed areas of the country. The 1945 Distribution of Industry Act designated Development Areas — in parts of Scotland, South Wales, and North East and North West England — where special aid to industry should be given. Since that time various policy initiatives have been attempted, varying considerably in the extent to which the growth of the economy in the rest of the country has been curbed effectively to benefit the disadvantaged areas. The definitions of the areas to be aided have changed extensively, encompassing much larger parts of the country but attempting to identify within them much smaller areas with special needs. Political considerations have influenced these definitions, and cases have naturally been made for some quite unlikely places. Such special pleading has been aided by the recognition that labour market areas, particularly for low-paid or low-skilled work, are often very small. Hence in recent years it has been recognised that even within prosperous cities there may be inner-areas that are declining economically. Today, regional policy is considerably complicated by the development of special programmes for inner-city areas, including tracts of East London.

There are in operation, therefore, three kinds of measures: control over the location of industry to help to force new enterprises to go to depressed areas; a variety of subsidies to assist developments in many different kinds of areas; and various attempts to focus other manpower policies upon those parts of the country where they seem most needed. Hence, many of the special measures, which will be discussed below, are applied selectively taking into account regional or local employment problems.

Anti-discrimination measures

Just as it has not been possible in a brief account to do justice to regional and inner-city policies, so also only a perfunctory reference can be made to anti-discrimination measures. The Manpower Services Commission certainly acknowledges a concern with this area of policy, but it is not its direct responsibility.

Legislation against racial discrimination in employment was first enacted in Britain in 1968. However it is the Race Relations Act of 1976 that provides the current statutory framework. It provides remedies not only to those who are the direct victims of racial discrimination but also to those able to prove that selection criteria have been used that have a discriminatory effect. Another important feature of the new legislation is the powers it gives to the Commission for Racial Equality (CRE) to initiate its own investigations of and, if appropriate, legal action against discriminating employers. This enables it to deal with situations where the composition of a workforce, or the proportion of black people in senior ranks in a firm, suggest that discrimination has occurred.

The 1975 Sex Discrimination Act provides closely similar legal safeguards for women under the supervision of the Equal Opportunities Commission (EOC). Both the EOC and the CRE are small bodies set a large task. While there have been some notable court victories, particularly in the sexual discrimination area, neither organisation has yet made much visible progress in investigations that they themselves have initiated. It is hard to assess as yet the overall impact of this legislation on the pattern of racial or sexual discrimination in employment.

NEW INITIATIVES IN MANPOWER POLICY

Job creation and work experience

Since 1974 the government has developed some special programmes to attempt to combat rising unemployment. These have involved the creation of special temporary jobs, forms of training and opportunities for work experience, and subsidies to encourage employers to take on some workers or to prevent redundancy.

The main effort went initially into two ventures, the Job Creation Programme and the Work Experience Programme. The former involved the subsidisation of specific temporary jobs for both teenagers and adults; the latter provided for brief spells in enterprises designed to give young people a better understanding of working life. However, in 1978 these two were replaced by the Youth Opportunities Programme (YOP) for people in the 16–18 age group, and the Special Temporary Employment Programme (STEP) for unemployed adults aged 19 and over.

The main elements in YOP are courses to prepare young people for work and a range of work experience schemes. This involves the effective abandonment of the job-creation element in services for this group. Instead, as the MSC stresses:

> The major objective is to help unemployed young people to gain permanent employment as soon as possible. For this reason the programme is to be operated so as to cause minimum interference with the labour market. [MSC, 1977b, p. 3]

Hence the payment of wages, as under the Job Creation Programme, has been abandoned for this group. Instead there is a standard flat rate allowance. The scheme is designed for those who are unemployed for at least six weeks after leaving school, and it is intended that all who remain out of work over about nine months should receive offers of places on the programme. No young person is expected to remain on one of the opportunities provided for over twelve months.

Most of the young people who are helped by the YOP scheme will either go on 'work preparation courses' or secure work experience on employers' premises. By December 1978 about 11,000 places had been filled on the former, and 29,000 on the latter. (*DEG*, 1979). The development of the work preparation courses adds to the complications of the different alternatives open to young people immediately above the minimum school-leaving age. Similar preparation may be done at school or in further education colleges, but whereas the youngsters will acquire grants on the YOP courses, they will not if they remain in full-time education. It is this anomaly that has led to discussions about the development of a grant scheme for 16–18 years olds who remain in education.

'Work experience' may be acquired in voluntary, community-oriented ventures or with ordinary employers. The MSC has itself published a report (Smith and Lasko, 1978) on a follow-up study of some of the early entrants to the previous Work Experience Programme (WEP). This suggests that the young people involved enhanced their prospects of obtaining normal full-time work. However, a substantial proportion of WEP 'graduates' secured employment in the enterprises where they had been placed for 'work experience'. To what extent, therefore, did their employers merely secure free labour for a period, during which they were also able to train and socialise their future employees? In other words, it may be that a significant proportion of the expenditure on an activity like this may subsidise employment that would be available in any case.

STEP has taken over the role of the Job Creation Programme. It is expected to provide up to 25,000 temporary jobs a year (MSC, 1977b). Preference is given to those between 19 and 24 who have been unemployed over six months and to those over 25 who have been out of work a year or more. All employed in the programme are paid wages at the 'appropriate negotiated rate'. The programme is biased to the areas of the country in greatest need. The jobs involved are temporary, averaging about a year in length. They may be sponsored by any employers, but are paid for out of public funds. While MSC staff administer both YOP and STEP, they do so with the assistance of local boards selected from employers, trade unionists and others regarded as representing relevant interests and sources of expertise.

While it would be wrong to assume that this job-creation programme will run into similar problems to its predecessor, some of the issues raised by the Parliamentary Committee that studied that should be mentioned, since it draws attention to difficulties inherent in such initiatives (House of Commons, 1977). The Job Creation Programme provided 'short-term jobs of social value' for unemployed persons. Jobs were expected to provide training where practical, to benefit the local community wherever possible and to pay the normal local wage rate for such work. There is also some concern that these temporary jobs should not replace 'normal jobs'. Hence the implementers of this programme were faced with a series of constraints and conditions, some of which seemed to be in conflict with each other. Jobs had to be worthwhile to the workers and to the community, but also temporary and not substitutes for jobs that would otherwise have been done.

It is not surprising that the Parliamentary Committee found a lack of sponsors from the private sector, particularly in view of the expectation of community benefit but no profit to the firm involved. In the local authority sector, where at the time of the Committee's investigation most jobs were found, the MSC itself commented on the problem that the programme financed 'relatively low priority local authority jobs at a time when authorities are having to cancel or defer more important work because of public expenditure constraints' (House of Commons, 1977, vol. II, p. 6). The Committee also commented on problems with the other organisations using the scheme — those from the voluntary sector, which it said had difficulties in managing such work, tended to 'go for the money without having properly thought out' how to use it, and faced some difficulties because these special employees were often doing work for money that others did for nothing.

Again, therefore, while the official claim is that the cost of job creation is the subsidy involved plus administrative costs minus the unemployment benefit that would have been paid to the person, an alternative view is that a significant number of the jobs are 'created' at the expense of jobs that would have been available in any case at no cost to the government. Private sector job creation is clearly open to this objection. In the public sector the position is more complicated, since the question is whether it is better simply to add to public expenditure, in a labour-intensive field, or to subsidise a special temporary job. The latter has political advantages when it is deemed to be undesirable directly to boost the size of the public sector. The emphasis upon the temporary nature of the measure may be important, but is it merely a temporary expedient? This is an issue to which I shall return.

Subsidies

Another kind of measure adopted to deal with high unemployment is a subsidy. In Britain, various devices to subsidise regional employment have been tried in the past, but the last few years have seen some new uses of subsidies. We may distinguish subsidies used simply to reduce unemployment from subsidies to try to benefit specific groups within the labour force. An example in the first category was the 'temporary employment subsidy' first introduced in 1975. By 1979, it was available, at a rate of £25 a week for a year and £10 a week for a further six months for each worker whose redundancy was avoided, to firms that deferred ten or more redundancies. This scheme ended on 31st March 1979 and was replaced by a scheme for subsidising short-time working that has many similar features. In February 1979, 73,000 jobs were being subsidised by means of the temporary employment subsidy.

There have also been a variety of experiments with subsidies to help specific groups of people. A recruitment subsidy for school leavers was tried, but ended when the Youth Opportunities Programme came into operation. Small manufacturing employers, in development areas and in some of the declining inner-city areas, with under 200 employees, have been able to claim subsidies of £20 for six months for each new job they create. This scheme was planned to end in March 1979, but has now been extended to 1980 and opened to firms in some other areas. Since its inception about 21,000 jobs have been supported. There is also the limited scheme, which has already been mentioned, to subsidise employers who take on disabled people. In summer 1978 another subsidy experiment was started. In three areas — Merseyside, Tyneside and the Leeds district — a subsidy of £20 a week was made available for up to twenty-six weeks for employers willing to take on adults living in those areas and unemployed for over a year.

The evaluation of the impact of subsidies is difficult, and only a limited amount of research has been done on this subject (see Haveman and Christiansen, 1978). The main difficulty is that there are inevitably what the economists call 'displacement effects'. Political claims tend to be made that each job created or protected by means of a subsidy is a direct contribution to the reduction of unemployment and that its cost to the Exchequer is the subsidy minus what might have been paid in unemployment benefit. However, the real effect may be rather different. Jobs may be 'created' or 'saved' at the expense of others elsewhere, and schemes of this kind are open to abuse by employers in search of subsidies for their activities. The OECD comments as follows on the British temporary employment subsidy:

> Some of the subsidised workers would have been employed anyway and some will displace unsubsidised workers. The lower the ratio of additional net employment to the number of jobs subsidised the larger will be the cost per net job created. It is impossible to determine the size of this ratio with confidence or to identify the extent to which it varies over time. The Department of Employment survey of firms' opinions suggests that 30 per cent of firms have identified a displacement effect in respect of jobs in competing firms. This is not necessarily the same thing as saying that 30 per cent of *jobs* represent displacement; the survey also suggests that the displacement effect increases over time. [OECD, 1978a, p. 68]

The displacement from 'competing firms' may of course be outside the country. Various EEC countries have experimented with subsidies, but there is a suspicion of the trading advantages individual countries may be seeking to gain by this means. This is one of the factors that brought to an end the wholesale regional subsidy operated in Britain, the 'regional employment premium', which sought to correct inter-regional imbalances in unemployment, and was described as 'regional devaluation'.

Hence, subsidies tend to be seen as justifiable if they are temporary or if they are designed to benefit some specific disadvantaged area or group, thus achieving social, if not economic, aims. However, two questions must be raised about this use of subsidies: At whose expense do the subsidised workers gain? Is there a danger that employers will come to regard certain kinds of people as only acceptable if they are offered a subsidy? These are two problems about the use of active manpower policy for social ends in a situation of high unemployment that will be explored in the concluding section of this chapter.

MANPOWER POLICY AND SOCIAL SECURITY

The income support available to a person who becomes unemployed varies considerably, and is largely determined by previous work experience. Thus someone who has been in steady, reasonably well-paid work for a number of years will receive unemployment benefit, including additions for any dependants. For the first six months of unemployment the basic benefit will be increased by earnings-related supplement, which may bring the weekly amount up to 85 per cent of previous earnings. This is calculated on the basis of contributions paid in the previous tax year. In addition, someone who is laid off as redundant from a job he has held for over two years will receive a lump sum redundancy payment, calculated by means of a formula taking into account his previous weekly earnings and the number of years he was in that post. Finally, since unemployment benefit is not taxable, the newly unemployed person may expect to receive an income tax rebate.

However, if he remains unemployed, his income from contributory benefits will fall by the amount of the earnings-related supplement after six months and end altogether after twelve months. In due course, therefore, the unemployed man is likely to require means-tested supplementary benefit to support himself and his family. The amount of this benefit is calculated by taking into account family responsibilities and rent levels, with corresponding reductions for other sources of income. One of the particular disadvantages for the unemployed claimant is that his supplementary benefit payment remains at the 'short-term' rate regardless of how long he remains unemployed. This is by contrast with the sick person, who acquires a long-term rate of benefit (in winter 1978/9, £6.30 more for a man and wife) after two years, and the pensioner who goes onto that rate when he first gets supplementary benefit.

The example described above is of someone who loses a job he has held for some time but then remains out of work. The position of someone who experiences repeated spells of unemployment is less satisfactory. Not only do workless spells diminish the earnings-related supplement entitlement, but the flat rate unemployment benefit is also calculated on the basis of numbers of contributions paid in the previous tax year. Moreover, after a year long spell of unemployment, which 'exhausts' the contributory benefit entitlement, a person has to work for at least thirteen weeks to requalify. Hence, someone with a recent previous record of unemployment is much more likely to need supplementary benefit as soon as he becomes unemployed.

Other groups who will not be able to secure unemployment benefit are the formerly self-employed and new entrants to the labour market who have not previously paid insurance contributions. The position of a married woman is also complicated. She may have availed herself of the option, now being phased out, given to married women not to pay ordinary insurance contributions, in which case she will get no unemployment benefit. Even if she has been a contributor, moreover, she will not be able to claim an increase in benefit in respect of the needs of her children or husband. Moreover, she will not normally be accepted as a claimant for supplementary benefit — she is deemed to be her husband's 'dependant'.

There is a variety of other situations in which unemployment benefit is likely to be refused. If a person is out of work as a consequence of a trade dispute, unemployment benefit will not be payable, even if he is not himself a striker. If he is deemed to be at fault for losing his job — he left voluntarily or was sacked for some form of 'industrial misconduct' — unemployment benefit may be refused for up to six weeks. Similarly, if he is found to have refused a job that it is reasonable to expect him to take, unemployment benefit may be stopped for up to six weeks. Disqualification from receipt of benefit in these circumstances is becoming more rare, the operation of such sanctions being incompatible with the modern Job-Centre 'philosophy'. In all these cases in which unemployment benefit is refused, individuals may still secure supplementary benefit for their families, and partially for themselves, but, the payments will be at less than the full rate.

The Supplementary Benefits Commission (SBC) is itself able to operate further sanctions against those unemployed people who are considered unwilling to take work deemed to be available to them. In the last resort they may prosecute someone for failing to maintain himself and his family. They may also ask an appeal tribunal to direct that a man should attend a 're-establishment centre' as a condition of receiving benefit. They may also use their discretionary powers to operate what have been called the 'four-week rule' and the 'thirteen-week rule'. On account of high unemployment these are not, at the time of writing, being operated, except in the summer in seaside areas where seasonal employment is available. The 'four-week rule' is applied to single, healthy, unskilled men (and exceptionally women) aged between 18 and 45. In places where there are deemed to be plentiful job opportunities for such people, they are interviewed after four weeks on supplementary benefit. If they are considered to be making insufficient efforts to find work, their benefit is stopped. The 'thirteen-week rule' represents a similar procedure — much more rarely operated — for other fit persons under 45 regardless of whether or not they have dependants.

The responsibility for these sanctions against the unemployed on supplementary benefits is usually in the hands of executive officers known as unemployment review officers (UROs). These officials are expected to keep all unemployed supplementary benefit recipients 'under review', calling them from time to time to interviews at which their efforts to obtain work are discussed with them. At these interviews they may threaten the use of the sanctions described above, or they may seek to advise claimants on ways to find work and overcome any problems that make it difficult for them to become employed. They may themselves collect information on available jobs and may make contacts with employers on behalf of the unemployed. Operating styles vary from officer to officer — they combine coercion with a concern for claimants' welfare in differing mixtures.

Under the pressure of heavy unemployment the SBC cut back its use of UROs. However, in 1979 the incoming Conservative government decided that this activity should be increased in order to prevent abuse of the social security system. I have argued elsewhere (Hill, 1974) that it is invidious that those who have the greatest difficulties in finding work, the long-term or frequently unemployed who are heavily dependant on supplementary benefit, get this special and potentially coercive attention from unemployment review officers. The UROs' access to information about jobs is bound to be inferior to that of his employment service colleague, yet there is a danger that once unemployment is prolonged the more expert manpower service washes its hands of people and passes them on to the UROs.

However, it may be argued in defence of the SBC that it is precisely because the MSC shows little interest in the low-skilled, long-term unemployed that the UROs are necessary. They have found that UROs do have some impact upon the rate at which those whom they investigate return to work. The government has recently claimed, on the basis of this evidence, that UROs are 'cost effective'. What however this assumes is that URO activity has some real effect upon levels of unemployment. It may be in reality that, overall, those encouraged or coerced back into work are merely replaced on the social security rolls by others who are displaced. Even if this is not the case, pressure upon the unemployed to enter work plays a role in enforcing low-wage work and diminishing the bargaining power of some of the country's most disadvantaged workers.

The reader will want to decide for himself whether abuse of the social security system is a problem deserving of political concern when the economy is unable to generate work for over a million people. There has been extensive controversy in recent years about the impact of the social security system upon the behaviour of the unemployed. It is suggested that the long-term unemployed are deterred from seeking work by the high levels of supplementary benefit relative to the lower earning levels. This argument is used, in the face of the evidence that the unemployed are the most impoverished of all supplementary benefit recipients, to justify both the maintenance of the UROs and the refusal to pay the long-term supplementary benefit rate to the unemployed. The team of civil servants who reviewed the supplementary benefits scheme have argued that the latter injustices should cease and the SBC has endorsed that proposal (DHSS, 1978); the government has rejected it.

The difficulty of testing the hypothesis about the impact of benefit levels upon the willingness of the long-term unemployed to seek work is that they are the group of job-seekers who are least attractive to potential employers. They are typically low skilled, often in poor health and very many of them are either totally new entrants to the labour market or relatively near to retirement (see Hill, *et al.*, 1973). At a time when jobs are scarce they are logically the ones who will be passed over. When they are offered jobs, the rates of pay involved are naturally at the very bottom end of the income distribution. It is therefore true that some, but the SBC stresses (SBC, 1977) relatively few, of the unemployed are securing more money out of work than anyone is able to pay them to work, in a society in which minimum pay is determined by union bargaining and government regulation of minimum wage levels in some trades. It is also true that a rather greater number would, if they took work, secure only a little more than they obtain on benefit. Moreover, their calculations about the advantages of going to work are complicated by the obscure maze of means-tested benefits available, and the interactions between benefit systems and the tax system. Many may, therefore, be very unsure about the actual income implications of any specific job offer, very ill informed about their rights to family income supplement, rent rebates and so on, and therefore disinclined to move from the relatively static security of supplementary benefit.

But is this problem of deterrence a consequence of benefits that are too high, or wage levels for some jobs that are too low? If short-term supplementary benefit rates are lower than some earning levels, is it reasonable to expect people to go to work for less than subsistence income? And since there is a scarcity of jobs to go round, does it matter that some people are not trying very hard to get work?

It has also been suggested that the very high benefits available to some of the newly unemployed also affect job-seeking behaviour. It has been argued that the introduction, in the mid-1960s, of earnings-related benefits and redundancy pay contributed to an increase in unemployment at that time. Economists have sought, by comparing other evidence on the state of the economy with data on unemployment, to test this hypothesis. It seems possible that these new benefits did have a slight effect upon employment durations amongst the short-term unemployed. They were, in a sense, designed to do this. They reduced the impact of redundancy and helped workers to avoid hasty relocation in inappropriate jobs. However, the difference they made was marginal and in the long run the only effect of the particular cushioning of the newly unemployed may be to increase slightly the job prospects of rather longer unemployed people. Since they have their maximum effect near the beginning of a spell of unemployment, they have no effect upon the phenomenon of long-term unemployment, and it is this that is of growing significance at the present time. Overall, the arguments about the deterrent levels of benefits are really red herrings in the debate about the contemporary problem of unemployment.

SHARING THE WORK AVAILABLE

Attention to the demographic factors that are increasing the size of the labour force and to the technological factors that are reducing industry's capacity to absorb workers has led to the examination of policies that will reduce the size of the labour force.

Logically, you may think, the labour force is made up of those in employment plus the unemployed. However, first, the employed labour force contains a reserve of people who are not in full-time work, or are not doing as much work as they would like to do, and are thus not — as far as they are concerned — fully employed. Therefore, one of the consequences of any increase in work opportunities is an increased participation by these people. Second, in Britain, the unemployed are identified as those who are registered for work at Job-Centres or Employment Exchanges. But since the MSC has in no way a mono-poly of information about job opportunities, there is no need to register with them in order to obtain work. Moreover, when jobs are scarce, registering for work may seem a singularly pointless exercise. If you want to apply for unemployment benefit, supplementary bene-fit or a credit of national insurance contributions, it is necessary to register for work. But if you have no entitlement to such benefits, then it is quite likely you will not register. In Britain it is particularly married women who fall into this category (see DE, 1972). Hence our potential labour force is rather larger than the official figures suggest. The significance of this complication is well expressed by the OECD:

> Another implication of continuously high unemployment is its dis-couraging effect on the behaviour of the peripheral labour force — minorities, migrants, second family workers, youth, the involuntarily retired. These workers enter and leave the active labour force as economic opportunities rise and fall. But it would be an over-simplification to assume that this unstable employment behaviour results from affluence and that a prolonged denial of labour market

access to those groups should not give rise to particular concern. Simply because these workers have left the labour force does not necessarily mean that they have done so willingly and their discouragement in finding a new job may be associated with considerable economic and social hardship. [OECD, 1978a, p. 9]

There are various ideas that are being examined for work-sharing or reducing the size of the labour force. Some of them are already being tried. For example, there is a 'job release scheme' which enables workers to retire up to a year early on a special allowance. This is payable if their employer takes on someone from the unemployed register. The various programmes for young people and in particular the efforts to encourage continued full-time education may also be seen in some lights as efforts to keep them out of the labour force. Ideas for a shorter working week, longer holidays and earlier retirement are being actively canvassed by trade unions.

However, attempts to reduce unemployment by reducing the size of the labour force may have a variety of unintended consequences. Individuals who were assumed not to be seeking work may fill the vacancies created; people already in work may take on more work by means of overtime, second jobs and so on; and migrants may move in from other countries (this is certainly very feasible within the EEC). Another complication with measures to share the short supply of work available is that they clearly have no impact upon the amount of income created unless, of course, they lead to the more efficient use of the workforce, a development that is not normally implicit in work-sharing schemes. Hence, suggestions that there should be a shorter working day or longer holidays must tend to imply lower rewards. If individuals attempt to offset this by doing more overtime or taking spare-time jobs or even by more 'do-it-yourself' activities, they will tend to undermine work-sharing objectives. But it is equally true that proposals for early retirement, longer compulsory education, more further education, sabbaticals and so on all have costs that must be met from somewhere. It is therefore vital to face up realistically to the extent to which such ideas imply a transfer of resources from those who are employed. This limits their political feasibility and heightens the possibility that they will have unintended consequences as workers seek to protect themselves from reductions in disposable income.

CONCLUSIONS: ACTIVE MANPOWER POLICY IN A CONTEXT OF HIGH UNEMPLOYMENT

This discussion has shown that Britain has developed a much more sophisticated approach to manpower policy during the 1970s. But the new system, headed by the Manpower Services Commission, has had to try to frame policies to cope with rising unemployment. Politicians have been eager to be seen to be doing something about unemployment; civil servants have responded with an ingenious range of new schemes. Yet demographic trends have been against them, and the new 'orthodoxy' of economic management with its emphasis upon limiting public expenditure and curbing the money supply has offered them no support.

But can these measures effectively increase employment? There is an inherent conflict between effective job creation and the reluctance of our economy-managers to countenance general reflation. Hence the OECD argue that while, as suggested above, wage subsidies are essentially only a temporary palliative, the alternative of job creation is similarly of limited value: 'If there are constraints on general reflation work creation projects cannot make a significant impact on employment'. Thus they go on: 'they are probably most suited to creating employment in particular regions or for particular groups of workers where private demand is low . . .' (OECD, 1978a, p. 75).

There seems, perhaps as a consequence of reasoning of this kind, to be a shift in thinking about manpower policy from economic to social objectives. Brian Showler, reviewing the employment service in 1976, argued that 'its essential social role has not received the emphasis it deserves, given the considerable and growing social problems associated with the changing conditions of the labour market' (Showler, 1976, p. 94). While this broadly remains true of the mainstream job replacement and training service, the new programmes are characterised by an increasing concern to target help towards identifiable disadvantaged groups in the labour market.

If little can be done to reduce overall unemployment, there is clearly something to be said for measures that alleviate individual problems, and therefore share unemployment more widely. However, there are some specific pitfalls in attempting to do this, into some of which the present measures seem to fall. There is an ever-present tendency, in public and political discussions of unemployment, for 'demand' and 'supply' factors to be confused. This perpetuates the view that the unemployed are to blame for their own predicament.

Therefore, any measures that concentrate upon attempting to improve the attractiveness to employers of particular kinds of people tend to reinforce this perspective. Readers may well have heard comments upon the illiteracy of young people's application letters for jobs, and about their failure to dress adequately for interviews. Careers advisers and teachers therefore give increasing attention to 'grooming' youngsters for job selection. Now, of course, young people who write nice neat letters and put on suits and ties for interviews may enhance their own chances of getting work. But such efforts are unlikely to do anything to affect the sum total of vacancies open to youngsters as a whole. The current obsession with these issues does nothing to relieve youth unemployment. On the contrary, it may reinforce employers' perceptions of young people as uncouth and unemployable, and strengthen their resolve to take on older people instead. The development of work experience activities may be similarly perceived. Of course young people who remain unemployed for some time after leaving school may become thoroughly demoralised and cease to believe in their prospects of obtaining work. Accordingly, work experience may be better than unemployment. However, is it not strange that while a few years ago school leavers without qualifications of any kind had no difficulty in getting jobs, many of them are now deemed to need 'work experience' before they can be regarded as employable?

Hirsch (1977) has brilliantly demonstrated how competition for positions in society that are inherently limited in supply pushes up the qualifications demanded of aspirants. Those who operate selection processes inevitably discriminate between applicants in terms of formal qualifications regardless of whether or not they are necessary to perform the tasks involved. People come to believe that those qualifications are essential, and to assume that individuals without them will be incompetent. The process that Hirsch identified at the top of the social scale also operates where jobs are scarce at the bottom. Employers forced to select from a large number of applicants for almost any job seek any basis for discrmination — educational qualifications, participation in a training course, work experience (real or artificial), length of time out of work and so on. As they do this they begin to believe that the discrimination process is necessary, that those who fail in the competition must be inadequate. In this light some of the contemporary concern about manpower shortages may be interpreted as a consequence of the operation of inappropriately stringent selection criteria, or as the shifting of the responsibility onto the unemployed for what are in reality hopelessly inadequate wage levels.

There are parallels, in the contemporary obsession with training and work preparation for young people, with the rather longer running debate about the relationship between education and social mobility. Halsey has expressed the issue very clearly:

> Too much has been claimed for the power of educational systems as instruments for the wholesale reforms of societies which are characteristically hierarchical in their distribution of chances in life . . . The typical history of educational expansion in the nineteen fifties and nineteen sixties can be represented by a graph of inequality of attainment . . . which has shifted markedly upward without changing its slope. In other words relative chances did not alter materially despite expansion. No doubt, the higher norms of educational attainment contributed something towards raising the quality of life in urban industrial society — that, at least, is the faith of the educationalist. But in terms of relative chances of income, status and welfare at birth, the impact of the educational system on the life of children remained heavily determined by their family and class origins. [Halsey, 1972, pp. 7–8]

Now, popular emphasis has shifted from concern with the amount of education *per se* to the importance of vocational education, training and understanding of the world of work. Yet this has occurred at a time when work opportunities, and in particular opportunities in manufacturing industry (for which youngsters are alleged to be particularly ill equipped), are declining. But perhaps this vocational preparation raises 'the quality of life'? Or does it just raise expectations that are bound to be frustrated?

The argument developed here rests upon the supposition that however much is done for the groups in the labour market least able to compete, it will not be enough to enable them to advance at the expense of those currently more advantaged. That may be an unfair and pessimistic assumption. If it is incorrect, however, is it still appropriate to ask just how much will they be able to advance? To what extent do measures designed to compensate for labour market disadvantages enable individuals to gain only on others who are but marginally better placed?

This last argument also needs to be related to the case for subsidies for disadvantaged workers. These are, of course, small in scale at the moment. To what extent does the subsidised disabled worker actually merely displace other slightly more fortunate disabled workers. Does the subsidisation of a job for a long-term unemployed person actually reduce the job prospects for other long-term unemployed people, or displace from employment someone who has seldom been able to hold a job for long? These are complicated questions. If challenged to devise a research design to answer them, I would be at a loss. Yet it is important to bear in mind that there *are* such consequences of labour market interventions of this kind. It would certainly be unwise to imagine that the character of the distribution of job opportunities in our society can be transformed by this route.

But there is a rather more concrete problem about the use of subsidies to help particular disadvantaged group of workers. It has been pointed out that two significant subsidy experiments — both still at a very early stage — have aimed to help the disabled and the long-term unemployed. The case for such subsidies seems to rest upon one or other of two arguments. It may be argued in terms of the greater costs entailed in employing particular kinds of people. Such costs include slower work rates, greater sickness rates, needs for greater supervision or safety precautions, and sometimes the necessary conversion of equipment. But very often it may be disputed whether higher costs really are involved. It is misleading, for example, to assume that all 'fit' workers operate at 100 per cent of their capacity and that 'disabled' workers are necessarily unable to maintain comparable work rates. So it may be that in many cases the argument for a subsidy rests upon no more than a need to overcome employers' prejudices and to prove that the subsidised individuals can be effective workers. The present 'job introduction' subsidy for the disabled would seem to have been designed on this assumption. But do such subsidies buy off prejudices or reinforce them? May we not find that in due course, if the experimental schemes are extended, employers will expect the promise of a subsidy before they will consider taking on the disabled or the long-term unemployed? Their image as substandard workers will have been reinforced. Let us hope our policy-makers do not fall into a similar trap with efforts to combat racial or sexual discrimination. Once subsidy schemes are started they are politically difficult to stop.

The final point to be made about the various ways in which governments have sought to help or protect disadvantaged groups in the labour force is that they have had some difficulties in selecting those in particular need of help. They have identified so many different target groups that the interests of some may be in direct competition with the interests of others: young new entrants to the labour market; the disabled; the long-term unemployed; people in disadvantaged regions; and those threatened with redundancy. Pressure groups and politicians are eager to bring to the attention of government the needs of other disadvantaged groups: the elderly; low-skilled, middle-aged men with heavy family commitments; women; racial minorities; and so on. For example, governments have provided subsidies both to prevent redundancies and to help the long-term unemployed to obtain work. There seems little doubt that, overall, the efforts in recent years to protect workers from dismissal militate against any efforts to share unemployment around more widely. Again, Halsey's observations on education and social inequality are relevant; does the system reduce the advantage of those very well placed in the labour market in favour of some of the disadvantaged groups or are they in fact bound to be largely competing against each other?

These rather gloomy observations about the current attempts to develop social objectives for manpower policy must be seen against the background of much less than full employment. While undoubtedly the British employment service has grown more sophisticated in recent years and the new programmes it has developed give significant attention to the needs of disadvantaged groups, manpower policies cannot be substituted for effective macroeconomic efforts to secure full employment. Subsidies are regarded as most effective when they aim to protect special groups rather than when they are expected to boost employment in general. Yet the former use may reinforce prejudices against such groups. Special measures that aim to improve the 'marketability' of those against whom the labour market discriminates fosters the belief that our problems lie with the supply of, rather than the demand for, labour, and thus reinforce the tendency to 'blame the victim' for his own unemployment. Job creation could represent a revolutionary new form of public labour market intervention, but it is in practice inhibited by the belief that it is undesirable to stimulate public expenditure and increase public service employment. Job-sharing may well be important in the future, but it is doubtful whether we are yet facing up to the political problems entailed in the fact that it is likely to involve further income redistribution.

These are very negative conclusions. But we are deluding ourselves if we see measures of this kind as satisfactory substitutes for more all-embracing economic measures. As Lord Vaisey argued in his evidence to the House of Commons Expenditure Committee:

The sum total of these schemes seems to me to be cosmetic rather than genuine in its economic consequences. What they do in effect is to push employment around a bit without much net effect. They are in no sense a substitute for the substantial regeneration of British industry . . . [House of Commons, 1977, vol. II, p. 147]

It has not been the function of this chapter to argue how this should be achieved. It is hoped that its tone has not been so negative as to suggest that the employment service has no part to play in the revitalisation of the British economy. On the contrary, it is very important that the system of government training has been much enlarged in recent years. Moreover, the job-placing service clearly has a very active part to play in fitting people to jobs.

Clearly, as the goal of full employment has been effectively abandoned as a political objective some politicians, particularly Labour ones, have been willing to support minor palliative or cosmetic policies to prove that they are still eager, or able, to combat unemployment (see chapter 3, pp. 78–80). We must not be misled by these activities into forgetting that the roots of our economic problems lie elsewhere than in the fit between the nature of our labour force and the requirements of our employment system. Above all, we must not be diverted by those who want us to misunderstand the real problems, or who are happy to produce a 'reserve army of labour', into blaming the unemployed for their unemployment.

CHAPTER 5

Unemployment in an Unequal Society

Adrian Sinfield

INTRODUCTION

Unemployment has to be examined as a characteristic of the society in which we live, not just of those members of it who happen to be out of work at any one time. It is a particular risk where employment has become the main way of getting a living, for few poeple have any regular and socially approved means of raising resources other than their labour power. Yet the very fact that employment is established for those without private means as the normal and legitimate way of life, and of supporting oneself and any family, places those who are out of work in a suspect and ambiguous, if not deviant, position. Market economies, however, rely on the ready availability of a labour reserve of unemployed, and unemployment serves a range of functions within capitalist societies. With increasing numbers out of work, the paradox appears all the greater: while unemployment comes to be regarded as all the more inevitable, if not necessary, being out of work seems to have become more reprehensible and less to be tolerated.

The dominant role of economists in discussions of unemployment appears so firmly established that it is generally forgotten that they only came to accept the subject as a proper concern to be tackled by economic policies in the second decade of this century (Harris, 1972, p. 6). Discussions of the problems of being out of work were common among the working class and in national and local policy debates long before the term 'unemployment' came to be used by economists in the 1880s (see especially Williams, 1976, pp. 273–5 and Garraty, 1978, chapters 1–4). In recent years, most discussions of unemployment and the unemployed within the other social sciences have tended to be confined by political and other concerns that have focussed attention almost exclusively on the supply side of the labour market. In particular, how much are incentives to work affected by the general experience of being unemployed or by the specific financial benefits received? How much hardship or poverty accompanies being out of work? How adequate are benefits in replacing earnings? And how much delinquency and hooliganism is the 'work' of unemployed, alienated youth?

Responses to questions such as these have largely overlooked the wider implications of unemployment and insecurity, and one consequence has been the failure to develop a systematic analysis of the sociology of unemployment. The description by a sociologist in the 1930s of 'liability to unemployment or insecurity of tenure' as 'the distinguishing feature of the proletarian estate' calls attention to the remarkable nature of this neglect by a profession seen by both its protagonists and opponents as centrally concerned with the nature and significance of the social division of labour and the structure of inequality in society (G. A. Briefs, 1937, quoted in Lockwood, 1958, p. 55).

Yet it is difficult to think of many more appropriate subjects in which to pursue the connection between 'the personal troubles of milieu' and 'the public issues of social structure . . . the essential tool of the sociological imagination and a feature of all classic work in social science' set out vividly and cogently by C. Wright Mills over twenty years ago. Indeed, Mills himself provided unemployment as his very first illustration: when many are out of work, 'both the correct statement of the problem and the range of possible solutions require us to consider the economic and political institutions of the society, and not merely the personal situation and character of a scatter of individuals' (Mills, 1959a, pp. 8–9).

Connections between unemployment, the unemployed and the wider society are evident throughout the book. In this chapter particular emphasis is placed on the unequal distribution of unemployment and insecurity, its consequences over time for different classes and its significance for the maintenance of the existing social structure. The development of a variety of institutional practices in the labour market that protect some groups and erect barriers for others are considered in relation to the differences of power that exist within the market. Among these arrangements are the public and private employment services and the various state programmes for income support that may influence the experience and duration of unemployment and shape the public and official perceptions of it and the deserving nature of different groups of unemployed. The actual experience of being out of work and any long-term effects can only be fully considered within the broader context provided by the earlier discussion, and so these are examined at the end of the chapter.

One major criticism of studies of unemployment since the end of the 1930s has been that they tend toward 'the piling-up of data . . . for the most part . . . descriptive statements or statistical summaries with few attempts at intensive analysis' (Ferman, 1964, p. 513). This verdict on research in the United States still applies, and with equal force to most of the work undertaken in Britain; it should however be added that even studies of this type tend to be lacking in other market societies, the main exception being West Germany with the emergence of much higher levels of unemployment in the 1970s. One particular shortcoming of the research has been the general lack of sustained, comparative analyses of the nature and impact of unemployment, and its significance in the wider society at different levels of demand for and supply of labour. In consequence, the effects of changes in demand and supply on the experience of being out of work, and on perceptions of unemployment and reactions to it, are given particular attention.

WORK, EMPLOYMENT AND UNEMPLOYMENT

The need to examine unemployment within an analysis of employment and work, and the ways in which work and workers are regarded in a capitalist society with a persisting class structure, cannot be sufficiently emphasised. The organisation and distribution of work and the allocation of reward, power and social honour among occupations significantly affect who are best protected from unemployment, who are most vulnerable and who are most likely to remain out of work. Unemployment therefore is not 'a kind of inevitable exhaust' of the 'economic engine . . . it is also a social process powered by the values we hold and the choices we make' (Liebow, 1970, p. 29) — and, it should be added, by the norms and conventions that have become institutionalised in our society, generally reflecting the values and choices of dominant groups in generations past.

The treatment of those out of work — the extent to which the needs and rights of some groups receive greater recognition than those of others; the forms of stigma and those most likely to be stigmatised or labelled as deviant; those declared most in need of special assistance or, alternatively, control and surveillance — is very much influenced by the value placed on work in general and the status of some jobs and their holders compared to others. The reality and the fear, or threat, of unemployment and the denial, reduction or restriction of income support are major, if not principal, means by which the state reinforces the work ethic. And of course the nature of that ethic, its reproduction and the maintenance of its force by parents, schools, employers, trade unions, employment and social security staff are an essential part of the framework within which the experience of unemployment has to be considered.

Emphasis on the need to study unemployment within the context of a work-orientated society where employment provides the main access to reward, privilege, security and participation for those without private means does not indicate any necessary acceptance of current forms of economic activity through employment. Indeed, the experience of unemployment, and its general increase, has led some to question the existing structure of employment and its dominance of patterns of life in an industrial society, the extent to which its prevailing forms are functional to the economy, society and the individual, and the ways in which it serves to maintain ruling interests.

How industrial societies have dealt with or reacted to the problem of unemployment provides an important indication of the ways in which any country has dealt with the experiences of industrialisation and continuing technical and economic change. Some nations have 'abolished' unemployment, but there seems to be very little information on what has been achieved, by what means, to whose benefit and at what cost (though see Ferge, 1979).[1] Views continue to differ on the functions of unemployment in a capitalist society, the amount that is needed for the 'smooth running' of the economy and the extent to which the level or distribution of unemployment is in the power of individual governments to control. Its persistence is acknowledged by the institutionalisation of measures to compensate or assist those out of work, albeit with generally careful attention to the maintenance of work incentives.

Some capitalist societies, however, have managed to operate with lower levels and somewhat different patterns of distribution of unemployment than others with similar rates of labour force growth or decline in economic demand. Britain appears to have moved over the last decide to a generally higher level of unemployment than most Western countries. In the mid-1960s it had a greater proportion of long-term unemployed than countries with roughly similar or even higher overall rates of unemployment. As jobless rates have risen and remained high, prolonged unemployment has increased faster in most countries, but Britain still appears to have a much greater concentration of its unemployed than the United States, for example where more of the labour force experience some unemployment in the course of a year but generally for shorter periods (see chapter 6, pp. 177–80, and Introduction, p. 10).

THE UNEQUAL DISTRIBUTION OF UNEMPLOYMENT

The unequal impact of unemployment has already been given considerable emphasis in the introduction to this book. Its distribution, as well as its scale, is central to any sociological analysis of the issue of unemployment, influencing both who bears the heaviest burden and the ways in which the public, the state and significant groups within society perceive and react to both the issue and the troubles it may bring. If all of us were experiencing unemployment ourselves once every six years, eight spells a lifetime or just more equally than at present (with only 3 per cent of the labour force bearing 70 per cent of the weeks of unemployment a year — Metcalf, 1980, p. 24), the problem would be very much more likely to be treated by those in power with as much priority as inflation — a view that may be borne out by the apparently greater concern with unemployment as a political issue in the United States through the 1970s.[2]

Despite the very uneven distribution of unemployment across the labour force, there are few data that enable an analysis even by the conventional approximations for class. The most recent evidence, for men only, shows that one in ten had some experience of unemployment during the previous twelve months in the mid-1970s (see Table 5.1 and the sources cited there). Men in unskilled and semi-skilled manual work were twice as likely as the skilled to have had some time unemployed; men in manual work as a whole were twice as vulnerable as the non-manual; and among these the intermediate and junior or routine non-manual had twice as great a risk as professionals, employers and managers. Analyses that distinguish the unskilled from the partly or semi-skilled show the former to have a particularly high rate (see also Bosanquet and Standing, 1972).

'For women the effect of occupational status is not so regular' (Harris and Clausen, 1966, p. 115). Table 5.1 shows that the un-

Table 5.1 *Unemployment by Socioeconomic Group*

	Men unemployed in the previous 12 months 1975, 1976, and 1977 %	Men Unemployed within the previous 12 months 1968–69 %	Women 1968–69 %	Men With any unemployment 1953–63 %	Women 1953–63 %
Professional, employers and managers	4	0	–	15	28.8
Intermediate and junior non-manual	8	5	4	29.6	44.1
All non-manual	(6)	(5)	(4)	(21.4)	(41.1)
Skilled manual	9	7	3	31.5	60.9
Semi-skilled manual	18	9	8	39.4	56.8
Unskilled manual		18	5	57.7	49.7
All manual	(12)	(9)	(6)	(36.8)	(56.4)
All	10	7	5	31.8	47.4
Total sample size	25,563	1,717	1,057	8,528	6,513

Sources: for column 1, '*General Household Survey* data for 1975, 1976 and 1977 for males aged 18–64', *Social Trends, 1980*, Table 5.19; for columns 2 and 3, Townsend, 1970a. Table 17.4; and for column 4 and 5; Harris and Clausen, 1966, Table 97.

skilled female manual worker had about the average rate in both
studies, with the partly skilled being more vulnerable in both, and the
skilled being most vulnerable in the earliest study. It also shows that
women had more unemployment than men over a decade of generally
low unemployment. These data only serve to reinforce the need for
more and better evidence on the labour force experience of women in
Britain — in most market economies unemployment is higher among
women (see chapter 6, p. 177).

Measurement by incidence is of course only a partial indicator of
the distribution of unemployment. Its duration and recurrence, and
its effect on individual and family resources over time, all need to be
taken into account. The unskilled particularly 'live in the shadow of
unemployment' (Townsend, 1979a, p. 601). Forming 9 per cent of the
male labour force with no time out of work in the last year, they
comprised 17 per cent of those with one–nine weeks unemployed and
as much as 39 per cent of those with ten or more weeks. Professionals,
managers and employers formed a slightly larger proportion of the
male labour force with no unemployment than the unskilled, but
'scarcely featured at all among the unemployed', let alone the long-
term unemployed. By the time of the larger General Household
Surveys from 1975–1977, experience of unemployment in the previous twelve months had risen from 7 per cent to 10 per cent: even
then the percentage for professionals, employers and managers was
only 4 per cent, compared to 18 per cent for the unskilled. Unskilled
and semi-skilled manual workers were also three times more vulnerable than others to spells of unemployment recurring within a year
(*Social Trends 1980*, Table 5.18).

The risk of unemployment also varies over working life for different
classes. The higher non-manual salaried employee may experience
some difficulty in first entering work and be forced into early
retirement, but the unskilled often remain vulnerable throughout
their four decades in the labour force: their most secure period may be
perhaps ten or fifteen years from the age of 25, although more work
needs to be undertaken on the differing distribution of unemployment
by age and occupation over longer periods of time, and so across very
different levels of economic demand. Unskilled school leavers entering the labour force three, or even two, decades ago both expected and
experienced a very different degree of security and freedom from their
counterparts today.

The difference between classes may be increased by differences in
their treatment when they are dismissed or made redundant. Senior

management, administrators and professionals have been much more likely to be given sufficient, or at least a longer, time to find a new post while being kept on full pay; and this has tended to apply even on dismissal or sacking. In recent years, legislation and agreements between unions and employers have extended protection in terms of advance notice and time off to look for work to more workers who lose their jobs, especially through redundancy, and particularly those with longer service with a company. The threat of unemployment for these workers therefore less frequently becomes a reality, and this protection is a considerable advantage when employers generally prefer currently employed applicants to those already out of work. Ironically, this greater help may mean that every successful job-change, with little or no unemployment in between, not only serves to reduce any sense of common cause with those harder hit by unemployment; it may positively encourage further social distancing and lead the more fortunate to assure themselves and their friends that jobs are there to be found if only those out of work looked hard enough. 'People with advantages are loath to believe that they just happen to be people with advantages' (Mills, 1959b, p. 14).

Unemployment may also help to determine, or at least maintain, a particular occupational position. Norris argues powerfully that many of those he called 'sub-employed' (with at least one month's unemployment in the last twelve) were in unskilled work because of previous unemployment. They were 'more likely to have experienced downward and erratic skill mobility', while those who had not been out of work 'were much more likely to have been upwardly mobile in skill terms' (Norris, 1978, p. 342). In Peterborough in the early 1970s, those previously out of work tended to have lower wages, lower skill jobs and and worse working conditions (Blackburn & Mann, 1979, p. 266; see also North Tyneside CDP, 1978, p. 53, and Metcalf, 1980, p. 25). Given increasing or persistently high unemployment, those out of work may be forced even further down into poorer and less secure jobs, especially if they have a disability or declining health. 'A man does not become an unskilled worker: it happens to him' (Dahrendorf, 1956).

POWER AND THE RESPONSES TO REDUCED DEMAND

While the amount of work available may be basically a function of economic demand, including the management of the economy by the state, this does not automatically determine how employment is organised and allocated across the potential labour force in terms of the number and types of jobs and the security attached to them. Any attempt to explain the distribution of security and insecurity and the patterns and practices of displacement and unemployment must take account of the power of the different groups involved in the labour market — employers, workers and the various intermediaries, including the trade unions and agencies of the state.

In general, the employer as the buyer of labour has more power, advantage and control than those who need to sell their labour power, and the higher the unemployment the further the balance tilts in the employers' favour: 'employer hiring requirements tend to rise — the definition of an "acceptable" worker is tightened up' (Reynolds, 1951, p. 73). The strengthening of the employers' position by higher unemployment goes much further than greater control over recruitment, and the advantages accruing to them within the workplace seem bound to moderate concern among employers over the wider social and economic costs of increased unemployment. 'The first function of unemployment (which has always existed in open or disguised forms) is that it maintains the authority of master over man' (article in *The Times*, 23 January 1943, quoted in Beveridge, 1944, p. 195).

The possibility of unemployment, the risk of lost security and seniority, results in much 'job stagnation' among those who have doubts about their ability to secure a comparable job, and the effect will be more widespread with rising or persistent unemployment. One in three employed men in North Tyneside said that they had stayed in jobs rather than 'increase the risk of unemployment by moving to another job'. Others avoided becoming unemployed again by accepting downgrading to lower paid or less satisfying work (North Tyneside CDP, 1978, pp. 76 and 230). Both groups have had to compromise more and accept even less independence of their employer as a result of the deterioration in the labour market, putting up with jobs or controls which they might have been able to escape in better times.

The frustrations fostered among those who settle for work at this cost may create a more receptive audience for stories of an affluent life on the dole spent by others, apparently more fortunate and less constrained by the fears or anxieties that keep workers in jobs. By contrast, when or where unemployment has dropped and demand is high, workers are more able, and more likely, to leave jobs and risk a period out of work because the range of opportunities is much greater, and those 'moving voluntarily . . . are more likely to improve their position than those obliged to change jobs' (Hunter and Reid, 1968, p. 24). This underlines the fact that the presence of unemployment impinges upon the labour force at large and not just those currently out of work.

At any level of overall demand, there may be a declining market for particular products or services; and these changes, as well as technological and other developments, may lead employers to seek to reduce their labour costs or change the structure of their labour force. The result may be reduced overtime, increased short-time and specific measures of work-sharing; natural wastage and no fresh recruitment; selective pay-offs or mass redundancies; or a combination of these with some 'labour hoarding' of those seen as most difficult to replace when demand picks up. Which strategy or group of strategies employers follow — or are encouraged or compelled to follow by their financial backers, private or public — will not simply be determined by the nature of the particular problems currently facing them or by the present level of unemployment or demand in the economy. They will also be influenced by past experience and by views of future prospects for the economy, the industry, the company and its particular product; by judgements of the quality, adaptability and pliability of their local labour force; by their assessment of local and national trade union reaction and strike records; by trends in labour costs; by established traditions of paternalistic labour hoarding or ruthless asset-stripping; by expectations of governmental aid and by many other factors. The role of the state, both in its overall management of the economy and in specific support to certain industries or forms of enterprise or development, may be very influential.

The ability or willingness of a company to attempt to ride out a recession will be affected by the resilience of demand for its products and by its own strength. A major employer, such as the large multinational enterprise, may be able to operate more independently of local or even national fluctuations in the business cycle than small firms, but it may be less immune to sharply rising energy costs than to political changes within any one country. With economic and political changes, nationalised industries and the public sector in general may become a major reducer of job opportunities and quickly dismiss earlier proposals that they should become a final protection against unemployment as 'the employer of last resort'.

The consequences for the local community as a whole, as well as the company's workers and the future of a particular industry, may vary considerably according to which decision is taken. A cutback on recruitment restricts opportunities for younger workers particularly, and encourages or compels mobility of that age-group needed to preserve the future of a community. A reduction in apprenticeships will have long-term effects on the industry in terms of the extent of training among the next generation of workers, leading to the problems created, for example, by the lack of skilled bricklayers in the building industry, which particularly suffers from being used as a tool of government economic policy.

'Natural wastage' is a revealing term in its attribution of some normal and legitimating characteristics to the man-made change of enforcing retirement at the earliest pensionable age, or even earlier by some form of severance pay. The privatisation of the economic, social and other costs paid by those who might otherwise have remained much longer in the labour force receives little attention in a society when rising youth unemployment reinforces views that the old should anyway be making way for the young. But the greater poverty and deprivation in their later years of those suddenly or prematurely retired may come to place a greater burden on extended family relationships and on local social services (Townsend, 1979a, chapter 19; Walker, 1980).

The extent and patterns of labour hoarding, rather than labour shedding, vary considerably even within single industries: from 1959 to 1975 rates in the engineering industry were more than twice as high in some sectors as others. But by cutting the number of hours worked a significant part of the cost of hoarding may be transferred from the employer to the workers — as much as 25 per cent in mechanical engineering between 1967 and 1973 (Wabe, 1977, pp. 47–50). Even reduced overtime may bring particular difficulties in Britain where so much trade union wage bargaining has been concerned with pushing up overtime rates and cutting the length of the basic week (Whybrew, 1964). Families' incomes fall sharply with the loss of overtime, and many are plunged into poverty on basic wages alone, while others may suffer significant deprivation and move out of their trade or area.

Over 100 years ago the community around the New Lanark mill set up by Robert Owen was held together because its workers were kept on at full pay for the years that the American Civil War prevented supplies of cotton from reaching them. It must have been a remarkable and most unusual act of cooperative socialism or paternalism then — and appears so again today as the meaning of labour hoarding changes from the retention of valued and valuable workers against a renewal of demand to the failure to shed labour efficiently and so raise productivity and profit. The image of the good employer who looks after his workers is now in more open conflict with the good business-man who prunes his labour costs.

The creation of redundancies is becoming more common, more openly acknowledged and more condoned and even encouraged than at any time since the war. The 1964–70 Labour government's emphasis on the need for redeployment, with the increasing talk of 'shake-out', made keeping on long-serving older workers in less demanding posts appear inefficient and unproductive paternalism. The introduction of a system of redundancy payments partly subsi-dised by the state, where length of service and age led to greater compensation for older workers, made changes in the 'last-in-first-out' convention, and the designation of older workers for pay-off became much easier. Opting for 'voluntary' redundancy was made more attractive to those longer with a company, reducing much of the tension and suspicion engendered by the selection of those to be paid off. For men no longer able to do the more demanding jobs or the overtime that brings up the basic earnings of manual workers, and without the protection of the incremental salaries of many white-collar staff, the chance of a nest-egg for their retirement offered by 'taking their redundancy' may seem much like winning the pools, although the average payment in 1979 was only £850. On Clydeside and other areas of mass pay-offs, it is reported that pubs are changing hands for 'astronomical sums' because of the good custom that is expected from the 'affluently' paid off, but the most general effect of major and multiple redundancies is its destructive or corrosive impact on a community (see for example Bulmer, 1978; Wilkinson, 1939; Jahoda *et al.*, 1972; Ginzberg, 1942; CDP, 1977; Martin and Fryer, 1972).

There is perhaps a general tendency to regard technological change more readily than other reasons as an acceptable cause of redund-ancies, although it may be more a means to reduce labour costs and the extent of trade union and employee power than to modernise the industry and make it more productive and competitive. Here research could start to throw much more light on the 'unemployers' and the creation of unemployment as well as on the experience of those who become redundant (Wood, 1977). Where and how great is the margin of freedom open to employers and employees in seeking to avoid bankruptcy and unemployment?

Some proposals to create unemployment, especially in the form of redundancies and plant closures, have been deferred, defeated or reduced in extent and effect as a result of action by those affected. The collective refusal to accept redundancy or plant shut-down has taken a variety of forms — for example, the struggles of Jimmy Reid and the Upper Clyde workers, the cooperatives of the Glasgow Express, Lucas Aerospace and Meriden Triumph motorcycles, the women leatherworkers who barricaded themselves in their Norfolk factory and the hovercraft builders in Millom (Bradley, 1978). The limited successes and the more general frustrations experienced by the 'militant' activists of the Amalgamated Union of Engineering Workers in Bristol in the early 1970s show the very different perceptions of the 'reality' of redundancy decisions that exist between employers and employees and within these groups (Dey, 1979).

A comparison of the patterns of redundancies, natural wastage, recruitment and the preservation of employment in the steel and mining industries in Britain and France over the last thirty years could cast valuable light on the roles played by management, unions and different parts of government. The more vigorous, prolonged and violent reaction of the French steel unions to announced redundancies — at least at some stages — may be related to the greater development of a secure, unionised employment in some traditionally heavy industrial regions in contrast to a larger, marginal and non-unionised industrial reserve obtainable from the poorer rural areas of south-west France or from the African colonies and ex-colonies, southern Europe and Turkey. The wide gulf separating the two groups may act to increase social distance and reduce the general dilemma for trade unions between their role in protecting the interests of their members within an industry or occupation and their more general political role as champions of the working class. The extent of divisions within the labour force may be maintained, reinforced or widened by the development of institutional barriers within the labour market.

THE DEVELOPMENT OF THE LABOUR MARKET

The economic bargaining and resisting power of different groups in the social structure has become institutionalised over time through a complex variety of institutional rules and traditional practices that tend to favour some groups of workers and exclude others, or at least push them to the margin as the less desirable part of a reserve army (Marx, 1930, pp. 694–716; Braverman, 1974, chapter 17). Analysis of the increasing institutionalisation of the labour market in the United States twenty-five years ago led Clark Kerr to conclude that 'the more secure are the "ins", the greater the penalty for being an "out" (Kerr, 1954, p. 105). Much recent research has suggested distinct, segregated labour markets within an area: the most common division is between a primary labour market, where employment is stable, well-paid, generally highly unionised and offering good opportunities for promotion, and a secondary labour market of dead-end jobs with poor working conditions and low pay, status and security (see, for example, Doeringer and Piore, 1971; 1975, pp. 70–1).

Discrimination by employers in the primary market and the resistance of the better-organised workers in the more desirable jobs to admit those who by their past work experience are seen as marginal or less desirable combine to maintain the divide; and the chances of crossing it may be reduced, some have suggested, by a mutual reinforcement between the attitudes of the poor and the working relationships within the secondary market (Feldstein, 1973a), although others have placed more emphasis on structural changes that create the barriers and separate the groups (Gordon, 1972). Most of these studies have been carried out in the United States, especially in inner-city areas characterised by high unemployment, a concentration of racial or minority groups and discrimination against them (though on European markets, see Castles and Kosack, 1973). The number of separate or segmented markets identified varies, and so do the criteria for differentiation, which have included industry, company, size of enterprise, occupation, age and sex (see for example Edwards *et al.*, 1975, part II).

In Britain there is generally less evidence of segregated labour markets, but there has been renewed interest in the range and form of institutional barriers that serve to stratify the labour force. Although by no means new (see for example Henry Mayhew, 1850, quoted in Thompson and Yeo, 1971; also Friedman, 1977, pp. 68–70), these may have taken on different and perhaps more persistent forms, militating against particular disadvantaged groups. There does, however, appear to be a long-established and persistent occupational segregation of the manual labour market by sex in Britain (Hakim, 1978 and 1979; Barron and Norris, 1976). Despite some limited changes, many of the barriers to women are unlikely to be removed until the demand for labour increases and remains high. There is also some suggestion of a separate youth labour market (e.g. Bosanquet and Doeringer, 1973).

In both the USA and UK there have been developments of some form of an 'irregular' or 'alternative' economy outside the sphere of regular financial transactions, also identified as the 'tertiary', 'illegitimate', 'underground', 'hidden', 'informal' or 'black economy' (Ferman, 1967; Ferman and Ferman, 1973; Ferman *et al.*, 1978; Gershuny and Pahl, 1980a,b; Bluestone, 1970; OCPU, 1978; Caplovitz, 1979; and CSO, 1980). On a self-employed, unofficial and informal basis, services are provided that undercut regular repair and maintenance firms, for example, in return for cash or some service 'off the books' or 'under the table' (Caplovitz, 1979, p. 93). Both seller and buyer derive immediate benefits from operating outside the formal exchange system, which would involve national insurance contributions, VAT and income tax declarations and payments; and the researcher delights in uncovering the more deviant and mordant example such as the 'casket salesman' in American ghettoes who retrieves buried coffins and restores them for second- or third-body sale to poor families (Ferman, 1967, p. 3).

While instances of the extent and variety multiply, work 'on the side' is not new. It is not clear how much this activity has grown, how long it continues and the degree to which its scale responds to the ebb and flow of jobs in the regular economy. We do not know how much its growth is a response to consumer demand or to the greater formal-isation of most employment, a function of cyclical changes in labour demand and supply, a temporary or persistent reaction to heavier direct and indirect taxation amid inflation, or a lasting rejection of the traditional work ethic by those preferring autonomy to the limited security and alienating routines of much employment. A detailed survey in the United States shows that most informal work is carried out for relatives or friends, and very often by people in employment outside their working hours (Ferman *et al.*, 1978). It seems unlikely that it provides an adequate alternative income for many out of work in Britain, although its current scale is a matter of great debate.

THE SIGNIFICANCE OF THE INTERNAL LABOUR MARKET FOR THE UNEMPLOYED

Stratification within the labour force is reinforced by internal labour markets where mobility, especially promotion, occurs mainly within the organisation after recruitment at one of the limited 'ports of entry'. The former tripartite structure of the civil service, with admission into the bottom of the clerical, executive and administrative grades and careers confined to movement within the grade, might provide an ideal type. In American industry the internal market may have become generally more important because of the long-established traditions of plant bargaining and seniority. But even in Japan, where lifetime service within one company is common, security is not ensured for all those working for the company. Much use is made directly, or indirectly through contractors, of a highly marginal and irregularly employed labour force, which has been increased during the recent economic crisis (*DEG*, February 1979, pp. 115–16; Taira, 1970, part II).

In Britain the growth of internal markets in the more technologically advanced industries, in administration and in the professions is likely to be further encouraged because of their advantages to management. Greater control of recruitment and promotion is possible with progress hurdles and 'ports of exit' to enable the easing out of recruitment 'errors'. In some shipyards, five months and twenty-three months are times for paying off the less desirable workers before certain legal rights to service or redundancy pay are gained. Some may find themselves trapped in a series of short-term jobs, and judgements that lead to such persistent insecurity become all the more important for individual workers as one company absorbs others in the same industry in the area (for example, Swan Hunter on the Tyne), or as the number of jobs in that occupation decline. Within any organisation, however, the level of security gained may vary sharply. The protection of an internal market has been a relatively recent development for many professionals who have given up self-employed autonomy and insecurity and often achieved permanent tenure (Perkin, 1969, chapter 3, session 4). Once some probationary hurdle has been cleared, the main anxiety may be the chance of promotion. Greater security also exists in many other higher non-manual posts in administration, and among some workers in the civil service, although it is generally much less in manual jobs.

For many skilled workers there may be security during apprenticeship but, once trained, the new tradesman may be the first to be 'let go' at any pay-off, with comments approving the opportunity to gain further experience elsewhere concealing the fact that the newly skilled worker costs much more on the same work than the trainee. Unem-

ployment may therefore be a greater risk for the skilled worker in the
first decade or so after training, until he is accepted as an established
worker with the company or finds a more secure but poorer paid and
lower status job outside his original craft. The importance of gaining
established status is evident in an industry like the merchant navy,
characterised by recurrent unemployment. The established seaman's
employment and re-employment may be determined at the 'seaman's
pool' where he signs to collect his state unemployment benefit and
any other payments — a privileged and valued status that saves him
from having to go 'on the dole'. The protected status of the 'blue-eyes'
or 'royals' in Tyneside shipyards may depend on the demand for a
specific skill, on personal reputation and ability, and on one's
contacts. Among the less skilled, seniority may be the only protection,
but decline in physical efficiency, let alone poor health, injury or the
change of foreman, may be a major threat to security that long service
may do little to avert. The procedures that have grown up and the local
role and power of the unions may do much to affect the extent to
which selection of those to be paid off is open and consistent.

Internal labour markets are not segregated from the labour market
outside the firm; they are also dynamic, responding to changes in the
demand for or supply of labour. As workers become scarce, employers
relax criteria for entry and increase the ports of entry to enable them
to meet their labour demands. The growing opportunities for job-
changing may also cause the removal of barriers as employers have to
replace the increasing number who leave voluntarily. Even so, in
Peterborough, when unemployment had been low for many years,
women and immigrants had rarely been able to enter the internal
markets for manual labour, and those in poor health, about 15 per
cent of the sample, were excluded altogether (Blackburn and Mann,
1979, pp. 282–4).

When the numbers out of work increase, 'the walls between establishments, rather porous in periods of peak employment, become
much thicker' (Reynolds, 1951, p. 73). Some ports of entry may be
closed and the unemployed admitted only to lower ones, and locked
out of higher, securer employment. School leavers taking dead-end
jobs find it very hard to obtain apprenticeships later because many
employers prefer subsequent generations of school leavers, expecting
them to be more educable — or at least more malleable and less
toughened or unionised — and more willing to manage on the low pay
of apprentices.

Other employers aim to attract 'better' job-seekers — whether this means younger, more qualified, or more compliant — to lower 'ports of entry', and so drive their usual applicants further down the market, displacing those below them. London Transport, for example, advertised for bus drivers: 'You don't need a University background to drive a bus — but it helps . . . a great deal if you are eventually looking for a management career, but feel like a rest from an academic way of life, or are having difficulty in finding a suitable position' (*The Guardian*, 28 June 1979). An excess of applicants encourages open or concealed forms of discrimination in selection. 'Credentialism' — the requirement, for example, of a school-leaving certificate for the most dead-end and least intellectually demanding jobs — effectively and impersonally works against those minority, racial or immigrant groups who receive less supportive or able schooling, on the rationale that even gatekeepers and floor sweepers have to be eligible for promotion in the internal market.

CHANGING DEMAND AND SOCIAL EXCLUSION

The shifting patterns of exclusion and inclusion, significantly influenced by the level of economic activity and by the value or attractiveness of certain groups to employers, indicate an extended hierarchy of security and insecurity across the labour force more than a specific division or divisions between segregated markets. At the top are those positions that convey social honour, high reward and power protected by established tenure or a service contract that guarantees continuing income after job loss (see below p. 156) at the bottom are the marginality, insecurity and poverty of many dead-end jobs, encompassed in such terms as 'sub-employment' for an 'underclass' who experience frequent unemployment until their periods out of work become more and more prolonged.[3]

Between the two ends of the hierarchy lie a great variety of jobs associated with very differing forms and degrees of reward and security. Some with great insecurity may offer high reward while they last, but 'the general structure of the labour market is predominantly hierarchical' rather than compensatory: 'jobs which are better than most on one characteristic tend to be better on others' (Blackburn and Mann, 1979, p. 86). In his study of poverty in the United Kingdom, Townsend found that men who had any experience of unemployment in the year prior to interview were twice as likely as the continuously employed to have had poor or very poor working conditions in their job and to have no entitlement to sick pay or a pension. They were also much less likely to belong to a trade union and to have the right to more than one week's notice (Townsend, 1979a, pp. 605–6 and Table 17.5).

Even in areas or times of high unemployment, the unskilled generally exceed the number of jobs available, and their abilities are not easily discovered except on the job. In consequence, recruiters fall back on general criteria such as appearance or length of unemployment, preferring the job-changer to those already out of work. As the choice available to employers increases, they are more likely to use the duration of unemployment as a rough guide for distinguishing among applicants — in 1979, in one town of average unemployment, some firms were saying that they would not consider any unskilled person out of work for more than two weeks. The labour market disadvantages of those already out of work are made worse during high unemployment because those who have to change jobs avoid work with little security even if wages are high. The unemployed will find not only fewer jobs opened up to them, but fewer still of the more secure ones (see for example Norris, 1978, p. 342).

The extent, therefore, to which certain groups are economically active, have a tenuous and marginal hold on some jobs or are excluded from the labour market altogether is heavily influenced by the success or failure of the economy in generating opportunities for employment and by the accustomed criteria for allocating this work. Those who find it more difficult to enter the labour force or to obtain jobs once they have become unemployed tend to be those people whom employers generally consider it less profitable, convenient or easy to employ, whether they regard them as less able or adaptable, or less compliant and insufficiently ready to accept existing patterns of work or discipline. Those without paid work therefore tend to be found disproportionately among the young and the old, the disabled and those in remote areas, and generally among the poorer and less powerful in society including radical, religious, immigrant and other minority groups, single parents with young children to look after and restrictions on their availability, those with mental hospital or prison records and so on. But they may also include those considered simply uncooperative or overactive in worker organisation or members of management who are too entrepreneurial and maybe threatening to senior colleagues (Hartley, 1980c).

This is not to say that these characteristics are the causes of their unemployment (Sinfield, 1976a, pp. 223–5). For example, many jobs, even manual ones, are physically less demanding because of more mechanical and other aids, and more older people are fitter and in better health than twenty or thirty years ago. But a worker who loses his job after the age of 50, or 40 in areas of very high unemployment, will be lucky to get back to work unless he has especially valuable skills or good contacts. Whatever the cause of his becoming unemployed, his remaining out of work is affected by the preference or prejudice of employers, intermediaries in job centres, and maybe his own internalisation of ageist views as well as the level of demand. The emphasis has to be placed first on employers', or recruiters', perception of what is desirable in applicants for a post (Hartley, 1980c; Berthoud, 1979, p. 83; and Reynolds, 1951) rather than on the motivation of the individual (Sheppard and Belitsky, 1966).

All the many reasons why certain groups have not been acceptable or desirable as 'good' workers have tended to fade away in the past as unemployment dropped and remained low and production was held up by lack of labour. Those who might have been discarded or at least not discouraged from leaving were helped to stay on, and the pace of work eased or its demands adjusted for workers reaching the normal retirement age. Employers actively recruited women with children to support for part-time work, visited schools to compete for school leaves, installed special ramps and machines to enable disabled handicapped workers to participate, approached probation staff to attract those coming out of prison, provided training in the local language for foreign workers or set up recruiting offices abroad — as London Transport did in Barbados in the postwar years of relative labour shortage.

This point was brought home to me in the mid-1960s during a study of the long-term unemployed in ten OECD countries. The proportion out of work for six months or more varied across the countries from 20 per 1000 members of the labour force down to barely 1 per 1000 (in Britain it is now rising above 25 per 1000 compared with less than 5 then — Sinfield, 1968, p. 26). What was considered surplus labour in countries of high unemployment became essential manpower in those of labour shortage: a variety of programmes and strategies were being initiated by employers and the state to attract into work people who were regarded as so handicapped, marginal or unemployable in the other countries that it was argued that they should properly be excluded from the statistics of unemployment.

Historical and comparative perspectives help to make us more aware of the ways in which changes in the demand for and supply of labour influence the social construction of definitions of the labour force in general and the unemployed in particular, and the legitimation of states of dependency. The age at which people wish to retire, and others may think it appropriate for them to do so, is significantly affected by the extent to which their long experience is valued or they are seen as keeping younger, and maybe more productive, workers out of a job. The speed at which women return to the labour force after childbirth is influenced by job opportunities and the readiness of employers to permit flexibility in working hours and to provide crèches and other facilities; or, in traditional working-class areas outside the textile towns, by the fact that their husbands are securely in work, and so there is less opposition to married women working.

The state of the economy is of course not the only determinant of movements in and out of the labour force. Changes, for example, in the labour force participation of women are occurring despite an economic environment that in many ways is making these much more difficult to achieve, but it is important to recognise that the level of the demand for labour, and the reactions to this, help to influence the extent to which the surrender, adoption or designation of the status of dependant is seen as legitimate and deserving, or illegitimate and undeserving, by individuals, communities and organisations including the many different offices of the state. Indeed the state's role in designating certain states of dependency acceptable ('early' retirement) or reprehensible ('scrounger' or 'work-shy') is particularly influential as these statuses become reinforced and institutionalised by different official measures that both derive from and have an impact on the state of the labour market.

THE JOB-BROKERS

Any analysis of institutional forces operating in the labour market should take account of the operation, scale and growing variety of state and other forms of 'intervention' in the labour market, including the whole range of manpower and income support policies. These have a significant effect on what jobs there are, on which job-seekers get what type of work and how quickly, and on the standards of living of those left out of work and the perceptions of the value ascribed to work and the social meaning and status of being out of work. This and the following section illustrate briefly the influence of job-broking and income support measures (for a fuller analysis of these and other labour market policies, see chapter 4).

For the employment service 'the gravest difficulties stem from conflicts of interest among [its] clients, which it must somehow mediate in order to survive', so 'its procedures must always represent a working compromise among conflicting interests and pressures' (Reynolds, 1951, p. 72). Each employer naturally expects the best applicants available, and the unemployed are also in competition with each other; but above all there are the opposing interests of the two groups. Policies and practices best serving employers will not necessarily best help those seeking work, although they may well help some to the exclusion of others.

In the 1970s the development of new purpose-built Job-Centres, often in central shopping areas, physically separated job-filling from dealing with benefits for the unemployed, which generally continued in the old Labour Exchanges that from their earliest days 'HM Office of Works had the desire to place . . . in those parts of the industrial towns which had the least savoury reputation' (Beveridge, 1953, p. 78). The display of vacancies on boards at the front of the job-shops now allows an element of self-service for anyone interested in finding new work, whether employed or unemployed (*EG*, February 1980, pp. 122 *passim*.; MSC, 1979a). It has been argued that this change has favoured the job-changer and worked against those becoming demoralised because of the length of their unemployment whose regular context with placing staff has been cut off. There has been official admission that two-thirds of those unemployed between one and two years and three-quarters of those out of work for more than two years had never been submitted for a job, although it is not at all clear that his has only occurred since separation of job-shop and benefit office. The service continues to be 'in a dilemma. It works for employers rather than the unemployed' (Metcalf, 1980, p. 25).

In what ways, and to what extent, does the employment service's dependence upon retaining the goodwill of employers in order to obtain knowledge of vacancies lead staff to select some job-seekers for submission before others? How far does this reduce any official resistance to notifying jobs that are below Wages Council rates and provide poor, if not harmful, prospects? And how far do the criteria for submission to these jobs help to create or maintain inferior labour market chances for the more marginal or vulnerable who then become labelled as unsuitable for better work because they are always in and out of jobs? There appears to be very little evidence on these questions and on the extent to which staff reflect or even reinforce what they believe to be employers' preferences (for two perspectives in the United States, see Blau, 1963, and Cohen, 1965). One exception in Britain is the light thrown on the work of the Disablement Resettlement Officers: they appear to insist on their role as educators of employers and to resist — or are officially discouraged from — policing the quota system (which requires 3 per cent of employees to be registered disabled), even when it is flouted by more than half the nation's employers (Simpson, 1975; Bolderson, 1980; and the studies carried out for MSC, 1979b). With rising unemployment they seem likely to restrict rather than increase the number and type of job chances available to a group that is particularly vulnerable to prolonged unemployment once out of work (Jordan, 1979). Such a policy could perhaps be more helpful to the disabled in areas or times of labour shortage than amid high unemployment.

A more buoyant economy would generally reduce the extent of the service's dependence on the buyer, who would have to rely more on its help to find scarcer labour, but there would also need to be a clear and sustained change of policy. In the low unemployment years after the war, the service often appeared to maintain a primary responsibility to employers — in some contrast to other countries (Sobel and Wilcock, 1966, pp. 38 and 74; Sinfield, 1968, pp. 66–74; Reubens, 1970). The prohibition of private employment agencies, as in Sweden, strengthens the position of the state service. More comparative analyses would show how far different systems of job-broking maintain or modify differences in the abilities of different groups to obtain work and how these operations affect or preserve public and official perceptions of the unemployed and encourage differential treatment of those seen as more, or less, deserving.

In the United States, political parties as well as trade unions have more involvement in job allocation, probably strengthening yet further the market position of the more established and securer workers in unions against minority immigrant and ethnic groups. Even within official services, stratification and division can often be particularly important. In one city in upstate New York in the mid-1960s the state employment service had separate offices for different occupational groups, ranging from the higher white-collar one (where its own local administration was based) with an attractive reception area, well-furnished with armchairs, carpets and glass and chrome coffee tables covered with magazines, through various linoleum-floored offices in different parts of the city to a shopfront with a few wooden benches and tables. From around six in the morning employers would drive up, shout out the numbers wanted and pick the men out from the groups waiting inside or outside. This 'office' appeared to close by eight each morning, with those unselected drifting off disconsolately: officials appeared to regard them as 'bums' and unemployables. The county welfare department believed the state service so little interested in these 'hard-to-place', generally black, unemployed that they were paying a private agency to get claimants off benefits and into work — often jobs of an insecure, dead-end type that soon left them out of work again.

In Britain, the division of services to help the unemployed find work, or at least to reduce their dependence on public support, has developed at national level. The long-term or recurrently unemployed who may expect to gain the poorest jobs — those sometimes described as the sub-employed — may receive most attention from the Unemployment Review Officers (UROs), although these staff are formally part of the income support system (see chapter 4, pp. 111–12). Their official functions 'in the interests both of claimants and of public accountability' (SBC, 1977, p. 50) serve to underline the ambiguity of their role as 'the guardians of work'. For those with long unemployment or a 'poor' work record, they may act as controllers of access to work, training and other opportunities and provide information of jobs or speak on behalf of the unemployed to counter unwillingness to employ somebody long out of work, disabled, with poor English, black, immigrant, or old. But they also serve to maintain the ethic of work by encouraging, cajoling or frightening some unemployed into work that is not likely to be as good, well-paid, secure or safe as that notified to the Job-Centres for those seen as more suitable or deserving, or just as 'ordinary' unemployed without any special problems.

The UROs have self-deprecatingly described their own work in helping or chasing men back to back amid high unemployment as 'shuffling the pack'; and some of them have objected to chasing up the 'poorly motivated' when so many people are keenly seeking work. Except perhaps marginally, they cannot add to the number of jobs; but what sort of work with what pay, security and opportunities a man is enabled to obtain may have long-term effects on his life-chances. The criteria for dealing a card to one claimant rather than another, whether he is seen as more worthy of help or of chivvying, become all the more important when there are few vacancies and length of time out of work is one of the most common yardsticks in recruitment. The very creation of these posts amid rising unemployment in the late 1960s, their maintenance when unemployment increased even further and the announcement in February 1980 of their strengthening by another 530 as a cost-effective measure — and the publicity given to these developments — deserve to be considered as an important part of the formal ways in which the state reinforces the general expectation that all who are able, and have no private means of support, should work to maintain themselves and certain specific dependants.

Operating generally at the other end of the social spectrum from the UROs is the Professional and Executive Recruitment (PER). Since 1973 it has been under strict requirement to achieve commercial self-sufficiency, charging employers for services that include preliminary interviewing and shortlisting. It is now 'unequivocally employer-orientated . . . entirely geared to finding staff to suit the employer . . . it does not attempt to find an employer to fit the candidate's needs', and less than half the people placed in 1977/8 were unemployed (Berthoud, 1979, pp. 92–3).

While both PER and UROs have become more directed towards reducing public, taxpayer-borne costs of unemployment, the social distance between their customers deserves emphasis because their very operation on either side of the basic state employment service serves to reinforce, even shape, differing perceptions of the needs of different 'classes' of unemployed. 'Work-shy' and 'malingerer' appear class-specific terms, and there seems greater readiness to account for lack of mobility or prolonged unemployment among senior white-collar staff in terms of institutional or employer-determined factors rather than the personal characteristics that tend to be stressed in accounting for the experience of low-status and low-skilled unemployed (see for example last chapter of Berthoud, 1979).

The admittedly crude picture emerging from such contrasts is of a stratified service that is all the more likely to limit the extent and direction of mobility when jobs are scarce. Professional and executive staff, for example, are generally helped to stay within these occupations, and those without clearly appropriate credentials have to break into these jobs by their own efforts. At the same time, the efforts of the UROs — or their very existence given the public view that they chase 'dole-dodgers', whatever they actually do — may result in others becoming more marginal and seen as less employable as they move from one insecure job to another with increasingly longer spells on social security.

In addition to the official intermediaries in the British labour market, there are of course many others, besides the now very limited help provided by the trade unions. Into the 1970s at least, some unions actually controlled the allocation of jobs: companies would contact the local sheet metal workers' union, for example, and not the state employment service. In other countries this practice is still firmly established as a benefit to both union and employer, encouraging union membership and possibly enabling more experienced selection and potential union sanctions on unsatisfactory workers. In Britain, private employment agencies have only recently been brought under some control, which is at least partly intended to protect job-seekers from certain forms of exploitation. In the major cities, and for certain occupations such as routine and junior non-manual, they may exercise a powerful influence, tending to help the younger and the qualified or qualifying, not the older, disabled or redundant manual worker. In the catering industry, they may come to depend on and exploit the marginal and insecure population of immigrants and the single homeless (NAB, 1966) for many of the poorest jobs.

The dramatic growth in agencies providing 'temps', especially in clerical, secretarial, and nursing jobs for women, may have worked considerably to the advantage of younger women and against others trying to bring up a family on their own or with some other restriction on their working hours and less mobility. The use of temporary staff also gives the employer more control over labour costs and reduces the number of workers to whom he is more committed and has to provide 'fringe' benefits; and in a bad labour market some of the 'temps' may face increasing insecurity as they fail to gain an established position.

WELFARE, CONTROL AND THE DIFFERENTIATION OF NEED AMONG THE UNEMPLOYED

One might expect the ways in which the state and other intermediaries allocate, and even create, jobs to have the strongest influence on perceptions of the unemployed and the legitimacy and urgency of their need. But 'income maintenance' schemes have come to exercise an extraordinarily powerful effect on public, political and administrative perceptions of what ought to be done about unemployment. The separate measures, with their very different mixtures of compensation and control, designate degrees of 'deserving' and 'undeserving', while providing very different levels of support that help to stratify the unemployed (for details, see chapter 4, pp. 109–14, introduction, pp. 21–3 and pp. 234–237).

These variations affect the return to work as well as the experience of unemployment. Some help to protect the unemployed from taking jobs with less pay, status and security, while others bring the modern stigmata of pauperism, locking them further into an 'underclass' of sub-employment and insecurity if they can find work at all. Poor benefits may compel the unemployed to exhaust any economic or social capital, demoralise them and their families, inhibit risk-taking and the will to compete for the few jobs available to many job-seekers, foster delinquent or criminal activity to increase resources, and hasten earlier withdrawal from the labour force. The effect may be all the greater when there are frequently announced drives against stroungers, the distribution of 'fraud awareness packages' to social security offices and increases in Unemployment Review Officers as part of public campaigns against abuse. The state's negative view of some of the unemployed becomes all the more evident when such measures are accompanied by cuts in special schemes to assist the long-term unemployed (see below, pp. 227–8).

To understand the effects of these programmes, one needs to examine not only whether there is poverty, however defined, but how changes in the source and extent of benefits, the conditions of receipt and the controls over behaviour touch the lives of the unemployed, their valuation of themselves and the perceptions of others — family, neighbours, officials, potential employers and also the wider society in its discussion of unemployment and the needs of the unemployed. 'The danger . . . of a generous plan of assistance' was stressed by Beveridge because of 'its effect on the minds of those in authority — governments, trade unions, leaders of industry' rather than any 'demoralising influence' upon those out of work (Beveridge, 1930, pp. 408–9).

In recent years the growth of schemes with different and over-lapping levels of benefit that provide a very wide range of support has helped to foster impressions of bounteous aid and to fuel concern over abuse and hostility — ironically, toward those unemployed on the lowest, and most restrictive, class of benefits. Political concern for the unemployed has thus become weakened: administrations concerned with public expenditure and the need to control wage demands and restrain the power of the trade unions feed upon and even nourish the opposition to benefits. While the growth of unemployment may be condoned, at best treated as regrettable but necessary, the state of being unemployed comes to be condemned. Even increases in the numbers out of work may lead to greater 'blaming of the victim' among many influential groups (Ryan, 1973; chapter 3, pp. 000–00).

The link between the structural issue of unemployment and the particular forms of income support is all the more important because of the significance over the centuries of the poor laws as the most evident area of the state's authority, power and control over most citizens. It has continued in its modern form to be the main means of preserving the work ethic, particularly for the poorly paid worker. The poor laws developed as the most punitive part of our family laws, and were an indispensable part of the overall system of labour legislation. Very often linked with legal prohibition of any form of wage bargaining and the formal establishment of *maximum* wage rates, they were heavily dominated by the fear of creating 'dependency' among the able-bodied out of work and the need to maintain incentives and work discipline (tenBroek, 1971; Mencher, 1968; Piven and Cloward, 1972).

The reforms early in the twentieth century, including unemployment insurance, drew on measures of trade union solidarity as well as Bismarkian tactics to fend off socialism. In sharp contrast to the 1834 Poor Law's intention to do something *to* the unemployed, these changes aimed to do more *for* them (though see Friedman, 1977, pp. 65–6). This prepositional difference reflected more a distinction made among those out of work than a change of attitude towards them all: 'strict discipline' for 'the able-bodied but chronically idle' experiencing 'recurrent distress' was being recommended by the poor law authorities even as they supported new schemes for 'the elite of the unemployed . . . respectable workmen settled in a locality, hitherto accustomed to regular work, but temporarily out of employment through circumstances beyond their control' (Royal Commission on the Poor Laws, 1909, pp. 1070–2 and 1114).

The continuation of the lower-status poor laws with such measures as the household means test and 'the less eligibility' of the wage-stop not only worked to confer stigmata on assistance programmes, their clients and often their staff: it also helped to legitimate unemployment insurance and its recipients as higher status and more deserving

(Deacon, 1976; Elks, 1974). The two schemes continue to have very different controls and surveillance, with different earnings limits for the claimants and their spouses, even though the basic assistance allowances exceed the flat rate insurance benefits for most unemployed with dependants.

Today, the longest and most frequently unemployed who have come from the poorest jobs are most likely to be dependent on assistance, while the higher paid, with least risk of both becoming and remaining unemployed, gain the highest levels of earnings-related insurance benefit, suffer from the least controls, and often receive redundancy payments for the loss of their job. The total impact of the changes of the mid-1960s was to widen the gaps among those out of work and set the long-term unemployed further apart from other recipients of state benefits, leaving them poorer as well as more subject to scrutiny and harassment (for details, see chapter 4, pp. 109–14). The recognition of separate and greater needs for others, however justified, had the effect of reducing the long-term unemployed, one of the poorest groups in our society, to their old inferior position and largely deprived them of the more equal status they gained under the flat rate benefit schemes of the low-employment years after the war. Redundancy payments have created a yet higher tier of most deserving job-losers whose compensation is secure whether they remain out of work or not; and by these individual benefits, sometimes topped up by employers, much trade union and worker resistance to redundancy has been removed (Dey, 1979).

In the United States, the division of power among federal, state and local agencies and the centrifugal tradition of states' rights and individualism have allowed even greater differentiation to grow and flourish. The most generous forms of support are private supplements to state insurance payments that result from union–employer bargaining. Most state insurance schemes derive from private plans designed in the 1920s Taylorist drive for greater business efficiency. In 1935 'the "European" approach, with its emphasis on the workers' economic needs, lost out to an "American" approach . . . which looked to the employer, often encouraging him to "prevent" unemployment' (Nelson, 1969, p. viii). Employer-only financing envisaged not just economic man, but economic employers, rationally able to dominate market forces, and embodied a variety of contribution devices intended to provide incentives to employers not to pay-off workers. This pre-Keynesian conception of the causes of unemployment has led to large employers appointing staff to contest benefit claims and generally advise on employee reduction in ways that have involved the smallest charge to the employer's insurance account. This has reinforced other tendencies toward secondary labour markets and the maintenance of an insecure and temporarily employed industrial reserve, including less-skilled black or minority workers, women with children to support on their own, disabled older workers with redundant skills, teenagers in inner-city areas and others who rarely qualify for insurance benefits.

Exclusion from the better jobs is further increased by assistance programmes that still owe much to the English poor laws of 1601 and 1834. Less than half the American states provide federally aided assistance for unemployed parents with families, and help for single unemployed is at best limited and restricted, often repressive, humiliating and stigmatising. Even in the federally assisted schemes, states set their own levels of need and then pay only a fraction of this for all or part of the year (see especially May, 1964, chapters 1 and 2, 'Go to the Ant, thou Sluggard . . .', and 'Newburgh: The Catalyst'; also Elman, 1966; Steiner, 1966 and 1971; Sinfield, 1976b; and SRS, 1979).

My own limited comparative analysis has made me very conscious of the constant grafting on to old systems of new schemes embodying different perceptions of justice and desert, of the causes of unemployment and of the merit and function of relief. The ideas institutionalised in the older programmes are not replaced, and the persistence of means-tested schemes may actually serve to keep notions of 'wilful idleness' among the lower classes alive, active and influential.

THE PERSONAL IMPACT OF UNEMPLOYMENT

Consideration of the impact of unemployment upon the lives of people out of work, their families and the wider community has been left to the end of this chapter because it can only be fully understood or analysed in the context of the earlier discussion. Emphasis is placed upon the variations in the experience of being out of work, the significance of changing demand for labour and perceptions of this, and the importance of access to resources in moderating the effects of unemployment.

There is general agreement that people out of work 'are not simply units of employability who can, through the medium of the dole, be put in cold storage and taken out again immediately they are needed.

While they are in cold storage, things are likely to happen to them'
(Pilgrim Trust, 1938, quoted in McGregor, 1979, p. 122). Studies of
the unemployed and accounts by people out of work or others working
with them provide many vidid insights into the experience (for the
former, see especially Bakke, 1933; Marsden and Duff, 1975; Aiken *et
al.*, 1968; Jahoda *et al.*, 1972; North Tyneside CDP, 1978; for the
latter, see Gould and Kenyon, 1972; Cohen, 1945; and Hannington,
1936). There has, however, been fairly little systematic and sustained
analysis of variations in the impact of what is a far from uniform
experience (Ferman, 1964). Unemployment is 'often a double loss'
(Hartley, 1980b): it may bring both the lack of the activity of work,
which provides a structure for the daily life of the individual and the
community, and the lack of the exchange relationship of employment,
which gives access to earnings and status.

The experience of unemployment varies greatly. A skilled fitter,
joiner or electrician in the shipyards, accustomed to being laid off
between jobs when there is quite evidently no work to be seen in the
yards, may welcome the break. To avoid heavy forfeit payments on
late delivery of a ship, the last few weeks or months may have involved
many hours of overtime over the whole week, and he will now have a
chance to relax with his family, catch up on some gardening, turn his
skills to repairs and improvements in his home, using perhaps the
greatly increased earnings of the last few weeks. Known and well-
regarded by the foreman, he will treat the first few weeks as a holiday
with every expectation of a recall when new orders arrive. Neighbours
and others in the community whose steep streets look down on the
empty shipyards recognise the interruption in work as part of the
established routine of the trade.

This is likely to be very different from the introduction to unemployment for the worker made redundant by the closure of a company
or its local branch — a common occurrence in high unemployment
areas as many big firms retain considerable flexibility in their labour
costs by expanding and contracting at their margins, exploiting the
opportunities for cheaper factories and other state subsidies in these
areas (CDP, 1977). The reaction for some may come close to 'the
psychology of unemployment' claimed in a review of studies during
the depression years:

> first there is shock, which is followed by an active hunt for a job, during
> which the individual is still optimistic and unresigned; he still main-
> tains an unbroken attitude. Second, when all efforts fail, the individual
> becomes pessimistic, anxious and suffers active distress; this is the most

crucial state of all. And, third, the individual becomes fatalistic and adapts himself to his new state but with a narrower scope. He now has a broken attitude. [Eisenberg and Lazarsfeld, 1939, p. 378]

— though see also the five stages identified by Bakke (1960, p. 113).

Analyses of the social and psychological impact, however, need to recognise a greater variety of reactions to allow for different precipitating causes of unemployment, varying demand for workers according to their occupation, level of skills, age, etc. and differing possession of and access to social and economic resources (Sinfield, 1968, pp. 61–8). While the early shock may fit the unexpected redundancy or disability, any optimism is likely to depend on the level of local demand, the age and health of the worker and the transferability of skills. The fatalism, or lack of openly expressed frustration, may be the initial reaction of those becoming accustomed to the repeated experience of unemployment to which those in the least secure and poorly paid work appear particularly vulnerable. Active distress may be greater among those forced by disability, declining health or lack of demand for their experience and skills to look for less rewarding and lower-status jobs or to contemplate many years of passing their time on the dole until they can claim the established status, and higher benefits, of retirement.

By contrast, the first experience of unemployment for the young school leaver may initially seem like his last school holidays, especially if his friends are out of work with him. With spending money maintained by his family, there may be a general sense of freedom at the release from a school where teachers have abandoned teaching for occupying or simply controlling those they expect to go into unskilled work (Willis, 1977).

The departure of friends into work and the evidence of their increased resources may bring a sharper realisation of the problems and the cutting-off of opportunities as he is pushed down into looking for poorer work than he had hoped for, missing the many apprenticeships with a fixed age of entry. Even if the market improves, it is the next generation of school leavers who will benefit, while his experience of the initially better-paid but less skilled jobs reveals how insecure and deadening many of them are. Movement between them becomes the only way of varying the monotony of many work routines that exploit the young unskilled. While jobs are plentiful, this may be a useful strategy, perhaps the best way to find out the better employers and the most tolerable jobs. Employers may prefer this mobility to disruptive or even destructive attempts to relieve the dreary monotony:

it saves them from having to make the job more attractive, provided that enough labour is available, and enables them to cut labour costs by replacing only when necessary.

Meanwhile the family and others may at least condone the job changing – 'they're only young'; 'they'll learn' or 'they'll have to settle down soon enough' — provided that the spells out of work are short and the jobs are available. When the competition for fewer jobs becomes greater, movement becomes riskier and many employers will prefer those with little or no unemployment and few changes of job: the job-changing 'becomes deadly' as the teenager spends longer in the labour market (Phillips, 1973, p. 416; see also Carter, 1966; Oxford University, 1975; Keil *et al.*, 1966; Reubens, 1977).

Being out of work may also be very different for married women in a society where expectations of their continued and obligatory parti- cipation in the labour force are still very different from those of married men and where even fewer of the jobs available to women offer any continuing career prospects. While this inequality persists, the unemployed wife may well lose less status and feel less to blame or blamed than would her husband on becoming unemployed. If he has secure and well-paid work, she may suffer less loss of income or access to it, especially given the much lower earnings of women. But her own power and control over resources and her own life within marriage and family may be significantly affected; and the total resources of many households may be brought down severely as many more families need two earners to keep them out of poverty – the proportion of families in poverty or near-poverty with men in full-time work would be increased by over 50 per cent but for their wives' earnings (Townsend, 1979a, p. 631; see also Hamill, 1978).

The extent of speculation must, however, be stressed because least of all is known through research about the effects of unemployment on women, whether single or married, with or without children (though see Eisenberg and Lazarsfeld, 1938, p. 375). Society, or influential groups within it, tends to regard the employment, not the unemploy- ment, of mothers with children as a social problem, preventing them from carrying out their unpaid roles as providers of social services for immediate and extended family and many others in the community, and so throwing an 'unnecessary' burden on the official services (Finch and Groves, 1980). Thus, long-established assumptions about women's work in the home and the duties of a mother impede recog- nition of unemployment among women as a problem (Land, 1979), which depends upon prior acknowledgement that they have a legitimate right to work in the employed labour force during peacetime. The lack of sufficient employment reinforces opposition: new factories in a depressed area 'only' bring jobs for women, and married women 'take' men's jobs. Wives of unemployed men often stress the problems of going out to work: 'what man can rest easy when his wife's in work and he's not?' or 'it's not right to be out at work when your man's not'. Both formal and informal pressures to find and stay in work are at present greater for husbands, and there is less stigma for wives who remain out of employment – and correspondingly less anxiety over their needing incentives or direction from officials (although it is barely a decade since mothers bringing up children on their own were more openly urged by assistance officials to find a job and stop claiming benefit).

These brief illustrations of the variation in the experience of unemployment, however stereotyped and in need of qualification they are, call attention to the importance of the level and nature of economic demand and the ways in which the unemployed and others perceive the experience. The demand for labour not only affects the incidence, length and occurrence of unemployment, and the official and other views of who should or should not be looking for work; it helps to shape the very character of the experience of being out of work. The lack of jobs changes the search for work into a monotonous routine that is itself depressing and often humiliating; the significance of luck, and 'who you know' not 'what you know', in finding work may diminish the unemployed workers' own respect for their skills and length of experience. Increasing numbers in the labour market, including many coming into the area in search of work, or the return of most friends and neighbours to work, affect the morale and confidence of those still unemployed.

The recurrent lay-offs from the shipyards mentioned above may be tolerable when the breaks are short and the wages in the yards are above the local average, but they bring greater anxieties when the industry is in decline. Older men fear that they will be overlooked at the next recall, especially if their health or general fitness is in question. Those whose skills are obsolete find long and useful service no longer gains them alternative work, and others who are regarded as troublesome, vociferous or just active in organising may be left out of work. The very competition for work and the vulnerability of all the unemployed to individual selection or rejection may weaken solidarity in many ways and reduce willingness to support the weakening powers of older men, to adjust the work routine and its speed for the disabled worker or the young and inexperienced, to stand up for more independent workmates, or to accept 'foreigners' whether distinguished by race, language, length of residence or simply by coming from the other side of the Tyne.

Beliefs about the extent of job opportunities, and whether they are increasing or diminishing, also affect the general tenor of views in society as a whole, in the local community and in the immediate family about the extent to which those out of work are victims of external forces to be supported and helped, or more responsible and to be blamed and stigmatised. The increased sympathy with the sharp rise in unemployment in the winter of 1962 was followed by criticism or dismissal of the smaller number remaining out of work by the end of the next year – 'just the dregs left on the dole' as one town clerk said to me. But there has generally been even harsher criticism of the unemployed in recent years, despite the declining job opportunities and the consensus that prospects for the unemployed will only worsen for the next few years at least. Even within families, as income falls and any savings disappear, sympathy may give way to tolerance and then tension and friction. Being left on the dole may become evidence of personal failure for the unemployed and those close to them; and these feelings and their implications are not easy to dismiss or discuss.

The importance of access to adequate resources is brought out by the ways in which some are able to protect themselves in advance from much of the risk of unemployment, indicating their greater power and control. Some employers, managers and key staff may secure service contracts that are virtually 'fireproof'. Whatever happens to the job or the firm, a salary may be guaranteed for many years with a share in any growth of sales or profits, a generous pension, the opportunity to take over company cars and other so-called 'fringe benefits' at considerable discounts — and the whole protected by discreetly planned 'tax efficiency' or 'tax mitigation' with the help of the growing body of company and individual tax advisers. But the scale and availability of these types of contract remain among the more concealed of the growing underworld of 'perks'.

Escape from the personal troubles of unemployment may also be achieved by finding an alternative source of income and an acceptable way of occupying one's time, without the stigma or loss of social honour that generally accompanies being supported by the state, whether 'on the dole' or in some public works. Many unemployed openly express a desire for a smallholding, corner–shop or small business where they can be their own masters — less vulnerable, they believe, to the risk of unemployment as well as the other controls of an employer and his agents — but very few have the resources to achieve this. More recently there has been increasing discussion of the greater intrinsic and extrinsic rewards and satisfactions of work found in the 'irregular' or 'alternative' economy by those who have escaped from both unemployment and employment (see references on p. 136 above). It is less clear how often this is a permanent move rather than a temporary resort for those with appropriate skills, more enterprise or boldness, some times continuing on a large scale what they already did in their spare time while employed; and there is also doubt about the extent to which one form of insecurity is being exchanged for another with no protection against illness, injury or the need to retire.[4]

The greater protection of service contracts and the 'escape' into an alternative economy both underline the importance of access to resources. Managers may generally be better protected from much of the hardship of unemployment; but 'self-esteem was not lower amongst the unemployed [than employed] managers and did not decline with longer unemployment' in a study of eighty-seven unemployed middle and senior managers (Hartley, 1980a). Some redundant staff on a management training course saw the break from the executive 'rat-race' as 'a superb opportunity to rethink their lives and start anew', but they had generally felt less involved or interested in their previous jobs, had not been subject to a forced redundancy and felt much less stress as a consequence (Fineman, 1978, p.334). There are also reports of successful changes of direction, such as the semi-skilled worker from the Midlands now fully absorbed in nature conservancy in the Lake District. One senior executive with many years in top management, first interviewed on television during a long and admittedly painful period out of work, eventually took over the running of a children's home with his wife. In a subsequent programme they both spoke of the greater sense of fulfilment and happiness on a much reduced income, and the opportunity provided by the husband's unemployment to reassess what they sought in life.

But for the great majority, the loss of the activity and involvement of work, and any rewards of status and privilege that attend it, may be considerable (Daniel, 1974, p.149). Even when income remains high, there may be significant deprivation and distress (Berthoud, 1979, chapter III). One manager could not bring himself to tell his wife or anyone else of the loss of his post and continued travelling to London by the same train until his season ticket expired. For some, 'early retirement' may be an acceptable and effective cover that maintains an honourable status, but at a cost of reduced living standards, especially in later years. Such a withdrawal from the labour force is unlikely to have allowed, for example, the usual replacement of household equipment and furnishings undertaken in the years before normal retirement. Despite the many variations in the experience of unemployment, therefore, the main theme that emerges from both official and independent research, from large or small studies, is the bleak, generally unrelieved picture of deprivation, lost opportunity and poverty among those out of work and their families — especially when the only wage earner is out of work a number of times or, even worse, for a prolonged period (Townsend, 1979a, Chapter 17; Clark, 1978; Hill *et al.*, 1973; introduction, p. 23–25).

Families with dependent children tend to be the worst off, needing to cut back more on expenditure and 'to borrow money and sell possessions to a greater extent than those without a dependent family' (North Tyneside CDP, 1978, p. 213). Their relatively greater deprivation is made worse by the more urgent nature of many demands on families' incomes (see especially Clark, 1978). While some needs can be put off till re–employment, winter shoes and coats for growing children or extra heating for babies cannot be. The greater risk of poverty and hardship among unemployed families contrasts sharply with the strongly held and widespread view that unemployed men with families are least hard–hit by the loss of earnings. Given the combined impact of publicly expressed disapproval — or at least lack of sympathy — and the financial pressures, and the ways that signs of poverty themselves become excluding or isolating stigmata, it is not surprising that reports of strain or tension within the family are more common when unemployed men have more family members dependent on them (North Tyneside CDP, 1978, p. 102; Newcastle upon Tyne City Council, 1980). 'Budget reductions and over-proximity caused frequent tensions between family members, occassionally leading to violence, divorce and family break–ups' (Colledge and Bartholomew, 1980, p. 11; see also J.M. Hill, 1978, p. 120).

It is part of the social construction of unemployment that attention to the troubles of those most vulnerable to the unequal risk of being out of work has remained very limited. yet a national study showed that poverty persisted 'for the much larger number [than the currently out of work] of those who have experienced spells of unemployment (however short) in the recent past' because they had either found poorly paid jobs or 'had become sick, or unemployed again' (Townsend, 1979a, p. 614). Most of the debate about incentives and the extent to which benefits out of work replace or exceed earnings has ignored the inadequacy of either income for many. When new groups have been hit by unemployment, they have been more likely to be seen as suffering hardship, and so the response to their personal troubles, in terms for example of adequate compensation, has been more likely to become a public issue. But the persistently unequal impact of unemployment, low earnings and poverty in or out of work is less likely to become a major public issue and tends to be seen as part of the 'natural' order that requires no policy intervention, let alone an urgent one.

This imbalance may be reinforced by standard methods of research. The acute deprivation and indignation of someone recently and unexpectedly made redundant, volubly aware of new problems and anxieties may be vividly caught in the snapshot of the single interview. But the same method may reveal little of the chronic poverty and the shrunken demands that are made on life by those who have been out of work many years. The disabled man, over 50 years of age and living alone in a high-unemployment area may appear to express a certain satisfaction with his uneventful life and low income because he has come to expect so little. Prolonged unemployment becomes for most 'a profoundly corrosive experience, undermining personality and atrophying work capacities' (Harrison, 1976, p. 34, and studies cited there; see also Colledge and Bartholomew, 1980, and Heimler, 1967, Chapter 7).

The tendency of those experiencing unemployment to suffer greater general deprivation than others in the labour force is brought out in the few studies that provide comparative evidence. In 1968–69 almost half of the men with any time out of work in the previous twelve months did not have household assets worth £200 compared to a quarter of the rest. They were also less likely to be accumulating assets or wealth in the most common way this is achieved in British society, by buying one's own house, and there was a greater risk of living in poor environmental conditons, having a lower household income and fewer consumer durables. In most respects those with more unemployment were even worse off, and much the same pattern also applied to women (Townsend, 1979a, Table 17.5 and pp. 605–6).

In Caplovitz's study of the impact of recession and inflaton in the

United States in 1976, 'those most vulnerable to rising prices were the people who suffered a sharp decline in income because they were unemployed'. They were much harder hit by what he calls the objective and the subjective inflation crunch, and by his three measures of mental strain, marital strain and balance of feelings, than the employed. Home owners were much less hard hit, but fairly few of the unemployed had the protection and security of owning their own homes. 'Those who suffered most from recession were the very ones suffering most from inflation' which emphasised 'the extraordinary human cost of the similarity of these economic events, which all economic theory predicts cannot happen at the same time . . . [T]hese economic catastrophes serve to exacerbate the natural cleavages in society between the more and the less privileged' (Caplovitz, 1979, pp. 42–3 and 176–8).

THE LONG-TERM IMPACT ON THE UNEMPLOYED AND THE WIDER COMMUNITY

The limited time perspective of much consideration of unemployment prevents fuller recognition of the significance of insecurity and being out of work for the unemployed and the wider community. Re-interviews in North Tyneside, twelve years after the first interview when all but three of the ninety-two unemployed had been in poverty, revealed the human erosion over time associated with unemployment and insecure work for that small sample: only a minority had 'fully escaped from poverty or low pay' by 1975 (North Tyneside CDP, 1978, pp. 245–7).

The costs of unemployment or sub-employment may extend well into the future but, in a society with persistent and widely accepted or tolerated inequalities, security and the opportunity for a satisfying, fulfilling career is generally so absent from the jobs of those most or longer unemployed that the loss of future is rarely considered. These people neither expect nor are expected to have careers in terms of the ordered upward progression that professionals, administrators and managers hope for themselves, so this loss is taken for granted by them — and, sadly, by most research too. The point is well brought out by Caplovitz when he concludes that the combined impact of inflation and recession 'wreaks havoc with the *present* lives of the poor and many working class families whereas it interferes with the *future* of the middle class families' (Caplovitz, 1979, p. 248). The uncertainty over present unemployment — how soon a job will be found and how long it will last, where it will be and how much it will pay — may well paralyse, or at least handicap, all taking of major decisions that could be affected by the need to move to a new job or to exhaust any family savings with prolonged unemployment. It may take many years to regain one's confidence and material security; and unemployment may reoccur before then, given the greater vulnerability of those once out of work to subsequent spells of unemployment (for example, M. J. Hill, 1978). And this second loss of work combined with economic deprivation can particularly undermine the worker (Aiken *et al.*, 1968 chapter VIII). 'For many,' as the Lynds said of mid-depression America, 'hopes have been hammered thin by unemployment and the necessity of living on relief' and 'the future is resisted as a threat' (1937, p. 475).

The long shadow thrown forward by the persistence of unemployment was recognised by Bakke in his study of Greenwich. Workers vulnerable to unemployment, he explained, do not lack foresight, but have to practice a different form of it. The 'ambition' or 'chosen' foresight of the securer and better-off enables them to plan aggressively for a better and more rewarding position. 'The emphasis' of 'forced' or 'security foresight . . . is not upon avoiding insecurity by climbing away from it' but it is doing one's best to consolidate and avoid slipping back and down (Bakke, 1933, pp. 43–44; cf. Lynd and Lynd 1937, p. 472). This constant awareness of the need to guard against insecurity may still influence many worker and trade union responses to employer proposals for greater productivity and the general relationship between employers and workers, just as many procedures, which the media and management today term 'restrictive practices', originated in measures to protect the jobs of union members.

'Folk-memories' of the depression are revived by rising unemployment, and this would seem to lend further support to views that collective bargaining is strengthened as a worker strategy by increasing unemployment (Burkitt and Bowers, 1979, p.13). More sustained bargaining may well lead to more wage negotiations so that, as Blackaby argues, 'the fall in employment since 1966 is a factor leading to a faster rise in money wages' (1976, p. 289). This may particularly apply in traditional working-class and industrial areas with many years of strong union activity. And wage demands may be further encouraged both by the unemployment of other wage earners in the household and by evidence of the greater security and privilege

of the extra benefits many managements provide for themselves; these
seem clear assurance that profit margins are not so low that any pay
increase will cripple the firm and jeopardise the workers' jobs (Pond,
1979). Yet current government policies are based on the premise that
rising unemployment will induce unions to settle for lower pay settlements in the hope of not pricing themselves out of a job.

Evidence from the United States also confirms that 'unemployment is not forgotten with the passage of time and can lead to a
misanthropic view of society and a pessimistic view of life' — the
'proper, albeit provisional, conclusion' drawn by Hyman from
opinon surveys in 1973 and 1974 with white males in work, aged
30–65. Interviews with workers in 1958 and again in 1960 suggest
more pessimism in 1960 among men in work in 1958 but then out of
work, and less pessimism among those who had the opposite experience; but both groups were less optimistic than those in work at both
interviews (Hyman, 1979, pp. 290–3). Experience more generally of
work insecurity and the 'chaos in modern labour markets . . . intrinsic
to urban–industrial society', according to Wilensky's 'guiding hypothesis, . . . fosters a retreat from both work and the larger communual
life' (Wilensky, 1961, pp. 523–4 and 539). Although his own sample
drew on 'the middle mass — a relatively secure population, well off by
American standards — only 30 per cent can by any stretch of the
imagination be said to act out half or more of their work in an orderly
career'; and Wilensky concluded that 'a vast majority of the [total]
labour force is going nowhere in an unordered way or can expect a
work-life of thoroughly-unpredictable ups and downs' (Wilensky,
1961, p. 526).

Intensive analysis of the labour market in the high-employment
city of Peterborough in the early 1970s would appear to provide
support for this picture in Britain. Blackburn and Mann 'believe
manual labour markets in general' are 'far less orderly and rational
than any of the economists would have us believe'. They stress the
'powerlessness and uncertainty' throughout unqualified workers'
lives: 'young workers are discontented and militant, family responsibilities and the experience of constraint teach them to comply in
early middle age, fear takes over later' (1979, pp. 289, 302 and 301).

Throughout the country the higher unemployment will mean a
reduction in work opportunities that may particularly affect those
entering or re-entering the labour force. Many sixth-formers leaving
at 18 will have to settle for jobs that once went to early school leavers
as they find graduates in the jobs they had learned to expect, and the

youngest may become still more vulnerable to unemployment or exploitation in casual jobs. With higher unemployment, many households will experience a reduction in their income as there are likely to be fewer members in work, and some of these may have less overtime or be reduced to short-time or even part-time work. These changes become all the more significant given the evidence on the need for two or more wage earners to keep many families out of poverty (e.g. Townsend, 1979a, p. 631).

The indirect impact on communities (see also pp. 20 and 234) may be severest in remote or inner-city areas hard-hit by unemployment and bankruptcies or by much reduced business for the self-employed and small traders with a consequent reduction in range and choice for their customers. A run-down of many social services, such as schools, housing and health clinics in 'D' villages, and a general devaluation of property are likely to increase migration by those most able to move, who are usually those with the most valuable skills and entering the family-formation years who are needed to maintain the life and renew the work of the community (Bulmer, 1978).

The effects of disappointed hopes, frustrated ambitions and the increased deprivation and poverty may emerge in many ways that may be exacerbated by other pressures and problems in society. Lack of work and housing may affect both the formation of households and the creation of families, leading to a drop in the birth-rate. The need to scramble for the fewer jobs fosters a more antagonistic and bitter atmosphere where newly arrived immigrants may be scapegoated for local problems and accused of taking local jobs; the hostility may be all the greater if the newness of the most recently arrived is prolonged and marked by differences in culture, language and race. The National Front today, like the Nazi blackshirts in the 1930s, may thrive all the more on these tensions (for the argument that the high-unemployment 1980s will be 'more dangerous' than the 1930s, see David Morris in *The Guardian*, 14 April 1980).

CONCLUSION

Throughout this chapter there have been references to the wider significance of rising or high unemployment in society: its function in maintaining worker discipline more generally, its role in discouraging job mobility and risk-taking in search of better jobs, its general reduction of economic opportunities and living standards, its impact on the 'public consciousness' or on significant groups within society in ways that tend to reinforce attitudes against the unemployed and lead to calls for less support and harsher measures for those out of work. The implications for the wider society were well brought out by the Swedish Royal Commission on Long-term Employment (sic) in its terms of reference in March 1974, when unemployment reached what was for Sweden the disturbing rate of 2 per cent: 'In a society where unemployment is accepted, great material and social gaps develop, resulting in the mutual isolation and alienation of different groups. Any social order not based on full employment must imply a restriction of living conditions and a squandering of human resources.'

But in Britain there has been little sustained research or discussion of these issues — in itself a reflection of the social construction of unemployment and the divorce maintained between public issues and private troubles. 'Full employment' or 'work for all' is no longer widely discussed as a social policy goal for a democratic society. Meanwhile, the level of unemployment remains a matter for debate by politicians, economists and industrialists largely as a means to some other policy goal — for example, the control of inflation or the trade unions, or to boost productivity.

In 1980 the connections between the structure of British society, the social facts of unemployment and the experience of the unemployed still need to be established. At present, discussions of unemployment and those out of work continue to be sporadic, fragmentary and limited. The assessment of the experience for individual, family and society remains isolated from wider consideration of its full significance for the careers and lives of those directly affected and for the sort of society in which we all live. The evidence there already is on the forms of human erosion, inequality and deprivation associated with unemployment constitutes a powerful case for a more systematic analysis of this link and a wider public debate on its significance. Failure to take up this challenge indicates a complacent acceptance of unemployment as a social and economic tax with very unequal impact that works to reinforce and even shape the inequalities of our social structure.

Notes

1. The combination of overmanning and labour shortage is reported in Russia and Eastern European countries. Yet very little seems to have been written on labour mobility and redeployment, despite brief

acknowledgements of 'a great deal of unplanned, often undesired, labour mobility' (Nove, 1980, p. 58). George Kolankiewicz of the University of Essex has reported the vigorous debate in the Polish weekly *Polityka* after the 'suggestion by a group of managers . . . that absenteeism, productivity and efficiency in Polish industry would improve "if we were to create a high stratum of unemployed whose very existence could compel others to greater precision and conscientiousness' ". In Russia 'a big campaign' has been mounted by the press 'against idlers and malingerers', who can be prosecuted 'under anti-parasitic legislation', according to Michael Binyon in *The Times* (16 January 1980).

2. At the end of the 1960s Ferman wrote that 'in American society there has been an acceptance of the proposition that unemployment is a price that must be paid to check inflation' (1969, p. 7). My impression is that during the last decade there has been greater concern over unemployment in the United States relative to inflation, both in comparison with the 1960s and with Britain in the 1970s. Over these last ten years unemployment has risen much more sharply in Britain than in the United States. The greater concentration of unemployment on the lower-paid and more marginal workers in Britain (Smee, 1980) might help to account for this as well as the particular impact of inflation, but the differential responses of market economies deserves more systematic analysis.

3. The US Department of Labour introduced the term 'sub-employment' in 1966 as 'a first approach to measuring the entire area of joblessness and employment hardship' (US Dept. of Labor, 1967, p. 75) including those in part-time work who wanted full-time jobs, those receiving wages that left them in poverty and those who were so discouraged that they dropped out of the labour force. With national unemployment at 3.7 per cent by the orthodox measure, sub-employment in the ten inner-city areas surveyed reached 34 per cent. This evidence was first published in a small pamphlet 'A sharper look at unemployment in U.S. cities and slums' and then later developed in 1967 (see 'Joblessness and poverty in urban slums' in US Dept. of Labor, 1967, pp. 74–100). In subsequent work in the United States a number of different indicators have been employed in the attempt 'to capture two major dimensions of labor market functioning that produce, and reproduce, poverty: first, the lack of opportunity for work; and second, substandard wage employment' (Vietorisz *et al.*, 1975, pp. 3–4, with a useful discussion of three separate indexes). Liebow (1967, chapter 2), Ferman (1967) and Gans (1968) also drew atten-

tion to the social significance of dirty work or 'maleplovment' and lack of work.

4. The traditionally high value attached to the small community-based and community-integrated enterprise may lead to more sympathetic research interest in the formation and development of alternative working relationships inside and outside the home. There may be a relative neglect of the possible obstacles to their growth and permanence — for example, the protection and security of those outside the formal insurance system and any dependants; the possible consequences of illegal activities and the means of coping with a decline in demand, obsolescence of skills and any inability to continue working, including illness, accident and the wish or need to retire. In short, is one form of insecurity in the proletarian estate being exchanged for another? Equally, of course, a writer may become too concerned with such anxieties given his own greater contact with the casualties of unemployment. Those who have successfully established themselves in an informal or alternative economy may not appear at all in studies of those who declare themselves unemployed.

CHAPTER 6

Unemployment in International Perspective

Constance Sorrentino

INTRODUCTION

Throughout the last few decades, there have been wide disparities in international rates of unemployment. During the 1960s unemployment rates across the major developed countries ranged from under 1 per cent to over 7 per cent of the labour force. International jobless rates in the 1970s have converged somewhat, but significant differences still remain. In 1978, for example, the lowest rate among nine countries studied was just over 2 per cent, while the highest rate was over 8 per cent. Since the 1960s, however, some countries that had been in the low range have moved up to the middle or to near the top of the international spectrum of unemployment rates.

This chapter presents an analysis of the differences in unemployment rates among nine countries — Australia, Canada, France, West Germany, Great Britain, Italy, Japan, Sweden and the United States. First, unemployment rates adjusted to a common conceptual framework are presented. The chapter then proceeds to a look at the characteristics of unemployment by age and sex on a comparative basis. Differences in duration of unemployment are then taken up. The concluding section presents a discussion of the non-statistical factors responsible for international differences in unemployment rates.

Throughout this chapter it should be kept in mind that unemployment is only one measure of under-utilization of the labour force. Under-utilization may also take the form of under-employment — such as persons in the labour force who work part-time for economic reasons or persons who must work beneath their skill or educational level. 'Discouraged workers', i.e., persons who would like to work but believe no jobs are available, also comprise a part of under-utilised labour that usually does not show up in the unemployment rate as measured by labour force surveys. However, such persons may show up in unemployment as measures by registration statistics. Persons may register as unemployed in order to collect benefits even though they believe they will not be able to find suitable work. It would be most useful to develop broader measures of under-utilization in making international comparisons, but comprehensive and comparable data on this subject have not yet been developed.[1]

THE INTERNATIONAL MEASUREMENT OF UNEMPLOYMENT

The construction of internationally comparable unemployment statistics has been the subject of studies by both the International Labour Office (ILO) and the US Bureau of Labor Statistics (BLS), and the procedures and definitions adopted are outlined in the Appendix. The adjustments made to the national data do not have a very large effect in most cases. Only negligible changes, or none at all, have been made in the official unemployment figures for Australia, Canada, Japan and Sweden (see Table 6.1). For Italy, adjustments have been small up until 1977 when a major revision was made in the Italian labour force survey.[2] From 1977 onward, there has been a rather large downward adjustment made to the Italian rate in order to exclude persons who have not actively sought work in the past thirty days. In the case of Germany, the adjustment to US definitions has usually resulted in a moderate reduction of the official unemployment rate. This is because the German registered figures include a number of persons who are working a few hours a week but are seeking more work. Such persons should be counted as employed for comparability with US concepts.

Upward revisions have been made in the British and French rates, except in recent years when official and adjusted rates have been virtually the same. In both countries this convergence is related to the fact that, as economic conditions worsen, more persons who are seeking work tend to register as unemployed rather than only to look for work on their own. Recent increases in unemployment benefits have also been a strong inducement for more unemployed persons to register. Furthermore, under the British Social Security Act of 1975, women who married after 6 April 1977 no longer had the option of not

Table 6.1 *Official Unemployment Rates and Rates Adjusted to US Definitions. 1960 and 1978*

Country	1960 Official rate %	1960 Adjusted to US definition %	1978 Official rate %	1978 Adjusted to US definition %
United States	5.5	5.5	6.0	6.0
Canada	7.0	7.0	8.4	8.4
Australia	NA	1.6	6.4	6.4
Japan	1.7	1.7	2.2	2.3
France	1.3	1.8	5.3	5.5[a]
Germany	1.3	1.1	4.3	3.4[a]
Great Britain	1.5	2.2	6.0	6.1[a]
Italy	4.0	3.8	7.2	3.5
Sweden	1.4[b]	1.4[b]	2.2	2.2

NA Not available
[a] Preliminary estimate
[b] 1961

Source: BLS

joining the national insurance system. Removal of this option has resulted in a substantial increase in female unemployment registrations. Previously, most unemployed British women had no financial incentive to register.

The adjustments to US concepts do not make a great deal of difference in the ranking of countries according to unemployment rates. The countries at the top and the bottom of the ranking are usually not affected (except for Italy, after 1977). However, the rankings in the middle of the array are often changed after adjustments are made. For example, in 1978 the British unemployment rate ranked fourth prior to adjustment to US concepts; after adjustments were made, the British rate was third from the top.

Table 6.2 *Unemployment Rates Adjusted to US Concepts, 1959–79*

Year	United States %	Canada %	Australia %	Japan %	France %	Germany %	Great Britain %	Italy %	Sweden %
1959	5.5	6.0	2.1	2.3	2.0	2.0	2.9	5.0	NA
1960	5.5	7.0	1.6	1.7	1.8	1.1	2.2	3.8	NA
1961	6.7	7.1	3.0	1.5	1.6	0.6	2.0	3.2	1.4
1962	6.5	5.9	2.4	1.3	1.5	0.6	2.8	2.8	1.5
1963	5.7	5.5	2.3	1.3	1.3	0.5	3.4	2.4	1.7
1964	5.2	4.7	1.4	1.2	1.5	0.4	2.5	2.6	1.5
1965	4.5	3.9	1.3	1.2	1.6	0.3	2.2	3.5	1.2
1966	3.8	3.4	1.5	1.4	1.9	0.3	2.3	3.8	1.6
1967	3.8	3.8	1.6	1.3	2.0	1.3	3.4	3.4	2.1
1968	3.6	4.5	1.5	1.2	2.6	1.4	3.3	3.4	2.2
1969	3.5	4.4	1.5	1.1	2.4	0.9	3.0	3.3	1.9
1970	4.9	5.7	1.6	1.2	2.6	0.8	3.1	3.1	1.5
1971	5.9	6.2	1.8	1.3	2.8	0.8	3.7	3.1	2.6
1972	5.6	6.2	2.6	1.4	2.9	0.8	4.1	3.6	2.7
1973	4.9	5.5	2.3	1.3	2.8	0.8	2.9	3.4	2.5
1974	5.6	5.3	2.7	1.4	3.0	1.7	2.9	2.8	2.0
1975	8.5	6.9	4.9	1.9	4.3	3.6	4.1	3.2	1.6
1976	7.7	7.1	4.8	2.0	4.7	3.6	5.5	3.6	1.6
1977	7.0	8.1	5.6	2.0	5.0	3.6a	6.2a	3.4	1.8
1978	6.0	8.4	6.3	2.3	5.5a	3.4a	6.1a	3.7	2.2
1979	5.8	7.5	6.2	2.1a	6.1a	3.0a	5.8a	3.9a	2.1

NA Not available   *a* Preliminary estimate based on incomplete data   Source: BLS

COMPARATIVE RESULTS, 1959–79

Canada had the highest unemployment rates, on the average, for the 1959–79 period, followed by the United States. These two countries have also experienced the most rapid growth in employment. In contrast, the Western European countries, with much lower average levels of unemployment than North America, had very slow growth or declines in employment.

Unemployment

North American unemployment rates have typically been far greater than those prevailing in other industrial countries, even after adjustment to a common conceptual base (Table 6.2). Over the past twenty years, unemployment in the United States and Canada has varied between 3.5 per cent and 8 per cent. In contrast, from 1959 to 1974, the highest unemployment experienced in Australia, Japan, France, West Germany and Sweden ranged from 2 to 3 per cent and the lows from 0.3 to 1.4 per cent. The highest rate in Great Britain was 3.7 per cent. Until recently, 4 per cent unemployment was considered to represent full employment in the United States. That figure, however, is considered to be extremely high in Western Europe and Japan, where full employment is often taken to be represented by 2 or even 1 per cent unemployment.

Since 1974, the adjusted unemployment rates abroad, especially in Australia, France and Great Britain, have risen to levels approaching and even exceeding those in the United States. For these countries, it is a new phenomenon to be in the same 'unemployment league' as the United States. German unemployment has also risen dramatically in recent years, but still remains under 4 per cent, a middle range by international standards. Italian unemployment has stayed under 4 per cent, but it is a bit higher than it was in most years of the 1960s. Japan and Sweden have both managed to maintain remarkably low jobless rates in recent years. Unemployment in both countries remains around 2 per cent. Even so, Japan's unemployment rate in 1978 was the highest since 1959.

Thus, for most of these countries, unemployment rates in the 1970s are substantially higher than those of earlier periods. This appears to be a long-term trend, rather than solely the result of the 'oil shock' of 1974 and its aftermath. Unemployment levels in many of the industrial countries have increased from cyclical peak to cyclical peak since the end of the Second World War. Growing supply–demand imbalances on the labour market are one reason behind the long-term rising unemployment trend. The fragmentary evidence available (OECD, 1973; Turvey, 1977) suggests that such imbalances are growing in a number of countries. In some countries, the changing composition of the labour force, with more women and young persons entering the labour market, has been an important factor in the long-term rise in unemployment rates.

The comparatively low Italian unemployment rate, and its lack of responsiveness to the slower growth of the 1970s, deserves some consideration. Unemployment does not fully reflect the degree of labour under-utilization in Italy. Agreements reached between management and labour have helped to share the burden of recession by encouraging partial rather than full unemployment. Consequently, the deterioration in the demand for labour is reflected more by a decline in working hours and a rise in the number of persons involuntarily working part-time rather than in overt unemployment. Similarly, Japanese jobless rates are not highly sensitive to fluctuations in the demand for labour. Japanese employers, with their tradition of lifetime employment, prefer to reduce working hours, transfer employees from one job to another within the same company and terminate contracts with part-time, seasonal or temporary workers who usually withdraw from the labour force until the job market improves.

Employment

At 3 per cent a year Canada has had the highest rate of employment growth since 1959 and is the only country with continuous employment expansion throughout the period (Table 6.3). Employment growth in the United States and Australia was also strong, while Japan was the only other country with employment growth exceeding 1 per cent a year. In Western European countries, in contrast, employment has grown very slowly or actually declined since 1959. In Great Britain, the growth rate was negligible: only about 1.2 million persons were added to he employment rolls in the two decades. France and Sweden grew by about 0.8 per cent annually, while Germany and Italy had declining employment trends. The recessionary period of 1974–75 had a strong impact on employment, which fell in six of the nine

Table 6.3 *Annual Average Employment Growth Rates, Selected Periods, 1959–78*

Country	1959–78 %p.a.	1959–74 %p.a.	1974–78 %p.a.
United States	2.0	2.0	2.6
Canada	3.0	3.1	2.0
Australia	2.2[a]	2.7[a]	0.6
Japan	1.2	1.4	0.8
France	0.7	0.8	0
Germany	−0.2	0	−1.1
Great Britain	0.1	0.2	0.1
Italy	−0.3	−0.6	0.7
Sweden	0.8[b]	0.7[b]	0.9

[a] Figures begin with 1964
[b] Figures begin with 1961

Source: BLS

countries, with the sharpest decline in Germany. Since 1974–75 employment has grown in all countries except Germany.

UNEMPLOYMENT BY AGE AND SEX

To understand the comparative impact of unemployment, one must look into the body of data below the aggregate unemployment rates. The discussion here will focus upon comparisons of unemployment by age and sex — characteristics for which reasonable comparable data exist (see Table 6.4).

Unemployment rates in most countries vary widely by age and sex. Teenagers characteristically have the highest jobless rates of any group in the labour force, followed by 20–24-year-olds. Workers in the prime working age group of 25–54 generally have unemployment rates one-half to one-third as high as persons under 25. The pattern for older workers (aged 55 and over) varies, but in most cases their unemployment rates are lower than those for workers in the prime age group. Women, with only a few exceptions, have higher unemployment rates than men.

Table 6.4 *Unemployment by Age and Sex, Adjusted to US Concepts, 1970 and 1977*

Country	By sex			By age					
	Both sexes %	Male %	Female %	Total %	Under 25 Teenagers[a] %	20–24 %	Total %	Over 25 25–54 %	55 and over %
				1977[b]					
United States	7.0	6.2	8.2	13.6	17.7	10.9	4.9	5.1	4.1
Canada	8.1	7.3	9.5	14.5	17.5	12.4	5.8	6.0	4.7
Australia[c]	5.2	4.3	6.8	11.1	16.1	7.2	3.0	3.2	2.2
Japan	2.0	2.1	1.9	3.7	4.8	3.5	1.8	1.7	2.5
France	4.8	3.3	7.2	11.8	NA	NA	3.5	NA	NA
Germany	3.7	3.1	4.6	6.2	6.9	5.7	3.1	3.2	2.6
Great Britain	5.5	5.5	5.6	11.4	NA	NA	4.3	NA	NA
Italy[d]	3.7	3.1	5.2	14.5	19.2	11.6	1.6	1.7	0.5
Sweden	1.8	1.5	2.2	4.4	6.7	3.2	1.3	1.3	1.2
				1970[e]					
United States	4.9	4.4	5.9	11.0	15.3	8.2	3.3	3.4	2.8
Canada	5.7	5.7	5.8	10.1	14.0	7.5	4.2	NA	NA
Australia	1.4	1.0	2.2	2.7	3.9	1.6	0.9	1.0	0.7
Japan	1.2	1.2	1.1	2.0	2.0	2.0	0.9	0.9	0.9
France	2.5	1.7	3.8	4.8	7.0	3.7	2.0	1.8	2.6
Germany	0.6	0.5	0.8	1.3	2.0	0.7	0.5	0.5	0.5
Great Britain	3.7	3.7	3.6	5.4	6.6	4.8	3.2	3.2	3.3
Italy[d]	3.2	2.8	3.9	10.2	11.9	8.8	1.5	1.6	0.8
Sweden	1.5	1.4	1.7	2.9	4.3	2.2	1.3	1.1	1.7

NA Not available
a 16–19-year olds in United States, France, Great Britain (1976) and Sweden: 15–19-year-olds in Australia, Canada, Japan, Germany and Great Britain (1971); and 14–19-year-olds in Italy
b March 1977 for France; April 1977 for Germany; 1976 for Great Britain and Italy
c Data not revised to new population estimates, which raised unemployment rate to 5.6 per cent
d Not adjusted to US concepts
e March 1970 for France; april 1970 for Germany; 1971 for Great Britain

Source: BLS

Young persons in the United States, Italy and Canada have long had very high unemployment rates. In 1970, youths under 25 in these countries had jobless rates exceeding 10 per cent; by 1977, they had exceeded 13 per cent. The high levels of youth unemployment for Australia, France and Great Britain shown for 1977 are a new phenomenon in sharp contrast to those prevailing in 1970. (The unemployment rate for British youth under 25 more than doubled from 1971 to 1976.)

Youth unemployment in Japan, Germany and Sweden remains much lower than in the other six countries, while Canada and Italy had the highest rates for persons under 25, that is, 14.5 per cent. This is not surprising for Canada, which also had the highest overall unemployment rate. However, Italy's moderate aggregate unemployment rate masks a severe youth unemployment problem.

Youth unemployment rates are, of course, affected by the overall job situation in each country. Therefore, comparative ratios of youth (under 25) to adult (25 and over) unemployment rates are shown in Table 6.5 for 1970 and 1977. These ratios may also be affected by the general level of unemployment, but they more accurately reflect the relative problems of youth unemployment among the countries. Italy had by far the widest youth–adult differential. In 1976, youth unemployment was nine times the adult rate. For the late 1960s and early 1970s the youth–adult ratio in the United States ranked second to Italy's. However, by 1974 Australia, France and Sweden had moved ahead of the United States, and by 1976 Great Britain was at virtually the US level. These comparative relationships persisted into 1977. In US recessionary periods, the gap between youth and adult unemployment rates usually narrows as young people are discouragd by poor job prospects from entering the labour force. In contrast, the youth–adult differential has risen sharply in recent years in Australia, France, Great Britain, Italy and Sweden, indicating a worsening relative position for young persons in the labour market. The differential has remained fairly stable in Canada and Japan, and declined in Germany.

Youth unemployment is generally short term in nature, reflecting the high turnover of youth in the labour market. However, when overall unemployment rises, the duration of unemployment generally lengthens, for youth as well as for adults. What was once seen as a brief period of transitional discomfort for youth is now becoming a prolonged situation of sustained hardship. In Great Britain, for

Table 6.5 *Ratio of Youth (Under 25) to Adult (Over 25) Rates of Unemployment, 1970 and 1977*

Country	1970	1977
United States	3.3	2.8
Canada	2.4	2.5
Australia	3.0	3.7
Japan	2.2	2.1
France	2.4	3.4
Germany	2.6	2.0
Great Britain	1.7 (1971)	2.7 (1976)
Italy	6.8	9.1 (1976)
Sweden	2.2	3.4

example, the mean duration of unemployment for youth under 18 was less than three weeks in January 1970. By January 1977, the mean duration had risen to over eleven weeks. This increase was greater than that for adults.

As a result of the growing magnitude and duration of youth unemployment, its effects are extending to high school and college graduates. In Italy, the number of university graduates seeking their first jobs has been rising. The educational reform of 1968 allowed unlimited access to university enrolment, and there are now about 70,000 graduates a year in comparison with 23,000 in 1962. The Italian economy has not been able to generate enough jobs for the influx of new graduates, who now account for about one-third of Italian youth unemployment. Rigidities in the labour market in the form of legal provisions tend to protect the employment position of those who are already employed. To a lesser extent, this has occurred in some other countries as well.

In most countries, older workers have lower than average unemployment rates. In 1977, of countries with data for persons aged 55 and over, only Japan had higher jobless rates for members of that group than for those in the 25–54 years group. In Japan, almost all enterprises now fix the retirement age at 55–58 years. Since social security payments begin at the age of 60, most workers reaching retirement age must seek work out of financial necessity, usually in lower paid jobs or self-employment.

Older workers in Italy have much lower unemployment rates than workers in the primary working ages, but then very few Italians over the age of 55 remain economically active, at least in a statistical sense, because of the substantial incidence of unreported or illegal employment in the official labour force surveys. Furthermore, many older Italians may disappear into the subsistence economy and become under-employed rather than unemployed.

In all the countries, except Great Britain and Japan, women were much more likely to be unemployed than men. French women had unemployment rates twice as high as those for French men, and the differential was also wide in Italy and Australia. Women were insulated from the harshest effects of the 1974–75 recession (OECD, 1976). Although unemployment remained higher for women than for men in most countries, the increases for women were slower, or at about the same rate, as that for men except in Italy and Great Britain where unemployment rose faster for women. In most countries, employment rose for women while declining for men during the recession. Women were somewhat shielded from the recession because business turndowns tend to be more severe in manufacturing and construction where there are relatively few women than in the service sector where female employment is heavily concentrated.

DURATION OF UNEMPLOYMENT

Data on unemployment by duration are not entirely comparable from country to country and they have not been adjusted to US concepts. Table 6.6 suggests that there are wide disparities in the duration of unemployment. The United States has a more short-term frictional type of unemployment and a relatively low rate of long-term unemployment compared to other countries. In 1978, over three-quarters of the American unemployed were seeking work for less than three months. Canada and Sweden also had a major proportion of their unemployment in this duration group; Australia and Japan followed closely behind. At the other extreme, only 14.5 per cent of the Italians were in this shorter-term category. Great Britain was in the middle of the array, with about two-fifths of its unemployed seeking work for less than three months. All countries except Germany have suffered a drop in the proportion of short-term unemployment since 1970.

One reason for the greater frictional unemployment in the United States and Canada, compared to Western Europe, may be the rapid

Table 6.6 *Duration of Unemployment, Selected Years*

Country and year	% of unemployed who have been seeking work for:			Unemployment rates %			
	Less than 3 months[a]	3 months or more[b]	6 months or more[c]	Total	Less than 3 months[a]	3 months or more[b]	6 months or more[c]
United States							
1970	83.8	16.2	5.7	4.9	4.1	0.8	0.3
1978	77.2	22.8	10.5	6.0	4.6	1.4	0.6
Canada							
1970	66.9	33.1	15.6	5.9	3.9	2.0	0.9
1978, 2nd quarter	56.0	44.0	NA	8.6	4.8	3.8	NA
Australia							
1970	88.8	11.2	NA	1.6	1.4	0.2	NA
1978	51.0	49.0	69.3	6.4	3.3	3.1	4.4
Japan							
1978, March	50.7	49.3	31.4	2.6	1.3	1.3	0.8
France							
1970, March	43.7	56.3	40.6	2.2	1.0	1.2	0.9
1977, March	27.4	72.6	52.6	4.8	1.4	3.4	2.5
Germany							
1970, April	30.1	69.9	50.5	0.5	0.3	0.2	0.2
1976, May	30.0	70.0	48.1	3.5	1.4	2.1	1.5

Great Britain[d]							
1971, July	NA	NA	28.2	3.3	NA	NA	0.9
1978, 4-month average[e]	40.9	59.1	40.9	6.2	2.5	3.7	2.5
Italy							
1960	27.0	73.0	42.8	3.1	0.7	2.4	1.4
1978	14.5	85.5	NA	4.5	2.2	2.3	NA
Sweden							
1970	78.2	21.8	9.8	1.5	1.2	0.3	0.1
1978	60.4	39.6	17.3	2.2	1.3	0.9	0.4

NA Not available

a Less than 15 weeks in the United States; less than 4 months in Canada; and less than 13 weeks in Great Britain and Sweden

b 15 weeks or more in the United States; 4 months or more in Canada; and 13 weeks or more in Great Britain and Sweden

c 26 weeks or more in the United States and Great Britain; 7 months or more in Canada; and 27 weeks or more in Sweden

d Data for the registered unemployed

e January, April, July and October.

Note: Except for the data for Great Britain, these statistics are based on labour force surveys and are fairly comparable from country to country. The British data are from the registered unemployed series and are less internationally comparable than the survey data

Source: Various national publications

growth in the labour force and in employment. A more rapidly growing labour force implies a larger proportion of recent entrants who have a high incidence of unemployment, though often of short duration. In addition, employers may be less reluctant to lay off workers when there is a steady flow of new workers into the labour market. The higher concentration of youth in the unemployment figures for Northern America also makes for a lower average duration of unemployment since young persons tend to have shorter unemployment durations than adults. Sweden has apparently managed to keep its long-term unemployment rates so low through its massive use of public works and labour market training programmes.[3]

WHY UNEMPLOYMENT RATES DIFFER

We have seen that North American unemployment rates have tended to be appreciably higher than those of most industrial countries, even after adjustments for differences in definitions and methods of data collection. Such differences accounted for only a small part of the gap in international unemployment rates. Explanations for the remaining differences may be sought in demographic, economic, legal and social factors.

The rest of this chapter examines some of the factors that may contribute to differences in unemployment levels across countries. In many ways the countries studied have more in common today than they did in the early 1960s. Some of these emerging similarities help to explain why international unemployment rates have tended to converge in recent years.

Supply of and demand for labour

In the absence of substantial changes in the composition of the supply of and demand for labour, increases in labour supply can normally be absorbed by increases in aggregate demand. The greater the rate of labour force growth, of course, the greater the potential difficulty in maintaining full employment. Trends in productivity also operate directly on labour demand.

It is commonly suggested that the rapid growth of the labour force in the United States and Canada has greatly increased the difficulty of maintaining full employment. Growth of the US civilian labour force alone called for about 25 million new jobs between 1960 and 1976 if unemployment were not to rise above the 1960 level of 5.5 per cent. With only 23 million new jobs actually generated, unemployment rose to 7.7 per cent in 1976. The lower unemployment rates of the European countries and Japan from 1960 onward were achieved during slow or negative growth of the labour force, and these countries created relatively fewer net new jobs than the United States and Canada.

Growth of the Canadian labour force outpaced all other countries, rising at an annual rate of 3.1 per cent between 1960 and 1978, and there was also a rapid increase in Australia. Labour forces grew by less than 1 per cent a year in France, Great Britain and Sweden. In Germany, however, the labour force declined, and this would have been greater but for the rapid influx of foreign workers since 1960. In fact, labour shortages developed during the 1960s in several countries, notably Germany and Japan, as the slowly growing supply of labour could not keep up with demand.

Population growth and trends in labour force participation rates are factors that underlie the different trends in the labour force among the countries studied. Since 1960, the civilian working age population has grown fastest in Canada (2.4 per cent a year), followed by Australia, the United States, Japan and France. Population growth was under 1 per cent a year in Germany, Great Britain, Italy and Sweden (Table 6.7). Labour force participation rates have been rising in the United States, Australia, Canada and Sweden because of large increases in female labour force activity, which has more than made up for the long-term decline in male activity rates. There has been less change in Great Britain, and a decline in the other countries.

The downward trend in male participation rates in all countries is attributable to earlier retirement and longer years of schooling. Underlying the rise in female participation rates in several industrial countries have been the lessening of job discrimination against women, increased availability of part-time work, decline in fertility rates, a high rate of increase in jobs in the service sector, and changing attitudes towards women's role in society. Sweden's high and rapidly rising female participation indicates a more active involvement of married women — 60 per cent in 1978 — in economic life compared with other nations.

The downward trend in female participation rates in Germany is

Table 6.7 *Labour Force Participation Rates, 1960 and 1978*

Country and Year		Both sexes %	Males %	Females %
United States	1960	59.4	83.3	37.7
	1978	63.2	77.9	50.0
Canada	1960	56.1	82.2	30.2
	1978	62.3	77.9	47.8
Australia	1964	58.7	84.2	33.4
	1978	61.1	78.9	43.8
Japan	1960	67.9	84.2	52.7
	1978	62.8	80.1	46.4
France	1960	61.8	84.3	43.0
	1977	57.2	71.4	44.1
Germany	1960	60.0	82.7	41.2
	1978	52.8	70.8	37.6
Great Britain	1960	60.7	86.0	38.7
	1977	61.7	78.1	46.8
Italy	1960	58.0	84.7	33.8
	1976	48.1	70.5	27.6
Sweden	1961	63.2	83.3	43.4
	1978	65.4	74.3	56.9

Note: Data adjusted to US concepts
Source: BLS

entirely due to a sharp drop in participation by teenage girls brought about by longer schooling. In Italy and Japan, however, female participation rates for all age groups fell after the war, largely due to the sharp decline in agricultural employment in both countries. Women who were economically active as unpaid family workers on the farm generally withdrew from the labour force when the family moved to the city. After this initial fall, a second stage of development witnesses a rise in women's activity rates. Italy and Japan have recently entered this second stage, which began much earlier in North America, Australia, Great Britain and Sweden.

The relatively rapid growth in working age population and the rising participation rates of women led to the relatively high rates of labour force growth in the United States, Australia and Canada. Low rates of population increase and declining or steady participation rates explain the low rates of growth in the German, Italian and British workforces. A major reason for the rapid increase in North America was the unusually high birth rates in the early postwar years. In most other industrial countries, in contrast, the ravages of the Second World War precluded any prompt return to normal family life and there was no comparable postwar baby boom. Projections for the United States and Canada indicate that the labour force will grow more slowly to 1990 than in earlier years, mainly because there will be a smaller number of youths reaching working age as a result of the sharp drop in the birth rate of the 1960s (Table 6.8). However, the teenage population is expected to increase in Western European countries (with the exception of Germany), Australia and Japan.

The 'demand' for labour might be defined as the sum of existing employment plus job vacancies, but no actual measurement of labour demand is prepared by any of the countries because adequate vacancy data are not available. Several factors may affect the demand for labour and consequently influence the ability of a national economy to provide ample job opportunities for its labour force. Certain factors, such as output, average hours and productivity, operate directly on labour demand, and others, such as investment, consumption and training, operate more indirectly. Table 6.9 indicates how two of these factors, output and productivity, have increased in the nine countries relative to growth in employment. Output is represented by real Gross Domestic Product (GDP), and productivity is represented by real GDP per employed civilian. Real GDP has risen most slowly in Great Britain over the entire period. Growth in the US economy was also relatively slow, while growth in Japan was over twice as fast. In 1974–78, however, the comparative picture changed dramatically. Growth in the European countries fell precipitously, while US economic activity remained at about the same pace. The downturn in Germany, Italy and Sweden was so sharp that these countries fell below Great Britain in terms of annual rates of change in GDP.

Several writers have investigated the causes of the differences in economic growth among the industrial countries. Angus Maddison (1964), in his analysis of the 1950s, concludes that the major cause was the pursuit by Western European governments of active contra-cyclical policies, which sustained high levels of demand and

Table 6.8 ILO Projections of Working Age Population and Labour Force, and Teenage Population and Labour Force, 1980–90 (1975=100)

Country	Working age population[a]			Labour force[a]			Teenage population[b]			Teenage labour force[b]		
	1980	1985	1990	1980	1985	1990	1980	1985	1990	1980	1985	1990
United States	107.1	112.2	116.7	107.9	114.5	119.9	96.6	84.4	82.4	90.7	75.3	69.7
Canada	110.2	117.4	124.8	110.7	119.7	126.8	101.4	83.1	88.5	95.9	75.1	76.1
Australia	109.9	118.9	129.1	109.5	118.7	128.3	105.9	105.1	121.0	100.5	95.1	104.4
Japan	105.4	111.0	117.4	105.6	110.9	116.1	103.5	111.2	127.2	99.2	102.3	111.9
France	104.7	109.0	113.2	105.5	112.2	116.3	102.2	101.1	103.9	97.4	92.3	90.4
Germany	103.8	106.7	107.3	104.4	109.7	111.2	114.5	107.8	83.8	108.1	96.9	71.5
Great Britain[c]	102.9	105.2	107.0	102.2	105.3	107.8	112.0	107.7	103.3	105.2	96.1	87.4
Italy	104.0	107.8	110.5	102.5	106.5	108.8	111.2	111.8	104.5	106.2	102.6	91.8
Sweden	102.9	105.8	108.3	102.2	105.2	108.6	106.6	111.4	111.3	101.0	101.0	95.8

a Age 15 and over
b Age 15–19
c Data for United Kingdom
Source: ILO (1977)

Table 6.9 *Growth in Real Gross Domestic Product, Employment and Productivity, 1960–78* (*average annual percentage change*)

Country	1960–1978			1974–1978		
	Growth in real GDP	Growth in civilian employment	Growth in productivity[a]	Growth in real GDP	Growth in civilian employment	Growth in productivity[a]
United States	3.6	1.9	1.7	3.5	2.3	1.2
Canada	5.0	2.8	2.1	3.3	2.0	1.3
Australia	4.2[b]	2.1[b]	2.1[b]	2.6	0.5	2.1
Japan	8.5	1.2	7.3	4.7	0.8	3.8
France	4.6	0.5	4.2	2.4	−0.1	2.9
Germany	3.8	−0.2	4.0	1.1	−1.2	3.4
Great Britain[c]	2.5	0.2	2.4	1.7	0	1.6
Italy	4.3	−0.2	4.5	1.6	0.8	1.1
Sweden	3.0[d]	0.9[d]	2.1[d]	0.5	0.9	0.4

[a] Real GDP per employed civilian
[b] 1964–78
[c] United Kingdom
[d] 1961–78

Note: Growth rates based on compound rate of change
Source: BLS

investment. In the case of Great Britain, however, growth was slow despite active fiscal policies because balance of payments problems caused restrictive policies to be pursued even when the economy was below capacity. US authorities, unlike their European counterparts, accepted fluctuations in activity involving absolute declines in output and substantial increases in unemployment as a fact of life.

Edward Denison (1967) believes that the European governments did not, on balance, do more than the United States to obtain growth. He comments that: 'the low standing of the United States in the "International Growth Rate League" is not an indication of poor economic performance, but an indication that there were opportunities to increase efficiency in European countries that did not exist to the same degree in the United States.' Most observers agree that differences in the distribution of employment and output among sectors account for a significant part of the difference in growth rates. As will be shown in the next section, the countries with the lowest long-term growth rates — the United States and Great Britain — entered the postwar period (and the 1960s) with the smallest percentages of the labour force in agriculture. The country with the highest economic growth rate, Japan, had the highest percentage in agriculture and experienced the largest shift out of agricultural employment. Now, however, the proportion employed in agriculture even in Japan is low enough that the changeover from that sector will no longer contribute to growth in the way it once did.

Other things being equal, increased output requires more employees. However, productivity growth may reduce the number of workers required for a given output. Since 1960, growth in productivity has been slowest in the United States. Thus a significant increase in employment could occur even with a relatively low rate of output growth. In Japan, rapid output growth was only partially translated into increases in employment because productivity growth was also rapid. Next to Japan, Canada had the highest GDP growth rate, generated by a very rapid rise in employment and a comparatively slow increase in productivity. In France, with a GDP growth rate almost as high as in Canada, output growth was mainly attributable to productivity increases, and employment growth was very slow. In Germany and Italy, output growth was generated entirely by productivity increases and employment declined. Thus, a relatively high rate of output growth does not necessarily indicate increasing levels of employment.

The United States had an unusually high rate of job creation from 1960 to 1978 in view of its relatively low rate of increase in GDP. Some countries, such as Japan, shifted their labour force from low productivity agriculture to high productivity manufacturing, whereas the United States had the greatest rate of increase in service sector employment, with many part-time jobs added to the total.

The relationship between changes in real GNP and changes in the unemployment rate has been formulated in 'Okun's Law'.[4] As commonly interpreted, Okun's Law says that each percentage point of real GNP growth in excess of 4 per cent will in the course of a year reduce the US unemployment rate by about one-third of a percentage point. In the same fashion, a rate of growth of less than 4 per cent will cause the unemployment rate to rise by one-third the deficiency in the growth rate. Thus, 4 per cent annual growth in GNP has come to be regarded by many US economists as approximately the rate of growth required to hold the unemployment rate constant. The reason the deviation of the unemployment rate is less than that of output is primarily that employers do not adjust their workforces proportionately with cyclical fluctuations in product demand and output.

Okun's Law is not immutable and the relationship between output and unemployment undoubtedly changes over time. The actual change in the unemployment rate can deviate substantially from the expected because of special factors, such as the stage of the business cycle. For example, Okun's Law works poorly in years marking the end of a cyclical expansion when labour tends to be in short supply and employers are reluctant to part with skilled workers.

Despite occasional lapses, however, Okun's Law offers a valuable rule-of-thumb and a helpful guideline for the forecaster. An international comparison of Okun's Law coefficients sheds some light on differences in unemployment rates across countries. Roger Kaufman (1978) has attempted such a comparison, calculating Okun-type equations for the United States, Canada, Japan, Great Britain and Sweden. The equations utilise the BLS unemployment rates adjusted to US concepts. Kaufman's equations show that the US unemployment rate, and to a lesser extent the Canadian rate, react much more quickly to output fluctuations than the rates for the European countries and Japan. The coefficients on current GNP, and GNP lagged one quarter, in the US equation are twice the size of those for the European countries and Japan. These differences, however, are practically eliminated over the medium and long run, Japan being the notable exception. Kaufman attributes the quicker response of US and Canadian unemployment to the smaller incidence of economic, moral and legal sanctions against lay-offs and discharges in North America compared to Europe and Japan. The general uniformity in the medium- and long-run responses occurs as rational economic behaviour, less restricted by short-run institutional constraints, comes into play. The Japanese exception is attributed to the unique lifetime employment system that makes the Japanese unemployment rate almost impervious to economic fluctuations.

Labour force composition

Differences between countries in the composition of the labour force are important in investigating why unemployment rates differ, since certain groups have been more prone to unemployment than others. The reason that many American economists now believe 5 or 6 per cent unemployment is a practical goal (in contrast to the 4 per cent goal of the 1960s) is partly based on the fact that women and teenagers now comprise a significantly larger portion of the US labour force than in the past. These groups presumably have fewer skills and looser attachments to their jobs than prime age males. Also, women and younger workers are more vulnerable to lay-offs than adult males because, on average, they do not have as many years of work experience. In recent years there has been increasing recognition that a woman's career prospects are endangered by her dropping out of the labour force and, consequently, women seem to be developing more permanent labour force attachments. Sweden is approaching a pattern of female participation by age similar to that of men, with no drop in labour force activity connected with birth and bringing up of children. In fact, for Swedish women with children under the age of 7, the participation rate is over 70 per cent, even higher than the activity rate for all women combined. Such forces are also at work in other countries and may increasingly have an impact on male–female unemployment differentials.

It was shown earlier that women in most countries had higher unemployment rates than men, and that teenagers had relatively high jobless rates in all countries. Thus it is relevant to consider the comparative trends in the proportion of the labour force accounted for by women and teenagers. Canada and Australia have had a comparatively large increase in the female work force during the period since

1960, and the United States also had a fairly rapid increase (Table 6.10). In 1977, Sweden had the highest proportion of women in its labour force. The United States ranked second, followed by France and Great Britain, with Italy by far the lowest. These rankings differed markedly from 1960, when five countries had higher proportions of women in the workforce than the United States. The United States and Canada have had a relatively high and growing proportion of women in the labour force. However, Sweden has maintained low overall unemployment rates even with a large and growing female component, and Italy has had both a low level and a declining trend in the female labour force, which has probably helped to keep unemployment down, since female unemployment rates have been 50–60 per cent higher than the male rates in recent years.

On balance, the overall effect of the demographic composition of the US and Canadian labour forces may be marginally to increase their aggregate unemployment rate compared with some other countries. The high and growing proportion of both women and teenagers in the labour force has exerted upward pressure on unemployment rates. Most other countries have not had to cope with as large or as rapidly increasing female and teenage components in the workforce. Recently, however, some European countries have had to contend with increases in these two components.

The industrial composition of the labour force is a factor of interest since workers in certain sectors of the economy are more often unemployed than others. In many developed countries (Japan and Italy are the best examples) small, family-owned businesses are found more frequently than in North America. The farms, small factories and commercial establishments owned and operated by family members have provided jobs and a substantial measure of protection from unemployment for a large segment of the labour force, though substantial under-employment and shrinkage of income may occur from time to time. Furthermore, in countries where this form of business organisation plays a significant role, there is more chance that a family member who loses his wage or salary job will return to working in the family business and thus not be counted as unemployed. In the United States, on the other hand, the economies of scale that can be realised in a large and fairly homogeneous sales market have been factors encouraging a consolidation of business enterprises, so that self-employment and family operations occur less frequently and the risk of unemployment is increased.

Unemployment is much less frequently associated with agriculture

Table 6.10 *Women and Teenagers in the Labour Force, 1960, 1971 and 1977*

Country	Women[a] As % of labour force			Labour force growth rate, %	Teenagers[b] As % of labour force			Labour force growth rate, %
	1960	1971	1977	1960–1977	1960	1971	1977	1960–77
United States	33	38	41	3.2	7	9	9	3.8
Canada	27	34	38	5.2	9	10	11	4.0
Australia	29[c]	32	36	4.1[c]	14[c]	12	12	0.8[c]
Japan	40	39	38	0.7	10	5	4	-6.3
France	36[d]	38	40	1.6[d]	8[d]	6	4	-3.1[d]
Germany	38	36	38	0	11[e]	8	9	-0.9
Great Britain	34	37	40	1.4	11[e]	9	8	-1.6[e]
Italy	31	28	30[f]	-0.4[f]	12	8	7[g]	-4.5[g]
Sweden	35[h]	40	44	2.3[h]	9[h]	6	6	-1.7[h]

[a] All working ages
[b] 16–19-year-olds in the United States, France and Sweden; 15–19 year-olds in Australia, Canada, Germany and Japan; 14–19-year-olds in Italy. Data for Great Britain are for 15–19-year-olds in 1960 and 1971 and 16–19-year-olds in 1977
[c] 1965 for proportion; 1965–77 for growth rate
[d] 1963 for proportion; 1963–77 for growth rate
[e] 1961 for proportion; 1961–77 for growth rate
[f] 1976 for proportion; 1960–76 for growth rate
[g] 1975 for proportion; 1960–75 for growth rate
[h] 1961 for proportion; 1961–77 for growth rate

Note: Except for Italy, data have been adjusted to US concepts. Growth rates (per cent per year) based on compound rate of change
Source: BLS

than with industry, partly because agriculture is less susceptible to cyclical change, but chiefly because a high proportion of workers in agriculture are self-employed or unpaid family workers. As indicated in Table 6.11, agricultural workers have been declining as a percentage of total employment in the industrial countries (see also Sorrentino, 1971). Italy, Japan and France had the highest proportions of workers, generally not susceptible to being counted as unemployed. Great Britain and the United States had the lowest proportions. However, it should be noted that Italy and Japan, the countries with the highest percentages, experienced a high rate of displacement from the agricultural sector in the period under review and have therefore had the added strain of providing other jobs for displaced farm workers.

Labour migration

The volume of migration in the western European countries has tended to fluctuate with the economic situation. Foreign nationals have flowed into many northern European countries when demand is high and have left when it is low, without seriously affecting unemployment levels. This flexibility of labour supply, particularly in France, Germany and Switzerland, had acted as a cyclical shock absorber, helping to keep unemployment rates low during recessions, although in 1974–75 the outflow was not as great as in past recessions. These cyclical flows of 'guestworkers' have no precise counterpart in the United States and Canada and are one of the factors explaining

Table 6.11 *Percentage of Total Employment in Agriculture*

Country	1960	1978
United States	8.5	3.7
Canada	13.3	5.7
Australia	NA	6.4
Japan	29.5	11.4
France	22.4	9.1
Germany	13.6	6.5
Great Britain	4.1	2.5
Italy	32.6	15.4
Sweden	15.5	6.1

NA Not available

why unemployment rates in some western European countries have been lower than in North America.

Almost all northern European countries have now placed bans or restrictions on new immigration, because of the social and political problems associated with migration as well as the 1974–75 recession. With rules of the European Community providing for a free flow of workers from one member country to another, efforts to stem the flow of migrants are aimed at countries that do not belong to the Community (e.g., Greece, Spain, Turkey, Yugoslavia). Many of the foreign workers remained in the host countries during the recent recession and slow recovery because they feared they would not be able to re-enter under the newly restrictive policies. Besides, increased unemployment and other benefits in the industrial countries exceeded any wages the migrants could hope to receive at home. This growing tendency for unemployed foreign workers to remain in the host countries contributed to the sharp rise in unemployment rates recorded in these countries during the recent recession and to the persistence of high jobless rates in the recovery. Foreign workers now present a significant unemployment problem in France and Germany in particular.

Income maintenance arrangements

Unemployment insurance and such income maintenance programmes as short-time payments and 'bad weather' compensation may have an important impact on unemployment statistics. Unemployment benefits may encourage workers to remain unemployed longer, while the other maintenance measures mentioned may serve to reduce recorded unemployment.

High levels of unemployment benefits payable for long periods of time allow workers to remain unemployed longer while they seek work with similar skill requirements and pay as their previous jobs. A major question recently has been whether high levels of unemployment benefits discourage efforts to find work quickly, thereby prolonging unemployment. Several research studies during the last few years have addressed this question (see Marston, 1975; Feldstein, 1973 and 1975; Grubel *et al.*, 1975; Green and Cousineau, 1976; Swan *et al.*, 1976; Cook *et al.*, 1976; Cubbin and Foley, 1977; Maki and Spindler, 1975).

⁻The OECD (1978b) analysed a collection of ten country studies on the effect of unemployment benefits on work incentives. For seven of the ten countries, evidence was found that, by lowering the cost to the unemployed person of looking for work, unemployment benefits have raised the level of voluntary unemployment. The United States study suggested that the presence of unemployment compensation raises the US unemployment rate by 0.7 per cent, mainly by increasing the duration of unemployment. Other countries in which a significant effect was noted are Canada, Ireland and Great Britain. The Maki and Spindler study (1975) for Great Britain suggested that introduction of the earnings-related supplement in 1966 induced an average increase in the unemployment rate of 0.6 per cent in the years 1967–72. The actual British rate of unemployment averaged 2.7 per cent in 1967–72, but would have been 2.1 per cent without the earnings-related supplement. A later study by the British Department of Employment, however, showed a much smaller effect (DE, 1976). (For further analysis on this point for Great Britain, see chapter two). Limited evidence of induced unemployment was found in France, New Zealand and Belgium, and no such evidence in Germany and Italy.

The OECD Working Party on Social Aspects of Income Transfer Policy (OECD, 1978b) did not feel that unemployment benefits are excessive, in spite of evidence that they may induce some additional unemployment. The Working Party pointed out that these benefits are intended to raise social welfare, and the fact that people prolong their job search by a few weeks may well improve the match between their skills and jobs and reduce labour turnover in the long run. Nevertheless, there is concern in some countries that induced unemployment may have become more significant, and it is clearly desirable that research be carried further.

Unemployment benefits twenty years ago were more generous and more widely available in the United States than in most other industrial countries. However, during the 1960s and 1970s, improvements in such benefits in the European countries, Canada and Japan have been significant. There is rather wide variation in the percentage of the labour force covered (Table 6.12). Sweden leads all countries with virtually all persons covered who complete the specified waiting period. About two-thirds of the Swedish labour force is covered by a government-subsidised system run by the trade unions. In addition, in 1974 Sweden established a 'labour market support' system extending coverage to all other persons, even new entrants to the labour market. The coverage in the United States, Canada and Great Britain is high in comparison with the remaining countries where a larger proportion of the labour force is employed in small firms or in agriculture, both of which are often exempted from coverage.

The maximum duration for which benefits are payable is a year or more in all countries except Italy. In addition, unemployment benefits are fairly generous in most countries, with all countries replacing at least half former earnings of manufacturing workers with two children.

The replacement ratio in Table 6.12 apply to workers formerly earning the average wage in manufacturing. All the countries except the United States provide for higher wage replacement rates for persons earning relatively low wages. In Canada, a benefit rate of 75 per cent applies to claimants with dependants and with earnings below one-third of maximum weekly insurable earnings. Similarly, Japanese workers at the low end of the wage scale receive 80 per cent of their former wage. Great Britain allows a maximum payment of combined flat rate plus earnings-related supplements equalling 85 per cent of former earnings. Sweden's trade union system permits a maximum benefit of about 90 per cent of gross earnings. In some countries, special payments are available for workers placed on short workweeks (Levitan & Belous, 1977; Henle, 1976 and 1978). During 1974–75, the introduction or improvement of compensation for partial unemployment permitted a fairly widespread resort to part-time work in several countries including Germany as a means of spreading a reduced volume of employment among the workforce.

For many years, statutory unemployment insurance or assistance schemes in France, Germany, Great Britain and Sweden have contained provisions covering payments for partial unemployment. Japan introduced such payments in 1975. In Italy, partial unemployment compensation is provided by a special institution, the Wage Supplement Fund. The United States and Canada do not have systems for short-time payments.

The systems vary significantly from country to country. The German system is neutral with regard to whether employers reduce daily hours worked or lay off workers for full days or weeks. The British system, currently the subject of criticism, encourages temporary lay-off or even dismissal of workers, rather than the use of shorter daily hours worked.[5] The systems in the other countries with short-

Table 6.12 *Unemployment Insurance Systems, mid–1975*

Country	% of labour force covered	Maximum duration of benefits (weeks)	Benefits as % of average earnings in manufacturing Single worker	Married worker with 2 children
United States[a]	82	65[b]	50	50
Canada	89	51[b]	63	63
Japan	45	15–50[c]	60	62
France	60	52–104[c]		
Regular system			50–56	57–63
Supplementary system			90	90
Germany	77	52	60	60
Great Britain	80	52		
Regular system[d]			19	41
Supplementary system[d]			38	60
Italy	51	26		
Regular system			9	22
Supplementary system			67	80
Sweden	100	60–90[c]	62–72	62–72

a Figures are representative of the majority of states

b Representas extended duraiton of benefits under national programme that take effect in times of high unemployment

c maximum duration depends upon age of claimant with duraiton rising with age

d Means-tested public assistance payments can substanitally raise these replacement ratios

Source: BLS

time compensation are closer to the German than to the British system, encouraging firms to retain workers during adverse economic conditions. Short-time payments replace 70–90 per cent of foregone gross earnings in Japan, 80 per cent in Italy, 60 per cent in Germany and about 50 per cent in France. Generally, financing is partly out of public funds and partly by the firms concerned.

The continental European and Japanese work-sharing systems spread the impact of an economic downturn. Under these systems, a firm that must reduce its total hours worked by 50 per cent can reduce each employee's workweek by 50 per cent. In contrast, a lay-off system (as in the United States and Canada) results in putting 50 per

...orkers out of their jobs, hence increasing

...ry adopts a work-sharing or lay-off system when
...e slack depends on that country's assessment of the
...isavantages of each system. Work sharing allows a
...distribution of the impact of a recession and the
...f an employer's workforce intact. Disadvantages include ... ...idities in labour markets, discouragement of firms and
workers from adapting to technological change and reduction of job
opportunities for new entrants. It seems that Western Europe and
Japan have opted for job security over job mobility; North America
places more emphasis on job mobility. American corporations continue to have, by European standards, an extraordinary freedom to
lay off workers when orders shrink. Lay-offs are common even in some
of the most heavily unionised US industries.

The American and Canadian systems of unemployment insurance
discourage work sharing because part-time workers are not normally
eligible for benefits; only persons totally without work can collect
unemployment benefits. Also, as collective bargaining agreements
now stand, it is most often in the employer's interest to resort to
lay-offs rather than reduced hours. Further, many North American
workers and labour unions look unfavourably upon short-time
schemes. Currently, a work-sharing system is being tried in the state
of California whereby those on economic part-time schedules will be
eligible for state unemployment insurance benefits. It is still too early
to tell whether the scheme will prove popular.

Most European countries provide special compensation for construction workers who lose work time on account of bad weather.
Workers do not sever their employment relationship in order to collect
benefits and are not counted as unemployed. In Germany, partly as a
result of the 'bad weather money' system, unemployment rates in the
construction industry are not appreciably higher than the overall
unemployment rate. In contrast, US and Canadian unemployment
rates in the construction industry are well above the national average.

Labour market programmes

Labour market policies constitute the measures used by government
to upgrade the skills of workers, to create jobs and to match people
and jobs. The general techniques of labour market policy have been

developed and used in both Western Europe an~
However, differences in economic environment, s~
institutional arrangements have had an impact ~
market measures and on the way in which they~
different countries (see chapter 4).

Labour market programmes began earlier and have becom.
widespread in many of the western European countries than in the
United States. An indication of the relative prominence given to
them is found in the ratio of a country's expenditures for such
programmes to GNP. Data for eight countries for 1972–77 show that
Sweden is the leader by far, spending over 2 per cent of its GNP on
labour market measures (Table 6.13). Germany and Japan rank
second and third respectively, with expenditures amounting to 0.7–
0.9 per cent of GNP in recent years. Rising US expenditures on labour
market programmes in the mid-1970s have put that country ahead of

Table 6.13 *Public Expenditure on Labour Market Programmes, 1972–77
(Percentage of GNP)*

Country and fiscal year	Training	Temporary employment maintenance or creation	Other[a]	Total
United States				
1972/73	0.10	0.13	0.17	0.40
1973/74	0.08	0.10	0.15	0.33
1974/75	0.12	0.17	0.17	0.46
1975/76	0.13	0.30	0.14	0.57
Canada				
1973/74	0.32	0.10	0.16	0.56
1974/75	0.27	0.08	0.13	0.48
1975/76	0.31	0.10	0.10	0.51
1976/77	0.29	0.12	0.10	0.51
1977/78	0.30	0.17	0.11	0.58
Australia				
1972/73	0.01	0.25	0.04	0.30
1973/74	0.02	0.02	0.04	0.08
1974/75	0.08	0.18	0.04	0.30
1975/76	0.11	0.18	0.05	0.34

able 6.13 *(cont.)*

Country and fiscal year	Training	Temporary employment maintenance or creation	Other[a]	Total
Japan				
1973/74	0.02	[b]	0.60	0.62
1974/75	0.02	[b]	0.61	0.64
1975/76	0.02	0.01	0.69	0.72
France[c]				
1972	0.15	[b]	0.02	0.17
1973	0.16	[b]	0.03	0.19
1974	0.17	[c]	0.03	0.20
1975	0.19	0.02	0.04	0.25
1976	0.20	0.02	0.06	0.28
1977	0.20	0.04	0.06	0.30
Germany				
1973	0.20	0.18	0.19	0.57
1974	0.21	0.22	0.22	0.65
1975	0.27	0.35	0.25	0.87
GreatBritain[d]				
1973/74	0.08	0.16	0.18	0.42
1974/75	0.10	0.19	0.16	0.45
1975/76	0.17	0.22	0.24	0.63
Sweden				
1972/73	0.39	1.39	0.54	2.32
1973/74	0.39	1.05	0.61	2.05
1974/75	0.32	0.63	0.61	1.56
1975/76	0.34	0.88	0.50	1.72
1973/77	0.61	1.16	0.52	2.29

[a] Includes expenditure on geographical mobility, employment services, aid to the handicapped and other labour market programmes
[b] Nil or negligible
[c] Percentage of GDP
[d] United Kingdom

Source: OECD (1978c) pp. 118–119

France and at about the same level as Great Britain. In 1970, British spending on manpower programmes was twice the US level.

Public works projects have been used in most countries to offset cyclical or seasonal declines in employment. In recent years, government-subsidised job creation in the private sector has emerged as an additional tool of manpower policy. For example, British temporary employment maintenance and job creation in the private sector from 1975/76 to 1979/80 directly involved an estimated 463,000 persons. Table 6.13 indicates increasing emphasis on job creation programmes (both public and private sector) in several countries in response to the 1974–75 recession. For example, US expenditures in this area jumped from 0.1 per cent of GNP in 1972–74 to 0.3 per cent in 1975–76. A significant rising trend also occurred in Canada, Germany, Great Britain and Sweden.

Governments have followed quite different strategies with regard to the mix between unemployment compensation and other employment policies. Sweden spent almost six times as much on employment and training programmes as on unemployment compensation in 1975. Canada, in contrast, spent almost five times as much on unemployment compensation as on other labour market policies. In the United States, France and Germany, expenditures on unemployment compensations were also higher than on labour market measures. In the United States, expenditures on unemployment compensation were about 30 per cent higher than the amount spent on labour market measures. These differences in policy were influenced by the levels of unemployment and the stage of development of labour market policies in each country. Germany normally spends much more on employment policies than on unemployment benefits (e.g. 2.6 to 1 in 1971), but the abnormally high levels of unemployment in 1975 caused spending on unemployment benefits to be almost twice as high as employment policy expenditures.

In Sweden, 'active labour market' policies are highly developed and provide a comprehensive system of institutions for retraining and relief. Sweden's training programme is the largest in the world relative to the size of its labour force. Also, Sweden is the only country that deliberately uses adult training programmes for counter-cyclical purposes. The Swedish programmes (as indicated in Table 6.14) have had a large impact on Swedish unemployment rates in recent years. Without them, unemployment potentially could have been 6.2 per cent rather than 2.2 per cent in 1978, for example.

Table 6.14 *Sweden: Effect of Labour Market Programmes on Unemployment, Selected Years, 1961–78*

Year	Unemployment adjusted to US concepts Number ('000s)	Rate (%)	Number of persons in labour market programmes ('000s)[a]	Unemployment plus persons in labour market programmes as % of civilian labour force
1961	52	1.4	15	1.9
1965	44	1.2	33	2.1
1967	79	2.1	48	3.4
1968	85	2.2	63	3.9
1969	72	1.9	65	4.1
1970	59	1.5	70	3.3
1971	101	2.6	83	4.6
1972	107	2.7	103	5.3
1973	98	2.5	112	5.3
1974	80	2.0	102	4.5
1975	67	1.6	94	3.9
1976	66	1.6	112	4.3
1977	75	1.8	165	5.8
1978	94	2.2	166	6.2

a Monthly average of persons in training for labour market reasons, work training programmes, public relief works, archive work and relief work for musicians, and sheltered and semi-sheltered workshops

Source: National Labour Market Board. *Arbetsmarknadsstatistik* (labour market statistics), various issues: and BLS calculations

Factors affecting youth unemployment

In times of both prosperity and recession, the United States has had youth unemployment rates that rank among the highest in the industrial world. The United States has also had a rather wide differential between youth and adult unemployment rates, although some countries have caught up or surpassed the United States in recent years. Canada has also had a relatively high youth unemployment rate, but a narrower youth–adult differential than the United States.

High youth unemployment has also existed in Italy for many years. As indicated earlier, the youth–adult unemployment differential is much more severe in Italy than elsewhere in the industrial world. Problems of teenagers in the Italian labour market are intensified by a high dropout rate from school (over half of Italian youths entering the labour market have not completed high school).

The relatively high youth unemployment rates in the United States have been attributed to several factors, including an inferior prevocational counselling system, minimum wage laws that do not exempt teenagers, and the relative dearth of apprenticeship programmes. It is also worth noting that the overwhelming majority of teenagers in the European and Japanese labour forces are full-time participants; relatively few work while they are still in school, partly because governments often provide stipends to students. In the United States and Canada, on the other hand, most teenage workers are also students, and this reduces their job attachment as well as restricts the types of jobs that they can take.

The position of youth in the labour market also reflects differences in fundamental attitudes and institutions. The emphasis of European education and labour market institutions on apprenticeship and vocational training tends to put the majority of young people into stable work-training relationships that discourage mobility. In the United States the importance of extended schooling has long been stressed because of the wider range of jobs open to persons with high school diplomas and college degrees. In short, the US system allows for greater mobility of labour and possibilities for career changes in later life. Thus, there is a trade-off between stability of employment in the early years versus the value of extended schooling and the information gained through job change and 'shopping around'. The different ways that countries view this trade-off have shown up in international differences in youth unemployment.

Teenage unemployment rates have remained high in the United States, Canada and Italy in recent years. The differential between teenage and adult unemployment has narrowed in the United States and remained stable in Canada. In contrast, Western Europe and Japan recently have had increases in teenage unemployment and a widening of the differential between youth and adult joblessness. Apparently, some of the problems experienced by North American youth are now coming to the fore elsewhere in the industrial world.

International differences in job security (discussed later), coupled with the recent recession, may contribute to an explanation of the severe youth unemployment problems currently facing many Western European governments. The traditional institutional arrangements that held down youth unemployment in the past (apprenticeship, vocational education, youth minimum wages) now appear to be vulnerable. It seems that many European employers are wary of hiring any new employees until they utilise the surplus labour they are holding due to strengthened job security arrangements. Also, the rise in wages paid to youth has outpaced the rise in overall wages. Moreover, the rapid growth of fringe benefit expenditures and compulsory state payments has added greatly to the costs of hiring the young. Increasing recognition of the adverse impact of the high costs of employing youth in relation to their productivity has led a number of European countries to experiment with subsidies to employers to hire young people.

Legal and social factors

Unemployment in several European countries has been curbed by legislation or labour-management agreements that shield workers from lay-offs. US and Canadian job security measures, by contrast, are much weaker. Where they exist, they are based on seniority and usually specify severance pay related to the length of service (see Jenkins, 1976; Yemin, 1976; and Braun, 1965).

In Germany, under a 1951 law, a legally valid discharge may be declared ineffective by the Labour Court if it is 'socially unjustified', that is, if it cannot be based on the characteristics or conduct of the employee or on important needs of the enterprise. Even if important business needs warrant the discharge, it is nevertheless 'socially unjustified' if the employer selected the worker for discharge with giving sufficient attention to the social factors involved. The procedures required under the 1951 law were made even stronger by the Works Constitution Act of 1972.

As a good example of how the German system works, one of the companies of the Thyssen group carried out a massive reorganisation, involving the loss of about 6000 jobs. The head of the firm's works council, which is an employee-run unit financed by the company, discussed problems with the employees, found jobs for many in other units of the company, and negotiated numerous problems with management. Not a single day was lost through labour conflict and no one suffered exceptional hardship.

Strict legislation also exists in Italy. Courts have applied tough standards to judge whether adequate justification exists for a dismissal; if not, a dismissed employee is entitled to reinstatement or an indemnity of five months' wages. If a lay-off is eventually made, the employer is required to take account of a number of factors including the family responsibilities and economic situation of the workers. In many firms, labour agreements also provide protection. At Fiat, where worker protection has been increasingly strengthened by labour contracts during the past few years, no reduction in the workforce is permitted.

A national agreement on security of employment was signed in February 1969 by French employers and all the trade union federations. This agreement, like the individual industry agreements that followed it, recognises the responsibility of the parties towards security of employment. In the case of prospective dismissals, the firms must consult with the plant employment committee and give due notice, endeavour to minimise dismissals and utilise intra-plant or intra-company transfers. Reductions of staff must be achieved as far as possible by attrition. The employer must give a dismissed worker priority re-employment rights for a year, guarantee seniority rights with the firm and assist him in obtaining all unemployment benefits to which he is entitled. In January 1975, the legal requirements for handling dismissals were further strengthened.

An employer's ability to lay off workers is also considerably restricted by Swedish law. Existing protection of employees was improved when the Security of Employment Act went into effect in 1974. This law virtually prohibits the dismissal of any employee except for the most serious misbehaviour. In Great Britain, the 1975 Employment Protection Act provides comprehensive new legislation regulating dismissals.

The recent recession has brought considerable improvement in job security provisions for workers in Western Europe. An OECD study (Gennard, 1979) of job security arrangements in France, Germany and Great Britain indicates that management prerogatives in dismissing labour have been substantially curtailed. This trend was found to have started in the late 1960s, but was considerably accelerated during the recession. There are several possible long-term disadvantages of increased job security: (1) it may induce firms to operate with a smaller labour force for producing a given level of output than would be the case with a mobile labour force; (2) the security of those in employment may be achieved at the expense of those who are out of work. In particular, it may considerably reduce the job opportunities for new labour market entrants, notably youth; (3) it may impede structural change and productivity growth by reducing labour mobility, thus making the economy more inflation prone.

Laws or labour-management agreements requiring advance notice of lay-off give workers time to look for another job prior to dismissal and allow for the placing of at least some workers in new jobs without a period of unemployment associated with the job search.

In the United States, most collective bargaining agreements do not contain clauses prescribing advance notice of lay-off. Moreover, those provisions that deal generally with advance notice of lay-off (43 per cent of the major agreements) normally specify only a very limited time period — in most cases less than thirty days.

Advance notification has been required by various laws regarding the dismissal of workers in Western European countries. One type of law obliges the employer to notify the employment service of the impending dismissal. Such laws exist in France, Germany and Great Britain. In Sweden, the Employer's Federation has an agreement with the Labour Market Board that requires a minimum of thirty days' notice to the employment service by employers preceding collective dismissals. Also, the Promotion of Employment Act (1974) contains rules of periods of notice to trade unions before production cutbacks can involve dismissals.

Another type of law calls for advance notice to employees prior to dismissal. France, Germany, Great Britain and Sweden have such legislation. For example, the Swedish law on Security of Employment requires a minimum of one month's notice, with longer notice (up to 6 months) as an employee gets older. In Germany, non-manual workers who have over twelve years' service must be given six month's notice prior to dismissal. Great Britain requires twelve weeks' notice after twelve years of service.

Besides laws, social customs and tradition play an important part in diminishing the threat of lay-off in Europe and Japan. Employers avoid dismissals if at all possible because they feel a high degree of responsibility for their regular employees and continue to provide employment, perhaps at reduced hours, when production declines. In addition, the employer may be somewhat afraid of loss of prestige among his fellow employers, because lay-offs might be interpreted as proof of his failure as a businessman. In Sweden, for example, companies reportedly try very hard to avoid the weakening of their reputation for job stability, especially since most major employers are located in small towns or cities where company practices are common knowledge.

Recognised 'regular' employees in Japan benefit from paternalistic attitudes on the part of employers that are unmatched by other industrial nations. In large Japanese enterprises, appointment to a regular job virtually assures employment until retirement, and the employer takes responsibility for maintaining the worker during periods of economic adversity. Japanese employers are allowed to shift workers from one job or one plant to another, so that the system is thus protected. Temporary or day lay-offs do not come under the unique in that it emanates more from tradition and implicit agreements than from law or collective bargaining agreements. Nevertheless, only 30–40 per cent of the non-agricultural labour force in Japan is thus protected. Temporary or day lay-offs do not come under the system. Even so, temporary lay-offs and permanent discharges appear to be much less frequent in Japan than in North America. Although some Japanese employers were forced to lay off workers during the 1974–75 recession, the great majority retained their excess labour. There are numerous stories of Japanese companies sending excess production workers out to sell their products door-to-door or to do landscaping around the factory.

In Western Europe and Japan, legal and social restrictions against lay-off are reinforced by the reluctance of workers to change jobs in search of improved wages or working conditions. In the United States and Canada, labour turnover rates in manufacturing are significantly higher than in Western Europe and Japan; mobility is often considered an attribute of the workforce even though the search for a new job may entail some unemployment. In contrast, the job attachment of

European and Japanese workers is much stronger, partly because of the belief that a change of jobs is likely to reflect unfavourably on a worker's dependability.

Other factors

Several other hypotheses have been suggested to explain international differences in unemployment rates. Some of these include the contributions and effects of: forms of economic organisation (i.e., free enterprise, socialism, etc); unionisation; the relative ethnic and racial heterogeneity of the populations; differences in seasonal, regional and structural unemployment; and international differences in the unemployment trade-off (Phillips Curve). Thus, this chapter is by no means a complete survey of all the factors that influence comparative levels of unemployment rates. However, I believe that the factors covered go a long way towards explaining why unemployment rates differ among the major industrial countries.

CONCLUSION

The presentation of unemployment rates on a common statistical base sets the stage for a second level of analysis that attempts to explain why international unemployment rates differ. Such explanations were sought in the economic, demographic, social and institutional differences that exist among the industrial countries. I believe that the relatively high levels of North American unemployment rates in comparison with the rates in Western Europe and Japan, until around 1974, were attributable primarily to large differences in rates of economic growth and labour force growth. Also important were laws and attitudes that restrict European and Japanese employers from laying workers off; worker mobility was much lower in those countries than in North America. In other words, frictional, job-changing type unemployment in North America, particularly the United States, was higher than elsewhere. The demographic and industrial structures of the respective labour forces were also factors, as were foreign labour migrations, especially for Germany. In Sweden, massive labour market training and job creation programmes were crucial in keeping unemployment low. Without them, Swedish unemployment would have approached the North American levels in some recent years.

It is evident that unemployment rates do not totally measure how well labour markets are functioning across countries. In each country under-utilisation of labour may take several different forms: countries that have a relatively low unemployment rate may simply be experiencing labour slack in a different form. For example, in the United States and Canada, during economic downturns, workers are typically laid off and become unemployed. In most of Europe and Japan, on the other hand, many workers move to a work-sharing arrangement ('short-time work') and remain employed. The American and Canadian systems of unemployment insurance discourage work sharing, whereas many of the European systems and the Japanese system are specifically designed to promote this practice.

It is misleading to look solely at unemployment rates, even those adjusted to a common base, and draw conclusions that one country is 'doing better' than another. Certainly, other factors must also be considered, such as the growth in the labour supply and the number of new jobs created. It has been shown that several countries with relatively low jobless rates have also created very few net new jobs since 1960, while others with high unemployment have created millions of new jobs. In addition, international differences in the duration of unemployment are significant. Comparisons based on long-term unemployment rates result in very different rankings in levels of unemployment from comparisons based on the overall rates. Thus, Great Britain, with high unemployment (at least in recent years), low rates of employment creation and a high long-term unemployment rate, would seem to have a much more difficult labour market situation than the United States, which has managed to create millions of new jobs each year and to maintain a much lower duration of unemployment, albeit with unemployment rates about the same level as in Great Britain.

Although there are still obvious and important differences in the labour markets of the countries covered in this international perspective, in several ways these countries are becoming more alike. Since 1974, there has been a convergence in international jobless rates, with France, Great Britain and Australia moving close to the US level and the German rate rising to a historically high level, though still moderate by international standards. One of the most important factors in this development has been the drastic change in relative rates of economic growth. The wide differences characteristic of the 1950s to the early 1970s no longer hold. American growth, in fact, has outpaced that of Europe since 1974, reversing the previous relationship. British growth, slowest of all in the postwar period, has been more like that of the continental countries since 1974. Japan, although still having the fastest economic growth rate, is not as far ahead as it once was.

Another important change in the post-1974 period has been a turnaround in demographic trends in a number of countries. A more rapid growth in the working age population will occur in the 1975–1985 decade for many European countries, making it harder to reduce unemployment, given the slower economic growth. Youth unemployment has been rising in most of Europe, and the teenage labour force is now increasing. Some observers have even noted a tendency in some countries for young people to take part-time jobs while attending school, as has been the case in the United States for many years. All of this is in sharp contrast with the situation in the 1960s and early 1970s when the teenage labour force was declining and youth unemployment was not considered a problem.

In the 1950s and 1960s, lower wages and savings gave workers very little to fall back on once they became unemployed. Unemployment insurance schemes in most of Europe and Japan were very limited and workers could not afford to take the risk of leaving and looking for a better job. With higher real wages and improvements in unemployment benefits, workers can now afford to remain unemployed longer, with a consequent longer duration of unemployment and higher unemployment rates. In several European countries and Japan, jobless benefits have been made much more generous and lengthy in duration; in Great Britain, although earnings-related supplements were introduced in 1967, there has been no change in the duration of benefits.

The countries with the lowest economic growth rates in the 1960–78 period — the United States and Great Britain — entered the 1960s with the smallest proportion of the labour force in the agricultural sector. The country with the highest growth rate — Japan — had the highest proportion in agriculture and experienced the largest shift of employment out of this sector. This contributed to both economic and productivity growth in Japan. Large shifts out of agriculture were also experienced by some of the European countries, notably Italy. Now the proportion employed in agriculture even in Japan has become low enough that the changeover from that sector will no longer contribute to growth as it once did. Furthermore, as the number of family-owned agricultural and business enterprises diminishes, the chances that a worker will become unemployed increases.

Finally, for some countries the foreign workforce is no longer as flexible as it was in the 1960s. Bans on the employment of foreign workers resulted in many staying in the host country because they feared they would not be able to re-enter later. Hence, foreign workers have added to the post-1974 high unemployment levels in several European countries.

These changes since 1974 suggest several reasons why recent international unemployment rates have drawn closer together. Convergence in economic growth rates and demographic patterns seem to be the two most important factors. Until a major impact has been made on the continuing problem of inflation, the prospects for reducing unemployment rates in the 1980s are not very bright. The rate at which costs and prices are rising presents a formidable constraint on policies to promote growth and, hence, to reduce unemployment. Yet, even if economic growth can be restored, there will remain a strong underlying tendency for unemployment to remain high in many of these countries. For example, the increase in the youth labour force that has already begun in some countries should continue well into the 1980s. The increasing labour force participation of women will also be a factor. Growing supply–demand imbalances on the labour market may intensify in the absence of programmes to mitigate their impact. Other long-term structural changes (such as the decline of agricultural employment) that have tended to push up national unemployment rates have yet to run their course in some countries. All these factors seem to point toward the conclusion that we may expect unemployment rates in the industrial countries to remain considerably higher in the 1980s than they were in the 1960s.

Appendix: The International Measurement of Unemployment

Production of internationally comparable unemployment statistics has long been a goal of the International Conference of Labour Statisticians, which in 1954 approved definitions of employment, unemployment and the labour force that are now widely acknowledged, though by no means generally observed (ILO, 1954).

In summary, the ILO definitions include as unemployed all persons who, during a specified time period, were without a job, available for work and seeking work. Also included are persons who had made arrangements to start a new job at a later date and persons on temporary or indefinite lay-off without pay. Persons in these two categories do not have to be seeking work. The labour force is defined as the sum of the employed and the unemployed. The employed consist of all persons who, during a specified time period, performed some work for pay or profit, including the self-employed. Unpaid family workers are included if they worked for at least one-third of the normal working time during the specified period. Persons with a job but not at work because of illness, vacation, strike, bad weather, etc. are regarded as employed. The armed forces may be included or excluded from the labour force.

The theory behind the ILO's standard definitions is that countries having different types of statistical systems can produce unemployment statistics that are reasonably comparable from country to country. In fact, however, relatively few countries strictly observe the international definitions, and, even among those that do, there is room for some divergence, since the ILO definitions permit a certain amount of flexibility. Therefore, adjustments in the figures for various countries are necessary if comparisons of unemployment levels are to be made.

The incomparability of national figures on unemployment is attributable to two chief causes: (i) differences in the systems for collecting data and (ii) differences in concepts or definitions.

(i) *Statistical systems*. The ILO identifies five chief systems for measuring unemployment, and all of these have been used at one time or another by the countries referred to in this chapter. At present, however, only two of the systems are in use by the nine countries in the preparation of official statistics. Australia, Canada, Japan, Italy, Sweden and the United States depend on periodic (usually monthly) labour force sample surveys; France, Germany and Great Britain rely on monthly counts of registrants at employment offices. Labour force surveys generally yield the most comprehensive statistics since they are designed to cover all persons seeking work, whether or not they register with employment offices. Also, changes in legislation and administrative regulations do not necessarily affect the continuity of the survey series, but may have a substantial impact on registration data.

(ii) *Concepts and definitions*. Even when the same type of data collection method is used, definitions of unemployment and labour force may vary across countries. Thus, labour force surveys may differ in regard to treatment of such groups as military personnel, students, unpaid family workers, discouraged workers and persons on temporary lay-off. Other sources of difference include reference periods, age limits and tests for current availability and work-seeking on the part of unemployed persons.

Adjustment for differences

A major effort to reconcile national differences in unemployment statistics was made in the United States in the early 1960s, when President Kennedy appointed a Committee to Appraise Employment and Unemployment Statistics. One of the chief undertakings of the committee was to compare unemployment rates for the United States and other leading industrial countries, adjusted for differences in coverage and concept. The detailed work performed for the committee (Myers and Chandler, 1962) has subsequently been improved and extended by the US Bureau of Labor Statistics (BLS) to yield a series of (approximately) comparable national rates covering the period 1959–79.

In the BLS procedure, the statistics of the other eight countries have been adjusted to achieve the closest possible comparability with those of the United States (BLS, 1978). The definitions used in the US labour force survey follow the general outline of the ILO definitions, but are more specific. The minimum age limit for the US survey is 16, a point left unspecified in the ILO definition. Also unspecified in the ILO definition was whether labour force status should be measured on a particular day or throughout a particular week. The US survey uses a week as its basic reference period, although unemployed persons have to take active job-seeking steps within a four-week period including the reference week. Only persons on lay-off who are waiting to be called back to their job and persons waiting to start a new job within thirty days do not have to actively test the job market to be classified as unemployed. Also, unemployed persons must be available to begin work immediately, except for temporary illness, and there is a survey question to test current availability. The US data are collected for the civilian population only. Persons in the armed forces are excluded from the employment and labour force totals.[7]

Fortunately, all the countries produce a good deal of supplementary information on unemployment in addition to their official unemployment rate. Such additional sources have been indispensable in adjusting the official data. For example, the three countries that use unemployment registrations as their official source of data also conduct periodic labour force surveys with many features in common with the US survey. Thus, for France, Germany and Great Britain, BLS uses the results of the surveys to obtain adjustment factors to apply to the registered unemployed series.

Often, even the survey data must be adjusted somewhat to conform to US concepts. BLS is able to make adjustments for many, but not for all, of the conceptual differences. In some areas, data are simply not available for adjustment purposes. Where adjustments have not been made, the remaining differences are believed to be minor, although the exact extent of these differences cannot be known. Instead of adjusting the data of all countries to the US lower age limit of 16, the age limits of other countries have been adapted, wherever necessary, to the age at which compulsory schooling ends. This was done because youths in several other countries complete their education and enter the labour force on a full-time basis at an earlier age (i.e., 14 or 15) than in the United States.

Notes

1. The Manpower and Social Affairs Directorate of the Organisation for Economic Cooperation and Development is doing some experimental work in the areas of setting up a standardised system for monitoring all facets of the labour market. However, much more data must become available before such a system can produce internationally comparable statistics on total labour slack.

2. The revision entailed the inclusion of more probing questions in the Italian survey questionnaire. This change resulted in a doubling of the reported unemployment count. However, over half the people enumerated as unemployed in 1977 and 1978 said that they did not take any active steps to find work in the past thirty days; therefore, they have been provisionally excluded by BLS for comparability with US concepts. BLS is concerned that a number of the 'inactive' work-seekers may be persons who are registered as unemployed but who do not regard their presence on the register as an active step to find work

in the past thirty days. When more information, including cross-tabulations, becomes available from the new Italian survey, a more precise adjustment may be possible, and the comparative Italian unemployment rates may be raised somewhat.

3. The data analysed here are cross-section data as of an average reference week. A distribution by completed spells of unemployment would show different results. Data for the United States illustrates this point. While only 2.8 million people were unemployed in an average week of 1969, 32 million different spells of unemployment occurred during the year. The distribution of completed spells is more heavily skewed toward the shorter durations than is the case with cross-section data. Thus, looking at data on completed spells of unemployment, unemployment duration appears to be much shorter on the average than had previously been thought to be the case. In 1969, an American who became unemployed remained unemployed, on the average, for about five weeks. The cross-section data, however, show an average duration of about eight weeks.

4. Named after Arthur Okun, member and later chairman of the US Council of Economic Advisers during the Johnson administration and now a senior fellow of the Brookings Institution in Washington, DC. The concept is more fully described in Okun (1962).

5. Reductions in daily hours worked are not compatable under the British system. Compensation for lay-offs under the heading of short-time work is borne in full by the employer for the first five days, and, subsequently, compensation is paid through the unemployment insurance system; however, earnings-related supplements are usually not payable to temporarily laid off workers. Therefore, persons wholly unemployed receive a higher level of benefit than persons temporarily stopped.

6. It should be pointed out that people on temporary lay-off, even if laid off for an entire week, are not counted as unemployed in the labour force surveys or registration statistics in Europe and Japan. This is because they are regarded as having a job to which they are likely to return; they do not usually seek other work and they receive compensation for their workless period. In North America, however, persons on temporary lay-off are counted as unemployed. It has been found that 'temporary' lay-offs often extend to the point that they become permanent, and American and Canadian workers on lay-off often engage in job-seeking activities.

7. At the time this was written, US definitions were again undergoing

review by a presidential commission appointed in 1978 (see Bregger, 1977). One of the recommendations is to include the armed forces in the US labour force figures (see NCEUS, 1979).

CHAPTER 7

A Most Unequal Tax

Brian Showler and Adrian Sinfield

INTRODUCTION

In the first half of 1980 the economic forecasts differ only in the degree of their gloom: all, including the Treasury, predict a rise in the officially registered numbers of unemployed to two million people and over within a year to eighteen months, or even sooner. The Cambridge Economic Policy Review Group has claimed that the maintenance of present economic policies will result in 3.5 million people unemployed by 1985 (Cambridge Economic Policy Review, 1980). While there is limited support for this view and much scorn poured upon it, the Group's role as Cassandra has depressingly been justified more than once in the past. After the March 1980 Budget the 'three experts of widely different economic opinions who advise the Treasury and Civil Service Committee of the House of Commons' have all concluded that unemployment will rise faster than the Treasury's own estimate and so the extra costs of the unemployment alone — in terms of lost taxes and insurance contributions and extra benefits — will leave 'little or no room for tax cuts if the Government holds to its present strategy' (*The Guardian*, 3 April 1980).

So far this year the main government measures specifically affecting the unemployed have been the very well-publicised 'government clampdown on social security fraud', including 530 extra Unemployment Review Officers 'to save taxpayers' money' (DHSS Press Release, 13 February 1980), and simultaneous, but understandably less-proclaimed, cuts in the budget of the Manpower Services Commission, which many ministers are said to regard as being far too powerful and independent. Amongst these cuts were proposals to extend special help to the long-term unemployed, and the major development and extension of existing schemes has been severely restricted. The March 1980 Budget also announced specific measures, discussed below, that will cut the resources of the unemployed over the next two years.

It is over seventy years since Beveridge's first book in which he sought to establish unemployment as 'a problem of industry' and not 'an act of God'. Today the debate over the causes of unemployment continues, though with little reference to divine intervention. The responsibility of the unemployed for their misfortunes — or affluent and easy taxpayer-supported comforts — seems to be a view that has gained more credence, ironically, as unemployment has risen and more families have had experience of at least one of their members being out of work.

In our view, the weight of evidence demonstrates unequivocally that the causes of the incidence and severity of unemployment are external to the person out of work. This is not to say that a few could not find work if they searched harder or reduced their expectation of wages, but this would only result in a redistribution of unemployment, not any reduction in the overall numbers out of work. Indeed one of the problems posed by unemployment is to understand the tendency in both public and official discussion to concentrate attention on those who are believed to be 'voluntarily' unemployed in the light of the facts we summarise briefly here (for sources, see chapters 1 and 6).

(i) The official total of unemployed has increased four-fold over the last fifteen years and is continuing to rise. There are now more people who have been out of work for over a year than at any time since the 1930s' depression.

(ii) There are many more people available for work than jobs available for them, and the job gap is widening. Many of the vacancies demand skills that the unemployed do not have and are in parts of the country where they cannot find accommodation. In addition, there is a substantial labour reserve of married women and many others not in the labour force.

(iii) Unemployment, which was so closely associated with poverty between the two world wars, has again become the single largest cause of the increase of poverty in recent years, even by the official calculations and standards.

(iv) In comparison to most other market economies we have experienced more and longer unemployment, with the burden concentrated most heavily on a smaller proportion of the labour force. At the same time, again in contrast to other countries experiencing increased unemployment, there have been no significant improvements in the structure and range of state benefits for the unemployed over the last decade.

The comparison of the pattern of unemployment with other countries in chapter 6 throws doubt on the rather easy assumption that we are simply the victims of an international recession. Even though there may have been a tendency for unemployment rates across the countries studied by Sorrentino to converge, the difference in 1979 ranged from 2.1 per cent in Japan and Sweden to 7.5 per cent in Canada. Britain, France and Australia, with rates around 6 per cent, have all experienced a considerable increase over the last twenty years, while Italy and Japan have reduced their rates.

Some of the apparently likely explanations of the harsher impact of recession on the British unemployed are not supported by hard data. Since 1960, other countries have had slower rates of growth in productivity *and* faster increases in the labour force, including women and teenagers, than us without such an increase in unemployment, and their rates have started to drop sooner; nor do we appear to have specially generous benefits for the unemployed or particularly low, or high, expenditure and activity on labour market programmes. Our low growth in real GDP, however, does appear to distinguish us from the other countries studied (see also Dean, 1979).

There is a marked contrast with the United States, which, on the standardised figures for 1979, has an unemployment rate identical to Britain but has been able to absorb many more people into the labour force and has been much more successful in creating new jobs. This has been achieved without any significant rise in unemployment over the years the rate in Britain has increased. Clearly much more needs to be done to examine the reasons for the different ways in which countries have coped with the impact of rising fuel prices and the other factors leading to a generally worldwide recession.

In Britain an acceptance of unemployment appears to have been growing steadily after two decades of low unemployment. Most groups in society now acquiesce in levels of unemployment that were regarded as unthinkable or just part of economic history less than a decade ago. While unemployment was low — much lower in the postwar years than anyone had dared to hope — successive governments were quick to claim this as their achievement and to compare their policies favourably against the efforts of prewar administrations Now that recent governments have failed or given up trying to reduce unemployment, the victims of unemployment seem more likely to be blamed than to receive further help. The few marches and demonstrations tend to be seen as political trouble-making, and the resigned and disillusioned silence of many unemployed is interpreted as the acceptance of unemployment and a reluctance to work — a view reinforced by the social distance in our class-bound society between most of those who make, debate and write about policies for the unemployed and the poorest of those out of work. Or it may simply be, as Alexis de Tocqueville commented, 'we so soon become used to the thought of want that we do not feel that an evil which grows greater to the sufferer the longer it lasts becomes less to the observer by the very fact of its duration' (quoted by Henry George, 1879, p. 286).

The greater concentration of unemployment, which has persisted despite the increase in levels of unemployment, reduces the visibility and political salience of the problems of those out of work. In the social divisions of unemployment the differing experience and support of different groups seem to reinforce the isolation of the unemployed, especially those most badly affected, from the rest of society. The increase in redundancies and the expectations of further job losses have so far seemed to concentrate the activities of most trade unions and the TUC on fighting or preparing to resist these, and there has been a failure to mount a more virogous and sustained demand for effective action to help those already out of work. The expected impact on employment opportunities of the publicly debated and feared 'silicon chip' acts to reinforce a general sense of impotence. In consequence there is a willingness to believe in some alternative 'culture of unemployment' that conveniently accounts for the persistently high numbers out of work. The emphasis on dole-dodging and scrounging has now become as effective a substitute for new jobs in dismissing the public problem of unemployment as the 'culture of poverty' was in rendering invisible the needs of the American poor in the 1960s without giving them any extra income or resources.

There is also a certain irony in the reforms and other developments in the labour market, social security, industrial relations and collective bargaining that have provided greater security and protection for some groups in the labour force. The very activity of establishing that some are more deserving than previously thought, and so entitled to better treatment, effectively delivers a kick to those further down the ladder of social repute, increasing the stigma and penalty of their exclusion without taking any deliberate action against them. This has long been the major hazard for any policy of incremental advance in any field, and the difficulties are all the greater in the labour market, given the increasing numbers out of work and the concentration of the heaviest burdens of unemployment upon a minority of the labour force.

'WORK FOR ALL' AS A SOCIAL POLICY

It is not only those out of work and those immediately dependent upon them who bear the costs of the workless state. It is 'also a nightmare for those . . . fortunate enough to have jobs. . . . It is a bitter commentary on our economic system' if it still has to depend on the fear of unemployment (Young and Prager, 1945, p. 17). To the human cost must be added the unproductive economic waste, which means less production of the goods and services that could improve the quality of life for all (see chapter 2, pp. 48–53).

The society with low unemployment, let alone full employment, is qualitatively different from one with high unemployment. A major social gain follows from much improved employment opportunities for the groups that are weaker and discriminated against in the labour market. Even the limited objectives of current equal opportunities legislation for women and for minority racial groups are much more difficult to achieve when those who have traditionally worked in an area are themselves having to compete for the diminished number of jobs. When 'their security is hostage', they will be less willing to accept new members of the labour force or make any adjustments to include, for example, people who are disabled or handicapped by ignorance of British working practices or the English language. In many ways a tighter labour market benefits the worker and the whole population. 'Unemployment makes us compromise with the quality of life' (FEAC, n.d.). Legislators are less ready to promote, and administrators less willing to enforce, legislation that compels employers to promote health and safety at work and to protect the environment for the community as a whole.

Throughout this book, as the reader may be only too conscious, considerable emphasis has been placed on the writings of William Beveridge, particularly *Full Employment in a Free Society*, published in 1944 very much as an alternative statement to the Coalition government's anaemic White Paper on *Employment Policy*. The latter, according to a National Fellow at the Hoover Institution, 'specifically defined the commitment to permanent full employment' in Britain (Dorfman, 1979, p. 157, note 4). In fact it was very careful to do nothing of the sort. By contrast, Beveridge argued powerfully for full employment as a social policy: 'jobs, rather than men, should wait' (1944, p. 21). This emphasis on the labour market as a seller's, rather than a buyer's, market embodies the basic principle in the argument for setting 'work for all' as a primary objective for society. 'A person

who has difficulty in buying the labour that he wants suffers incon-
venience or reduction of profits. A person who cannot sell his labour is
in effect told that he is of no use. The first difficulty causes annoyance
or loss. The other is a personal catastrophe' (Beveridge, 1944, p. 19).

The persistence of unexpectedly low unemployment for most of the
twenty years after the war meant that the debate on the meaning and
desirability of full employment, and the priority that it should be
given in contrast to other societal objectives as a social, economic,
political and moral goal never took place. Today this appears as one
of the great missed opportunities of the early 'welfare state' when
memories of the 1930s were still very much sharper. In consequence,
the discussion has remained largely frozen in terms of the values and
language of the 1930s and the early years of the war and has been little
developed in the light of the changes that have occurred since then.

Although most discussion of unemployment today refer with varying degrees of enthusiasm to a golden age of full employment in the
first twenty years of the welfare state, Beveridge would not have
hesitated to remind us that by his standard we have never met the
requirements for 'full employment'. In 1944 he defined this as 'having
always more vacant jobs than unemployed men, not slightly fewer
jobs. It means the jobs are at fair wages, of such a kind, and so located
that the unemployed men can reasonably be expected to take them; it
means, by consequence, the normal lag between losing one job and
finding another will be very short' (1944, p. 18).

The importance of this definition is that it sets objectives that go
beyond crude aggregation. Few are still prepared to claim that there
is no housing problem in Britain because there are more houses than
people looking for houses; it is recognised that the houses may be of
the wrong size, in the wrong place or just inadequate. Yet, explicitly
or implicitly, it is assumed in many discussions that we have reached
'full employment' when the number of jobs available reaches the total
available for work, irrespective of the skills required, their location,
the level of wages or the nature of the job.

THE QUALITY AND QUANTITY OF WORK
AND THE 'MICROCHIP'

In arguing for full employment and social investment in the United
States, Michael Harrington has said 'we are not, after all, in favour of
everyone having "a" job — any job — without regard to its impact on

the individual and the society. We want to create an economy of meaningful, useful work' (Harrington, 1976, p. 125). We have to develop principles and priorities for economic recovery and work for all that take as their objective the need to provide economic activity that is both socially useful and intrinsically rewarding to the worker. And, as 'the dirty jobs' strike of 1971 reminded society, we must not assume that its social value is enough to make work fulfilling.

While we have called attention to the human erosion that accompanies much unemployment, we have also emphasised the link that exists between poor jobs and poor security in work, the general problem of 'sub-employment'. 'Some kinds of *employment* also demean men and women, represent waste and contribute very little either to production or welfare and, through their very existence, make unemployment on the present scale possible' (Townsend, 1978, p. 17). Much of the employment in our society is unpleasant, unsatisfying, unproductive and unrewarding; other work, at best, is monotonous, tedious and unfulfilling. This is why it is necessary to bring together the debates about unemployment and the type of economic activity or work that a modern democratic society should aim provide, and relate these discussions to the changes that may follow from the application of microelectronics and other major technological developments.

The importance of establishing a wider debate on the coming changes is all the greater now that we are much more aware that technological change is not inevitable and uncontrollable in its impact. While it may be in the interests of many to convince us otherwise, it is possible to influence where these changes occur and to what use they are put. To take one example, we need to explore and exploit opportunities for transferring people within the social services from mechanical, form-filling operations that can be taken over with the help of the micro-chip and leaving them free to engage in more personal, caring work. The economic cutbacks have meant that in many social security offices more and more staff are engaged in the routine completion of forms for the increasing number of claimants, including the many more unemployed, while there has been a reduction in the visiting of elderly and other recipients of benefit to ensure that they obtain all the benefits and services that can be provided for them.

The ferocity, speed and form with which the micro-processor and other advanced computer technologies will hit society is a matter for considerable debate. Forecasts for 1990 range from the cautious

'identifiable reduction, especially in the service sector, in job opportunities for the relatively unskilled' of the Department of Employment's Manpower Study Group to the collapse of work with five
million unemployed, with appropriate levels of change throughout
society as well as the economy (*EG*, February 1980, p. 121, and
CPRS, 1978, compared to Jenkins and Sherman, 1979, and also CIS,
1979). The more recent commentaries suggest less cataclysmic but
nevertheless specific and substantial changes in certain occupations
and industries (see for example Jones, 1980).

No one is denying that many jobs will disappear and that at the least
there will be a significant redistribution and restructuring of employment. This of course has happened many times before with very great
differences in the rate, extent and impact of the change. The predictions of the job-destroying impact of automation and the first
computer revolution fifteen to twenty years ago turned out to be
largely unjustified and generally alarmist. The large-scale 'permanent displacement' forecast by many in the United States in the
early 1960s did not occur because many more jobs were created by the
technical changes to replace those that were lost, and the expansion of
demand 'under the impetus of the Vietnam war and tax cuts' brought
unemployment down 'to historically low levels' for that country
(Metcalf, 1980, p. 30).

However, the effect of the second computer revolution on jobs
seems likely to be greater this time. The unskilled and clerical sectors
that suffered losses last time may be even more severely affected, and
many of the routine non-manual jobs that were created then and
brought great numbers of women into the labour force will disappear.
Unqualified school leavers and women expecting to return to the
labour force after child-bearing may bear the brunt of the disappear-
ance of jobs. But the major determining factor is still the level at which
the economy is being operated. If demand continues to be restrained
by government policies as at present, then the impact of technological
change will be very much greater. And there is the additional danger
that British industry will be even slower to innovate than in the recent
past (Pavitt, 1980) and become less competitive still, and the demand
for labour fall more heavily as a result.

But a policy of work for all who want it entails a much fuller
consideration of the population of working age than current British
debates about the size of the labour force and the number of jobs to be
provided have tended to assume. In Sweden 'the aim is not merely to
create employment for today's job applicants — the people reflected

in unemployment statistics — but also to remove the various obstacles which today prevent many people outside the labour force from actively seeking employment.' This means that we do not treat those outside the labour force merely 'as a labour reserve to be mobilised when the need arises' (OECD, 1979, p. 202, quoted in Pond, 1980, p. 5).

Married women are probably the main group in Britain that is recognised as a labour reserve, including many in part-time work who would prefer to be working full-time. Earlier in the century, most women had to wait till wartime to be encouraged to add paid employment to their unpaid labour in the home, but since the early 1950s the proportion of married women at work has more than doubled and is expected to continue increasing. At least part of this growth in labour force participation is due to a decline in the number of women who have not married. There is only limited evidence of women displacing men from jobs, contrary to many assumptions; certainly up to 1971 'male inroads into women's preserves had not been counterbalanced by women's entry into typically male spheres of work' (Hakim, 1978, p. 1266). Women have moved into the growing service sector and into many routine white-collar jobs, both old and new. Forty per cent, very much more than in any other Common Market country except Denmark, only have part-time jobs (*Social Trends*, 1980, p. 123).

Any consideration of the potential number of people wanting to work must also take account of the man-made or socially designated age for withdrawal from the labour force. There are many who would prefer, and would be quite able, to continue working past some enforced age of retirement. Many jobs are, of course, of such an unpleasant and demanding form that older workers look forward to the standard age of retirement, and will accept early retirement on a reduced pension almost gratefully. The combination of rising unemployment and the fear of yet fewer jobs as a result of the new technological revolution has made us much too easily accepting of such a picture.

But within a long-term programme to provide work for all who want it, the raising or removal of the minimum age at which retirement can be enforced solely because of age can 'permit a smoother mix of labour and leisure across life' which may bring greater freedom and other benefits to all workers of any age (Burkhauser and Tolley, 1978, p. 457). Combined with opportunities for working part-time and with flexible and adequate pension systems that do not discriminate against those working past the standard age of retirement — as many state, occupational and private schemes do at present — this could provide valuable protection against the poverty and deprivation that hit many a few years after they have left the labour force.

Much of the debate about early retirement, or bringing forward the age for standard retirement, in the context of high unemployment is likely to be seen by future historians as remarkably opportunist. Not only are older people generally more healthy and able to work longer than ever before; many jobs are much less physically demanding and allow a greater flexibility to both employer and employee for part-time or full-time working. Yet the proportion of men aged 65–69 in the labour force dropped by over one-third between 1964 and 1971, and is estimated to have fallen even more steeply since then, with a similar but less severe decline among single women (Townsend, 1979a, p. 656). They have, as Blackaby says, 'simply committed the industrially unforgivable sin of growing old' (1976, p. 297; see also *EG*, April 1980, pp. 366–9).

There is a great difference between enabling people to opt for early retirement with adequate and flexible pension systems and allowing many to be chased out of the labour market on low incomes and with a high risk of falling into poverty for the last decades of their lives. The debate also ignores the social value and functions of being able to play a useful part in the general daily routine that characteristics most of our lives. It disregards the fear with which many people approach the formal retirement age, dreading the insistence on withdrawal that more firms and public employers are demanding to reduce their labour costs by so-called 'natural wastage'. The man eased out at 60 with an immediately attractive, but inadequately inflation-proofed, payment spends the rest of his years in a very different way from the 70 year old man who was recently taken on one side by his employer and told 'you know, I think you and I ought to have a very serious talk about how long you should continue — when you get to 80'.

THE DISTRIBUTION AND SHARING OF WORK

Some may argue that we should wait until the long-promised economic recovery begins before we start exploring some of the goals that many may regard as utopian. But the very way in which any recovery comes about — or, more immediately, the impact of the continuing decline is distributed — will itself have long-term effects offering very different chances to different groups in the labour force. On past experience, for example, those who have now been three or four years out of work will be amongst the last to return even in an economic miracle or war. They will continue to be among the least secure and most marginal members of the labour force if they do not drop out altogether. Every improvement in work opportunities therefore must try to counter the forces that militate against the most disadvantaged. Equally, more attention should be given to ensuring that those who are already most vulnerable do not suffer yet more severely and harshly from further declines in demand.

The immediate issues for public debate and policy-making can, we believe, be stated simply. If unemployment is not going to decline in the near future (and the main questions are where, how much and how fast it will increase), the debate needs to be about how the work that is available should be distributed, and how those excluded from any meaningful economic activity should be treated. We need to discuss the principles of justice and equity that should apply in the allocation. The present ways of sharing out what work there is, and the changes people will allow to alter that allocation, largely reflect the dominant values and the choices tolerated by those holding significant power in society. Any proposals to distribute economic opportunities more evenly, let alone to provide work for all, are bound to challenge established assumptions and the prevailing patterns of the distribution of work if they are to be of any real help to those now unemployed and the many others likely to lose their jobs in the future. Even a fairer distribution of the jobs there are will threaten the vested interests of those who have managed to achieve greater security and privilege.

It is within the broader context of these issues that the debate about a better, more equitable and wider distribution of opportunities for economic activity should be pursued. Within this, 'work-sharing' may be able to make a major contribution, but the term conjures up different connotations and meanings to different groups — a device to disguise unemployment, a means of sharing limited opportunities equally, or a tactic to enable employers to hoard the more valuable labour at a reduced cost till the crisis is over. The trade union movement has widely supported this option, and particularly a reduction in the standard working week. The AUEW in particular has long pursued this objective, most recently and vigorously in its pay and conditions claim in 1979.

There is little doubt that a strong case exists for a reduction in hours, particularly on the grounds of comparability with many white-collar workers. Its effect on the general level of unemployment is likely, however, to be marginal given that the usual negotiating stance is one that demands the same money income for reduced hours of work. Unless work-sharing is matched by a similar willingness and desire to share income and consumption more equally, it is unlikely to improve the job opportunities of those presently outside the labour market and more likely to stimulate further labour-saving measures from employers. Meanwhile, workers who see their own standard of living threatened by the multiple impact of inflation, rising taxes, rents and rates and further cuts in their social wage are going to be less willing to accept a further reduction through work-sharing.

There has been some decline in the total annual hours worked in terms of standard hours, overtime hours and numbers of holidays for most of the postwar period. The result, combined with a growth in part-time work, has been a fall in aggregate working hours — a drop of 6.9 per cent between 1967 and 1977 compared with a decline in employment of only 0.4 per cent (Timbrell, 1980, p. 16). But, as the author points out, this trend to increased 'leisure' was associated with generally rising standards of living and cannot justifiably be extrapolated into a period of falling national income. Whilst some further opportunity for work-sharing or even job-sharing in some particular industries and occupations remains, its impact upon aggregate labour supply seems bound to remain limited and uneven, and is unlikely to have any noticeable effect upon unemployment levels.

ACTIVE MANPOWER POLICIES

One strategy pursued with some spasmodic vigour by the Labour government of the 1970s was the development of an 'active manpower policy', expanding the traditional employment service functions of placing and retraining and introducing a range, or rather a patch-work, of new and temporary special programmes (see chapter 4). But the development of such a policy in the 1960s assumed the existence of appropriate macroeconomic policies designed basically to alleviate frictional or structural mismatches. A sustained level of high unemployment, let alone a gradual or sharp increase, makes the operation of many manpower policies much less effective, particularly for the more disadvantaged groups amongst the unemployed. 'The duty of the service will always be first to those who are least able to help themselves' (Permanent Secretary to the Ministry of Labour quoted in OECD, 1966, p. 118), but the criterion for success of most job schemes in the 1970s was basically a 'body-count' one based on reducing the rising numbers of unemployed as cheaply and quickly as possible as an emergency, and temporary, political measure. With manpower policies aimed predominantly at the short-term and young (under 18) unemployed, the dilemma is underlined. Given a limited, even declining, number of jobs, one vulnerable group gains help at the expense of others who may be even more disadvantaged, such as the disabled and the long-term unemployed.

Even before the cutbacks under the present government, those responsible for manpower policy had barely begun to confront these problems: with very small exception the schemes made 'little contribution to long-term employment' although they could no longer 'be dismissed for being only cosmetic' (Townsend, 1978, p. 18). Unfortunately, the slow move towards programmes that provide the more difficult and more expensive long-term help for the hardest to place has been checked by the massive cuts in the MSC budget.

At the end of April 1980 it was estimated that the total number of people being assisted by all the different schemes was 299,000, but the cuts of the June 1979 Budget and others since then were beginning to take effect (*DEG*, November 1979, pp. 1122–5). Many schemes, including the Small Firms and the Temporary Employment Subsidies, were no longer accepting applications and the age for men eligible for the Job Release grant had been put back from 62 to 64. The future of the Youth Opportunities Programme may be more secure than many other schemes, but the small increases announced will not keep up with the increasing unemployment among school leavers, which the Manpower Services Commission fears may double within a year (Eric Varley in *Hansard*, 5 March 1980, col. 498). The closure of some Skillcentres will bring a drop in the numbers receiving training through TOPS, and the Special Temporary Employment Programme — one of the few schemes aimed more towards the increasing numbers of long-term unemployed — has been cut back and concentrated in areas of high unemployment only.

In consequence, official reports that acknowledge, for example, the increasing scale of the problem of long-term unemployment have lamely concluded that the provision of adequate help is largely prevented by the adverse economic climate (*EG*, January 1980, p. 12).

Yet prolonged unemployment, when overall unemployment is high, can become a process of cumulative, self-reinforcing disadvantage. There is always the danger that the efforts of manpower policy to 'reallocate' the available jobs among different categories of unemployed put too much stress on the supply side and on the characteristics of the unemployed; in this way they may reinforce subtle forms of 'blaming the victim', especially when the unemployed remain out of work, despite 'training' in interview technique, tie-wearing and social skills. But, despite such difficulties, we would argue that the work of the employment services and other programmes should be directed more towards the needs of those liable to remain unemployed (see for example Reubens, 1970; Williams, 1967; Showler, 1974 and 1977).

Until a return to an economic strategy capable of providing the appropriate macro-foundations for the effective use of manpower policies, support should be encouraged for those policies that provide higher income support than social security benefits and help to offset the disadvantages suffered by those groups most vulnerable in the present recession. Even if a substantial turnround in the economy were to take place, policies to attack the entrenched position of long-term unemployment in Britain would continue to be required, but at present the most directly relevant scheme, the Special Employment Needs Programme, appears to have disappeared completely in the MSC budget cuts.

Manpower policy as such cannot provide any long-term contribution to tackling unemployment unless the government is prepared to finance labour market programmes of Swedish dimensions rather than cut them back. Even before the cuts, however, this would have required a four-fold increase at least in the proportion of GNP devoted to these programmes in Britain (based on Table 6.13). But, without an adequate demand for labour, measures to help the hard-to-employ will only make a limited contribution: this was emphasised by a detailed comparative review of the operation of special manpower programmes in the 1960s. The 'maintenance of overall unemployment rates at 2 per cent or less for years at a time may be the single most important factor in minimising the number of hard-to-employ and motivating a program to seek out the residual group who might appear unemployable . . . at 4 per cent unemployment' (Reubens, 1970, p. 384).

MACROECONOMIC POLICIES

Thus both work-sharing and unemployment-sharing through man-power policy have been shown in practice to have only limited effect in ameliorating the general and highly unequal consequences of the growth in unemployment. Attention must therefore focus upon the macroeconomic policy field in terms of assessing the rise and fall of employment policy in the earlier postwar period, and the prospects for its re-establishment. As Deacon and Showler have shown (in chapters 2 and 3), the genesis of employment policy was a halting process full of compromise: it represented a far from comprehensive endorsement of any Keynesian optimism about the abilities of governments to manage demand effectively enough to maintain what only later came to be regarded as an acceptable level of employment.

The immediate postwar period was one of acute labour shortage, which forced the government into considering quite extraordinary proposals, such as banning football pools and moving against the 'drones and spivs' to release labour for more 'essential' work (chapter 3, p. 65 and Deacon, 1980). The experience of low unemployment, both unprecedented and unexpected, gradually transformed the prevailing orthodoxy within government and amongst the electorate about the abilities of government to ensure a high and stable level of employment. For a few years the ability to do so was regarded as the prime political virility test and failure to pass was seen as certain to result in political suicide.

A thoroughly expansionary fiscal policy was, however, never given full rein throughout the 1950s and 1960s. The balance of payments constraint with fixed exchange rates was regarded as inviolable, and devaluation 'regarded as unthinkable right up to the point at which it became inevitable' (Coddington, 1980). While Britain was left at the bottom of the European GNP growth league table, economic management took on its infamous stop–go character. The unstable labour market this created left many workers vulnerable to insecurity and so liable to suffer even more severely as unemployment rose and remained persistently high.

In retrospect, however, the achievement of these years should not be underestimated. Whilst prices and wages exhibited an inflationary tendency, which was higher in some years than others, there was no discernible upward trend until the end of the 1960s. Similarly, between 1950 and 1966 annual average levels of registered unemployed ranged between 239,000 and 539,000 (excluding school leavers and adult students), although a mild but steady upward trend was apparent through the economic cycles. Thus for over two decades we came very much closer to full employment without an excessive degree of price inflation. Furthermore, although the rates of economic growth and productivity were comparatively poor, a significant amount of capital restructuring and labour force adjustment took place without a comparable increase in unemployment.

Doubts about the priority given to 'full employment' policies grew from the mid-1960s, and by the end of that decade balancing Britain's external trade account had replaced high employment as the most evident measure of government performance and perceived electoral appeal. By the mid-1970s this policy transformation gathered momentum, symbolised by the conversion of Sir Keith Joseph to monetarism in 1974 and by Prime Minister Callaghan's speech to the 1976 Labour Party Conference when he denied that the Keynesian option of expansionary fiscal policy to reduce unemployment was still available, and argued that in the past the principal effect had been inflation.

Coddington (1980) has described the Barber boom of 1972/3 as the first attempt in the postwar period to apply Keynesian expansionism apparently unconstrained by the external balance of payments account. All previous attempts at expansion, operating with fixed exchange rates, had been halted prematurely by a rapid deterioration in the balance of payments. This last dash for growth — however much of a panic measure — was thought to be untrammelled by the external account as the pound sterling was floating, and any upward pressures created by domestic expansion on imports would be offset by rising exports as the pound 'automatically' devalued. Furthermore, a domestic incomes policy was in operation in an attempt to slow down the impact of rising import prices on the domestic inflation rate. But British exports proved rather less responsive to price variations and the incomes policy quite unsuccessful in preventing the rapid absorption of increased import costs into product prices: the result was to further undermine export performance. The entry into the EEC in 1973 on highly unfavourable terms, the serious political confrontation over incomes policy with the miners in early 1974, and the unprecedented rapid increase in oil prices all reinforced the balance of payments problem and the inflationary pressures. They brought an end to growth and the start of major recession and stagflation through the mid-1970s. The climate of opinion by that time (greatly influenced by the experience of the Barber boom) made reflation an unthinkable option, and unemployment came to be seen as a lesser evil than inflation.

If a significant attack on unemployment is to be mounted in the 1980s, it will be necessary to establish 'work for all' as a matter of serious political, social and economic priority. This will require not only more effective income maintenance and manpower policies, but an active employment policy overall. We have already stressed that the high concentration of unemployment provides one reason why increased unemployment has not become a central public issue. By contrast, inflation is a near universal experience and has commanded much greater attention. As public expenditure cuts continue and extend the experience of unemployment to more professional and white-collar workers, and the pressures of capital restructuring spread the experience of redundancy and unemployment to more prime age, skilled and experienced male manual workers, the relatively silent acceptance of unemployment may change; but so far, redundancy policies have proved quite successful in 'buying off' major, sustained opposition to increased unemployment at national level.

The widening social impact of high unemployment will be accompanied by yet heavier public expenditure costs. The deliberately conservative estimates in chapter 2 show that the net loss in 1978 was at least 4 per cent of total public expenditure — and that was after excluding the costs of a high minimum level of unemployment. This figure takes no account of the huge revenue that could have been generated from the extra GNP available had full employment been achieved. By cutting the real value of short-term benefits and manpower policy measures, the present government has of course taken steps to reduce the public expenditure burden of any given level of unemployment. But this 'saving' will be completely swamped by the impact of rapidly rising unemployment and falling real output, which will increase transfer payments and reduce public sector revenue. The House of Commons Public Expenditure Committee in April 1980 openly questioned whether the income and expenditure estimates in the White Paper for 1980/1–1983/4 were viable, given the budgetary implications of total unemployment rising over two million by 1981 and even further beyond then.

But these costs, heavy as they are, are only the immediate costs of high unemployment. The total bill to the economy would have to include the future costs of even current unemployment, let alone its increase. How many of those in poorer health are being signed on for sickness and invalidity benefit? How many more than in a period of full employment are likely to go into mental hospitals and long-stay homes, or become homeless vagrants who never return to the labour force? How much more will be paid out for supplementary benefits and social services for those forced to retire early and involuntarily without any opportunity to build up savings? What will be the cost to employers of taking back workers out of practice from long disuse of their skills, with the greater risk of industrial accidents and their cost to the individual, the nation and the firm? These are simply examples of the long-term costs of prolonged and high unemployment that can be seen from past experience here and abroad. Of course they ignore the costs of human waste and erosion; but even this slightly wider accounting has been neglected by economists. We cannot say how many years' increase in GNP will be swallowed up simply in meeting the already incurred debts of current unemployment.

But given the current political climate, no government will be prepared to consider policies for reducing unemployment that do not significantly contain inflation. At present the Conservative government is attempting to control inflation by monetary policy with scant concern for the unemployment consequences; indeed, the evidently rising level of unemployment is recognised by many economists to be the key device by which the government expects to frighten the trade unions, whom they hold to blame for inflation, into accepting lower wage settlements in the hope of keeping their jobs and thus ceasing to fuel inflation by holding out for 'excessive' wage demands. Meanwhile, the majority of economists remain sceptical about the ability of monetary policy alone to achieve a reduction in the inflation rate, and there is little evidence to suggest any close short- or medium-term relationship between the money supply and the inflation rate. Even those economists who tend to accept a monetarist explanation of the causes of stagflation suggest that its resolution may not lie in a simplistic reversal of the causation process. Trevithick (1977), for example, argues that the causes of inflation have been basically monetarist in origin but goes on to argue that reducing inflation cannot be achieved by monetary policy alone, and that other policy options should be seen as complements rather than alternatives (see also Allsopp and Joshi, 1980).

The two principal constraints on any alternative Keynesian expansionary policy would appear to be those imposed, firstly, by the internal inflationary impetus and, secondly, by the external balance of payments and trade. The two policy options canvassed by the principal 'Keynesian' schools, the National Institute of Economic and Social Research and the Cambridge Department of Applied Economics, are incomes policies and general import controls respectively. While the complexities involved in devising and implementing incomes policies cannot be discussed here, the effectiveness of past policies remains highly debatable. The experience of the 1970s, however, would seem to suggest that, when such policies have received broad support from the TUC, they have enabled some control over inflation to be exercised and eventually some modest reflation to be attempted. Any balanced assessment of the evidence and theory of inflation must acknowledge some force to the argument that at least *some* part of the inflationary experience of the 1970s is the consequences of institutional, social and cost-push factors (see for example Hirsch and Goldthorpe, 1978). It seems improbable therefore that a reliance on an ill-defined and difficult-to-quantify policy of adjusting the money supply will prove sufficient. Incomes policy may well prove less costly in terms of unemployment and inequality as a means of reducing inflationary expectations, but it has to be recognised that a government determined to pursue inegalitarian fiscal policies is unlikely to be able to achieve the necessary compliance of the trade union movement in any such policy.

No matter how difficult, it does seem that some reform of the system under which we settle pay will be required if adequate reflation is to be achieved. But to attempt to force reform by creating fear through rising unemployment is both unfair and ineffective. It has already been argued that the balance of payments has been a persistent constraint on domestic economic expansion ever since 1945, if not before. That constraint is still present, despite floating exchange rates and a self-sufficiency in oil. In fact, this has helped to increase the sterling exchange rate in recent years, undermining British manufacturing exports, and reinforcing high import penetration. Some policy to arrest this tendency to de-industrialisation is essential. The strongest and most comprehensive policy would be one of general import controls, which is propagated with great vigour by the Cambridge school and supported by the TUC (Cambridge Economic Policy Review, 1980).

While such a policy is clearly anathema to the Conservative goverment at the time of writing, it is however not the only possible approach. Policies could be developed to promote exports and encourage the production of import substitutes by direct government investment. Alternatively, or at the same time, more use could be made of differential taxation and industrial and regional subsidies. But these too seem unlikely to be pursued by a government committed to non-intervention in the market and to substantial reductions in financial assistance to industry. Meanwhile, however, there seems no reason why the nation should continue many of its present fiscal policies that quietly and often substantially provide indirect support to importers. One apparently trivial example is the preferential tax treatment of company cars, which provides an indirect subsidy from the taxpayer to the car industry. An increasing number of companies are allowing senior management a choice of car: in preferring some of the more expensive foreign models, they are effectively directing a tax stimulus towards imports. Whatever the merits of present tax expenditure on fringe benefits, it seems odd that this form of indirect intervention in the market should be allowed by the government to stimulate foreign imports that threaten a very vulnerable British industry.

The Conservative government has so far kept the door firmly closed on the use of any policies capable of encouraging economic development, or at least helping to remove the constraints on any expansionist policy. Macroeconomic policy is therefore seen as essentially minimalist, and confined largely to a severe monetary deflation intended at some unspecified future date to purge the market system of its ills; and then, by some equally unspecified mechanism, economic health will be restored. Thus, just as Robbins in 1934 believed that the depression of the 1930s should have been sharper in order to provide a more thorough shake-out, the present government appears to believe that previous deflations in the postwar period have failed in their purgative effects simply because they have not been deep enough or long enough.

THE WELFARE OF THE UNEMPLOYED

Whatever the level of unemployment, the welfare of the unemployed and those dependent on them needs to be protected. This imperative seems even less disputable when there are many more out of work than jobs available, especially when the government allows, or even encourages, high unemployment as part of its economic, industrial or political strategy. Even the limited research of what now seem the halcyon days of the early welfare state indicated that benefits for the unemployed have never provided adequate compensation for the loss of work or kept families clear of poverty (for example, Townsend, 1973, chapter 5; Sinfield, 1970). At present, benefits are greatest and controls least for those out of work who have recently lost jobs with high earnings; the long-term unemployed, by contrast, are not even eligible for the long-term social security benefit, which raises the scale rate by at least 25 per cent.

Until 1979 the extension of this higher rate to the unemployed seemed the most favourable development likely in a generally hostile climate. This would only have helped those very long out of work but the extra cost was seen as too great, despite strong support from the Supplementary Benefits Commission itself. To put this in the context of the fiscal policies just mentioned above, the estimated cost in July 1977 was less than two-fifths of the £45m a year by which a Labour Chancellor of the Exchequer reduced his announced tax increase on company cars for 1976/7 — in response to pleas from business and management associations, and presumably both sides of the motor industry. Although the long-term rate is now to be paid to all other supplementary allowance recipients after one year, it seems even less likely to be extended to the unemployed. Instead, the March 1980 Budget introduced changes that will reduce the resources of the unemployed. The national insurance flat rate unemployment benefit has been deprived of the limited protection against inflation provided by price-indexation; combined with the failure to increase child benefit adequately, the total child support for an unemployed family has only been increased by a third of the current rate of inflation, and 'an unemployed two-child family faces a cut of £2.80 in the real value of their already meagre weekly benefit' in November 1980 (Ruth Lister in letter to *The Guardian*, 2 April 1980).

Further cuts have also been announced for later dates: benefits paid to the unemployed will be taxed from April 1982 and the earnings-related supplement to flat-rate benefit will be withdrawn at the same time, after some reduction from January 1981. The total effect of these changes will be to narrow the range of resources available to the unemployed through the state — not only *by* the state, as much of these are transfer payments largely funded through insurance contributions. The levelling-down of incomes will push many more unemployed below the threshold for means-tested benefits including supplementary allowance. In consequence, it is not at all clear that much, if any, government revenue will be saved, given the extra applicants for supplementary allowance and the extra staff demands on both social security and tax offices. In fact, it is believed that the previous governments considered, but quickly discarded, the idea of taxing unemployment benefits because of the major administrative difficulties involved for these departments and for employers, as well as for the unemployed themselves.

These changes are being introduced following the first official survey of the standard of living of the unemployed on the means-tested supplementary allowance scheme to be published since the war (Clark, 1978). This more than confirmed the picture of poverty and hardship among the unemployed presented by many earlier independent studies, and the Supplementary Benefits Commission itself has drawn attention to the greater deprivation of those out of work among its recipients, largely as a result of the more limited help that it provides for them (for example, SBC, 1978, p. 44 and 1979, p. 22; and its evidence to RCDIW, 1978).

But this evidence of inadequate benefits and poverty has received little attention because of the continuing concern that benefits out of work may exceed earnings in work. High rates of earnings-replacement in Britain are the accidental by-products of national insurance unemployment benefit and earnings-related supplement while accompanied by income-tax rebates, or of supplementary benefits and other means-tested benefits for those from lower-paid jobs who have not received the benefits already available to them while in work. All the evidence, official and independent, indicates that only a minority of the unemployed are in this 'better-off' position and the number is probably diminishing. The value of unemployment benefit plus earnings-related supplement for a two-child family fell further below the average net income of a manual wage earner during the 1970s.

The most generally acknowledged ways of tackling this problem are to increase the value of child benefits paid to families in and out of work and to lift the tax threshold for the lower paid. Promises that child benefits, which replaced family allowances and income tax allowances for child dependants, would be taken out of the public expenditure category have not been carried out, and child benefits will not fall further in real value as part of the expenditure cuts. At the same time the abolition of the lowest rate of taxation and the limited lifting of the tax threshold has done little to help remove the 'poverty trap' and may well have increased it, especially when the increased national insurance contributions are taken into account (*Low Pay Unit Bulletin*, April 1980).

Given that the unemployed are having to pay the penalty for an international recession and the nation's, or the government's, failure to control inflation, it might be argued that the object should be a fair compensation for the time out of work, meeting successive governments' declarations that the poorest and most vulnerable should be protected from the harshest impact of public expenditure cuts. Over twenty years ago, J. K. Galbraith (1958) suggested that higher levels of benefit should be paid while unemployment was higher and there were clearly insufficient jobs for those seeking them. The fear of weakening incentives should be least when there are far fewer jobs available than people seeking them. Alternatively, the duration of benefits could be extended temporarily while unemployment remains high — a policy that has grown up somewhat fitfully through a variety of temporary measures in the United States, only to be cut back in the 1980 Budget proposals. The disadvantage of both schemes is that the lower paid, including the disabled, the unskilled and the older worker, remain more vulnerable to becoming and remaining unemployed even when total jobless rates have fallen, and are more likely to need this support even when unemployment is lower.

The Beveridge Report of 1942 proposed that unemployment benefit should not be limited in duration, subject to acceptance of training or retraining after six months if required; and this period could be extended if unemployment were high (1942, paras 326–8). While the postwar government accepted the recommendation that sickness benefit, now invalidity pension, should be paid with no time limit once three years of contributions had been paid, unemployment benefit has always been limited and over a third of those out of work had drawn their full entitlement of a year at the last count in Mary 1979. Compensation in terms of full or near full income replacement is not now recognised in Britain as a legitimate social cost that the nation should accept for the unemployed.

THE CHALLENGE TO DEMOCRACY

On the evidence available, the policies of successive governments have failed to deal adequately or justly with either the social or economic consequences of high and persistent unemployment. In a society that lacks the will or the resources to reduce unemployment dramatically, the unemployed would appear to have a special case for particular compensation. Given actual policy and practice over the last decade, however, historians of the 1970s appear bound to describe them as a time when the unemployed were used to solve the nation's economic problems, the threat or reality of unemployment being seen as the best way to counter pressures towards inflation. Those worst and longest hit by unemployment have been compelled to pay a harsh tax on behalf of the rest of society in the fight against inflation. By allowing the numbers out of work to rise, and by cutting back benefits and other forms of help, the state, supported by the rest of society it would appear, is effectively saying to the unemployed, its conscript army in the war against inflation: 'with your help and at your cost, we shall win the war'.

Any general improvement in standards of living may have been halted, but inequalities appear to be widening, further encouraged by the most recent budgets. Forty per cent of the £3,500 m in tax cuts in the June 1979 Budget went to the top 5.5 per cent of taxpayers (Malcolm Dean, *The Guardian*, 26 March 1980). Analyses of the March 1980 Budget show that only those earning over £20,000 per year, or maybe £30,000, will clearly be no worse off (*Sunday Times Business News*, 30 March 1980, and *Low Pay Unit Bulletin*, April 1980). Against this background, the doubling of Unemployment Review Officers, the general encouragement to 'tighten up' that social security staff are said to be receiving, and the cuts in benefits and services planned or already implemented provoke a change of metaphor to describe national policy for the unemployed. In producing its White Paper on *Employment Policy*, the wartime Coalition government claimed to have 'declared war on unemployment' (*Hansard*, vol. 401, 21 June 1944, col. 214). It would appear that the present Conservative government is declaring war on the unemployed.

There have been swift changes of policy by governments in the past and 'the famous Heath U-turn expansion of 1972 actually reduced unemployment by almost half a million in eighteen months' (Walker *et al.*, 1979, p. 53). It seems unlikely on present evidence that even such a change would be accompanied by more helpful policies towards those who remain out of work, and we believe that there is a need to develop policies that will lead towards rewarding and secure work for all. At present, this country has neither a set of coherent policies to bring about a major reduction in unemployment nor any coordinated programme to reduce the impact of existing unemployment on those suffering its direct and indirect effects. The variation in the experience of unemployment may be great, but the predominant picture is one of the significant erosion of the quality of very many lives and considerable economic waste. People's worth and the wealth of the nation are devalued by unemployment.

Unemployment is hurting more and more people, creating and intensifying poverty. Indeed, it has become the principal cause of increased poverty in Britain. The hardships of unemployment are made all the less easy to bear by public campaigns against scroungers that — either directly or indirectly by their impact on the surrounding community — harass, humilate and demoralise the unemployed and their families, and often particularly their children. The costs of unemployment are not be measured simply by the lack of income, the unpleasantness or tedium of the experience, and the depression of the search for new work: they are borne by many of the unemployed for years after their return to work, and many careers never match up to previous promises or hopes. There is, further, a significant cost to the community as a whole: you do not have to lose your job to feel the effect of unemployment. The absence of sufficient opportunities for satisfying and rewarding work limits the careers and lives of many more people than are forced to draw the dole.

Such a conclusion is unfashionable and apparently unpopular to judge from most public debates on the subject. Our view, therefore, is all the more likely to be regarded, and perhaps dismissed, as special pleading. While we have sought to build on the work of the earlier chapters, we should emphasise that the other contributors to this book are in no way bound by our comments in this final chapter. But we would also stress that this book would not have been written had it not been for the belief of the contributors that the subject of unemployment was receiving less attention than it deserved. Today, as over a generation ago,

> there are still too many people who . . . fear that full employment will jeopardise their own freedom to do as they wish. [They are] either without any personal experience of unemployment or they have forgotten what unemployment meant to Britain and to other countries afflicted by it . . . It is one of the paradoxes of the capitalist economy that it endows unemployment with a function. Unemployment is politically dangerous. But it also serves to keep industrial discipline. [Young and Prager, 1945, pp. 12 and 62]

That at least still appears to be a widely held belief, although a virtual trebling of unemployment within seven years does not appear to have led to any changes that employers might regard as an improvement in industrial discipline. Nor is there any evidence of which we are aware that the earlier years of high employment were accompanied by a significant increase in industrial indiscipline. Indeed, a comparison of the two periods and what was achieved in them would seem to lend support to Beveridge's wartime reflection: 'it might be that cattle must be driven by fear. Men can and should be led by hope' (1944, p. 250). Beveridge was never under any illusion that changes to bring about full employment would mean restriction of the freedom of some in order to extend the benefits of security, now held and taken for granted by many of us, to the rest of the population (*ibid.*, p. 23).

In 1966, just before unemployment began to increase in Britain, there was discussion of job-ownership by the worker (see, for example, Eric Jacobs, the Labour correspondent of *The Times*, 15 July 1966, p. 15). This went well beyond the limited idea of a right to compensation on redundancy, introduced to encourage what was hopefully described as 'redeployment' and to reduce opposition to it (Fryer, 1973). It offered hope that workers might have greater control of their own careers: in a society that provided work for all they would be secure from the experience of unemployment — a state that is now condemned in the individual but tolerated, even regarded as natural, in the economy.

In the 1980s this challenge still faces us, for the ultimate test of any democratic society must be the quality of life that it enables its members to enjoy. In any society, the quality of the work that is available is a vital part of that quality of life. Without work — the opportunity to contribute to society in a useful way — the individual is cut off from society. The challenge is to find enough work of sufficient reward and value for all who want it. Until we do, the unemployed and our whole society are diminished.

Postscript – September 1980

Over the summer the more pessimistic economic forecasts have been supported by the continued sharp rise in unemployment to a rate of 8.4 per cent — more than one in twelve — out of work in September. The feared level of two million unemployed was passed in August, and now two and a half million seems very likely before the end of winter. The total of registered unemployed, seasonally adjusted and excluding school-leavers, is said to give the best indication of the underlying trend: the increase over the last twelve months has been more than 40 per cent. Since January the increase in redundancies notified has been so great that the year's total is likely to be at least twice, if not three times, the number for 1979. The seriousness of the recession is also underlined by the continuing drop in the number of job vacancies to well below half of the total reported a year ago: this 'confirms other bleak statistics including increased destocking, a fall in industrial output, lower consumer spending and a rise in company liquidations' (*Daily Telegraph*, 24 September 1980).

The government's main reaction has been to re-emphasise the monetarist policies to which it has been committed in its fight against inflation and to reaffirm the need for 'sensible' pay increases. Mr. Prior described the high figures as 'a measure of the seriousness of the underlying economic problems of the country, in particular the need to relate pay settlements more closely to increased productivity. These problems have been evaded for far too long' (Secretary of State for Employment, press release, 24 September 1980). The Department of Employment is said to be drawing up 'a package of measures' with the main effort placed on the Youth Opportunities Programme. But increased unemployment and short-time working are already pushing public expenditure above previous estimates; it is not yet clear how much extra money will be made available for the new measures given the reports of a further round of spending cuts in response to the government's embarrassing failure to control the money supply. Confident accounts of major policy changes continue to appear, but at present these appear less rather than more likely. Although the passing of the two million mark seized the headlines briefly in August, and unemployment has received some more attention with fewer references to scrounging and abuse than even a few months ago, there is also little clear sign of any sustained and organised protest from the Labour Party and the trade union movement.

Meanwhile evidence has continued to mount of the hardships and difficulties experienced by the unemployed and their vulnerability to poverty. Initial findings of the DHSS 'unemployed cohort' study show that the flow of men becoming unemployed at any one time is much more similar to the stock of men already out of work, even the long-term unemployed, than many previously thought. Interviews with 2,300 men who became unemployed in autumn 1978 found that their previous earnings tended to be 'far below the national average' at all age levels and 50 per cent came within the bottom fifth of the earnings' distribution. Very many had also had previous experiences of unemployment, one-half within the previous year, and — not surprisingly therefore — most had very little, if any savings (*EG*, August 1980, pp. 830–2). The significance of these findings has been reinforced by a Policy Studies Institute study report whose conclusions are pinpointed in its title, 'How Unemployment Makes the Poor Poorer' (D. J. Smith, *Policy Studies*, July 1980).

The poverty and other hardships of the unemployed have also been given considerable emphasis in the final Annual Report of the Supplementary Benefits Commission (Cmnd 8033, especially chapters 5 and 6): 'those out of work are entitled, as the casualties in a battle to get the economy right, to assured, adequate and accessible incomes' (para. 1.33). The Commission examines the recent policy changes (summarised in our concluding chapter) and concludes: 'to increase incentives while unemployment accelerates upwards is like trying to encourage someone to jump into a swimming pool while the water is drained out' (para. 5.28).

Bibliography

Please note that London is the place of publication except where indicated and that all official papers are published by HMSO unless otherwise specified.

AB [Assistance Board] (1945) *Report for 1944* Cmd 6700.

Adams, Leonard P. (1971) *Public Attitudes Toward Unemployment Insurance* (Kalamazoo, Michigan: W.E. Upjohn Institute for Employment Research).

Addison, P. (1977) *The Road to 1945* (Quartet Books).

Aiken, Michael, Ferman, Louis A. and Sheppard, Harold L. (1968) *Economic Failure, Alienation and Extremism* (Ann Arbor: University of Michigan Press).

Akerlof, G. A. (1979) 'The case against conservative macroeconomics: an inaugural lecture'. *Economica* 46.

Allsopp, Christopher and Joshi, Vijay (1980) 'Alternative strategies for the UK'. *National Institute Economic Review* 91, February, pp. 86–103.

Armstrong, Keith and Beynon, Huw (eds) (1977) *Hello, Are You Working? Memories of the Thirties in the North East of England* (Whitley Bay: Erdesdun Publications).

Ashton, D. N. and Field, David (1976) *Young Workers* (Hutchinson).

Atkinson, A. B. and Flemming, J. S. (1978) 'Unemployment, social security and incentives'. *Midland Bank Review* Autumn.

Bain, G. S. (1972) 'The labour force' in A. H. Halsey (ed.) *Trends in British Society* (Macmillan).

Bakke, E. Wight (1933) *The Unemployed Man* (Nisbet).

Bakke, E. Wight (1960) 'The cycle of adjustment to unemployment' in Norman W. Bell and Ezra F. Vogel (eds) *A Modern Introduction to the Family* (Glencoe, III.: Free Press).

Bakke, E. Wight (1969) *The Mission of Manpower Policy* (Kalamazoo, Michigan: W. E. Upjohn Institute for Employment Research).

Banting, K. (1979) *Poverty, Politics and Policy* (Macmillan).

Barlow Report (1940) *Report of the Royal Commission on the Distribution of the Industrial Population* Cmd 6153.

Barron, R. D. and Norris, G. M. (1976) 'Sexual divisions and the dual labour market' in Diana Barker and Sheila Allen (eds) *Dependence and Exploitation in Work and Marriage* (Longman).

Beckerman, Wilfrid (ed.) (1979) *Slow Growth in Britain* (Oxford: Oxford University Press).

Berthoud, Richard (1979) *Unemployed Professionals and Executives* (Policy Studies Institute).

Beveridge, William H. (1909) *Unemployment: A Problem of Industry* (Longmans, Green).

Beveridge, William H. (1912) *Unemployment: A Problem of Industry* (Longmans, Green).

Beveridge, William H. (1930) *Unemployment: A Problem of Industry* (revised with additions).

Beveridge, William H. (1942) *Social Insurance and Allied Services* Cmd 6404.

Beveridge, William H. (1944) *Full Employment in a Free Society* (Allen and Unwin).

Beveridge, William H. (1953) *Power and Influence* (Hodder and Stoughton).

Beynon, H. (1978) *What Happened at Speke?* (Transport and General Workers Union).

Blackaby, Frank (1976) 'The target rate for unemployment' in Worswick (ed.).

Blackaby, Frank (ed.) (1978) *British Economic Policy 1960–1974* (Cambridge University Press).

Blackburn, R. M. and Mann, Michael (1979) *The Working Class in the Labour Market* (Macmillan).

Blau, Peter M. (1963) *The Dynamics of Bureaucracy* (Chicago: Chicago University Press).

Blaug, M. (1968) *Economic Theory in Retrospect* Heinemann).

BLS (1978) 'International comparisons of unemployment'. *BLS Bulletin* 1979 (Washington D,: US Government Printing Office).

Bluestone, B. (1970) 'The tripartite economy: labor markets and the working poor'. *Poverty and Human Resources Abstracts* July/August.

Bolderson, Helen (1980) 'The origins of the disabled persons employment quota and its symbolic significance'. *Journal of Social Policy* 9:2, April, pp. 169–86.

Booth, A. E. (1978) 'An administrative experiment in unemployment policy in the thirties'. *Public Administration* 56.

Bosanquet, N. and Doeringer, P. (1973) 'Is there a dual labour market in Great Britain?' *Economic Journal* June.

Bosanquet, N. and Standing, G. (1972) 'Government and unemployment, 1966–70: a study of policy and evidence'. *British Journal of Industrial Relations* July.

Boulet, J. and Bell, A. (1973) *Unemployment and Inflation: The Need for a Trustworthy Unemployment Indicator* (Economic Research Council).

Bradley, Keith (1978) 'Industrial Democracy: An Analysis of the Scottish Daily News'. University of Essex PhD thesis.

Braun, K. (1965) 'European limitations on employee dismissal'. *Monthly Labor Review* January.

Braverman, Harry (1974) *Labor and Monopoly Capital* (New York: Monthly Review Press).

Bregger, J.E. (1977) 'Establishment of a new employment statistics review commission'. *Monthly Labor Review* March.

Brittan, S. (1971) *Steering the Economy* (Harmondsworth, Middx: Penguin Books).

Brittan, S. (ed.) (1975) *Second Thoughts on Full Employment Policy* (Centre for Policy Studies).

Brittan, S. (1977) *The Economic Consequences of Democracy* (Temple Smith).

Brittan, S. (1978) 'Inflation and democracy' in Hirsch and Goldthorpe (eds).

Bulmer, Martin (ed.) (1978) *Mining and Social Change: Durham County in the Twentieth Century* (Croom Helm).

Burkhauser, Richard V. and Tolley, G. S. (1978) 'Older Americans and market work'. *The Gerontologist* 18:5.

Burkitt, Brian and Bowers, David (1979) *Trade Unions and the Economy* (Macmillan).

Butler, D. and Kavanagh, D. (1975) *The British General Election of October, 1974* (Macmillan).

Butler, D. and Stokes, D. (1974) *Political Change in Britain* (Macmillan).

Butler, R. A. (1971) *The Art of the Possible* (Hamish Hamilton).

Cambridge Economic Policy Review (1979) 'Summary and policy assessment' 5.

Cambridge Economic Policy Review (1980) 'Summary and policy assessment'.

Cannan, E. (1932) 'The demand for labour'. *Economic Journal* 42.

Caplovitz, David (1979) *Making Ends Meet: How Families Cope with Inflation and Recession* (Beverly Hills: Sage).

Carr, E. H. (1951) *The New Society* (Mancmillan).

Carter, Michael (1966) *Into Work* (Harmondsworth, Middx: Penguin Books).

Castles, S. and Kosack, G. (1973) *Immigrant Workers and Class Structure in Western Europe* (Oxford: Oxford University Press).

CBI (1979) *Innovation and Competitiveness in Smaller Companies* (Confederation of British Industry).

CDP — Community Development Project (1977) *The Costs of Industrial Change* (Home Office).

CIS (1979) *The New Technology* (Counter Information Services).

Clark, Marjory (1978) 'The unemployed on supplementary benefit'. *Journal of Social Policy* 7:4, October, pp. 385–410.

Coates, D. (1980) *Labour in Power?* (Longmans).

Coates, K. (1979) *What Went Wrong?* (Spokesman Books).

Coddington, Alan (1980) 'Navigating the economic straits'. *The Listener* 2647, 31 January.

Cohen, Harry (1965) *Demonics of Bureaucracy* (Ames; Iowa State University Press).

Cohen, Max (1945) *I was one of the unemployed* (Gollancz).

Colledge, Maureen and Bartholemew, Richard (1980) 'The long-term unemployed: some new evidence'. *Employment Gazette* January, pp. 9–12 (summary of their report *A Study of the Long-Term Unemployed*, Manpower Services Commission, February 1980).

Cook, P. A., Jump, G. V. Hodgins, C. D. and Szabo, C. J. (1976) *Economic Impact of Selected Government Programmes Directed Toward the Labour Market* (Ottawa: Economic Council of Canada).

Cosgrave, P. (1978) *Margaret Thatcher: A Tory and Her Party* (Hutchinson).

Cowper, R. (1978) 'The skilled worker shortage takes a turn for the worse'. *Financial Times* 25 September.

Cox, Sarah and Golden, Robert (1977) *Down the Road: Unemployment and the Fight for the Right to Work* (The Writers and Readers Publishing Co-operative).

CPRS [Central Policy Review Staff] (1978) *Social and Economic Implication of Microelectronics* (National Economic Development Office).

Cripps, F. (1977) 'The money supply, wages and inflation'. *Cambridge Journal of Economic* 1.

Crossman, R. (1976) *Diaries of a Cabinet Minister Vol. 2* (Hamish Hamilton and Jonathan Cape).

CSO (1979) *National Income and Expenditure*.

CSO (1980) 'A glimpse of the hidden economy in the national accounts'. *Economic Trends* 316, February, pp. 83–7.

Cubbin, J. S. and Foley, K. (1977) 'The extent of benefit-induced unemployment in Great Britain: some new evidence'. *Oxford Economic Papers* March.

Dahrendorf, R. (1956) 'The unskilled labourer in British industry'. University of London PhD thesis.

Daniel, W. W. (1972) *Whatever happened to the workers in Woolwich?* (Political and Economic Planning).

Daniel, W. W. (1974) *National Survey of the Unemployed* (Political and Economic Planning).

Daniel, W. W. and Stilgoe, E. (1977) *Where are they now?* (Political and Economic Planning).

Daniel, W. W. and Stilgoe, E. (1978) *The impact of employment protection laws* (Policy Studies Institute).

DE (1971) *People and Jobs*.

DE (1972) *Unemployment Statistics: Report of an Interdepartmental Working Party* Cmnd 5159.

DE (1974) 'Characteristics of the unemployed'. *Department of Employment Gazette* March.

DE (1976) 'The changed relationship between unemployment and vacancies'. *Department of Employment Gazette* 84, October.

DE (1977a) 'Characteristics of the unemployed: sample survey June 1976.' *Department of Employment Gazette* 85, June.

DE (1977b) 'Some further characteristics of the unemployed'. *Department of Employment Gazette* September.

Deacon, A. (1976) *In Search of the Scrounger* (Bell).

Deacon, A. (1978) 'The scrounging controversy'. *Social and Economic Administration* 12.

Deacon, A. (1980) 'Spivs, drones and other scroungers'. *New Society* 28 February.

Dean, Andrew (1979) 'The labour market in a slow growing economy' in Beckerman (ed.).

DEG (1977) 'New projections of the future labour force'. June.

DEG (1979) Answer to a Parliamentary question, January, p. 46.

Denison, E. (1967) *Why Growth Rates Differ* (Washington, DC: Brookings Institution).

Dey, Ian (1979) 'A study of the formulation and implementation of policies relating to redundancy and unemployment by the AUEW district committee, Bristol. 1970–72'. University of Bristol PhD thesis.

DHSS (1978a) *Social Assistance: A Review of the Supplementary Benefits Scheme in Great Britain* (Department of Health and Social Security).

DHSS (1978b) *Annual Report for 1977* Cmnd 7394.

Doeringer, Peter B. and Piore, Michael J. (1971) *Internal Labor Markets and Manpower Analysis* (Lexington, Mass.: D. C. Heath).

Doeringer, Peter B. and Piore, Michael J. (1975) 'Unemployment and the "dual labour market" '. *The Public Interest* 38, Winter, pp. 67–79.

Donnison, D. (1976) 'Policies and priorities for supplementary benefits'. Unpublished.

Donnison, D. (1977) Chairman of the Supplementary Benefits Commission, quoted in account of BASW Annual Conference. *Social Work Today* 20 September.

Dorfman, Gerald A. (1979) *Government versus Trade Unionism in British politics since 1968* (Macmillan).

Dow, J. C. R. (1970) *The Management of the British Economy 1945–1970* (Cambridge University Press).

Economic Survey (1947) *Economic Survey for 1947* Cmd 7046.

Edwards, Richard C., Reich, Michael and Gordon, David M. (eds) (1975) *Labour Market Segmentation* (Lexington, Mass.: D. C. Heath).

EEC (1980) *Report on Social Developments, Year 1979* (Brussels: European Economic Community).

Eisenberg, Philip and Lazarsfeld, Paul F. (1938) 'The psychological effects of unemployment'. *Psychological Bulletin* pp. 358–90.

Elks, Laurie (1974) *The Wage Stop* (Child Poverty Action Group, Poverty Pamphlet 17).

Elman, Richard M. (1966) *The Poorhouse State: The American Way of Life on Public Assistance* (New York: Pantheon).

FEAC [Full Employment Action Council] (n.d.) 'Full employment' leaflet (Washington, DC: FEAC, approx. 1977).

Feagin, Joe R. (1975) *Subordinating the Poor* (Englewood Cliffs, NJ: Prentice-Hall).

Feldstein, M. S. (1973a) 'The economics of the new unemployment'. *The Public Interest* 33, Fall.

Feldstein, M. S. (1973b) 'Lowering the permanent rate of unemployment'. *U.S. Congress Joint Economic Committee* (Washington DC).

Feldstein, M. S. (1975) 'Unemployment insurance: time for reform'. *Harvard Business Review* March/April.

Ferge, Zsuzsa (1979) *A Society in the Making: Hungarian Social and Societal Policy 1945–1975* (Harmondsworth, Mddx: Penguin Books).

Ferman, Louis A. (1964) 'Sociological perspectives in unemployment research' in Arthur B. Shostak and William Gomberg (eds) *Blue-Collar World* (Englewood Cliffs, NJ: Prentice-Hall).

Ferman, Louis A. (1967) 'The irregular economy: informal work patterns in the urban ghetto'. Mimeo, Ann Arbor: University of Michigan.

Ferman, Louis A. (1969) 'The hard-core unemployed: myth and reality'. *Poverty and Human Resources Abstracts* 4:6, November/December, pp. 5–12.

Ferman, Louis A. and Ferman, Patricia R. (1973) 'The structural under-pinnings of the irregular economy'. *Poverty and Human Resources Abstracts* 8, March, pp. 3–17.

Ferman. Louis A., Berndt, Louise and Selo, Elaine (1978) *Analysis of the Irregular Economy: Cash Flow in the Informal Sector* (Ann Arbor: Insititute of Labor and Industrial Relations, University of Michigan—Wayne State University).

Field, Frank (ed.) (1977) *The Conscript Army: A Study of Britain's Unemployed* (Routledge and Kegan Paul).

Field, Frank (1979) *One in Eight: A Report on Britain's Poor* (Low Pay Unit Paper no. 28).

Finch, Janet and Groves, Dulcie (1980) 'Community care and the family: a case for equal opportunities?' *Journal of Social Policy* 9:4, October.

Fineman, Stephen (1978) 'The stressless redundancy?' *Management Decision* 16, pp. 331–7.

Folk, Hugh (1969) 'The oversupply of the young'. *Trans-Action* September, pp. 27–32.

Forester, Tom (1979) 'The great jobs hunt: trying to beggar regional neighbours'. *New Society* 3 May, pp. 252–5.

Foster, J. I: (1974) 'The relationship between unemployment and vacancies in Great Britain (1958–72): some further evidence' in D. Laidler and D. Pardy (eds) *Inflation and Labour Markets* (Manchester: Manchester University Press).

Freedman, R. (ed.) (1962) *Marx on Economics* (Harmondsworth, Middx: Penguin Books).

Friedman, Andrew L. (1977) *Industry and Labour* (Macmillan).

Friedman, M. (1977) *Inflation and Unemployment: the new dimensions of politics* (Institute of Economic Affairs).

Fry, G. K. (1975) 'Economic policy-making and planning 1945–70. A survey'. *Public Administration Bulletin* 18/19.

Fryer, Robert H. (1973) 'Redundancy, values and public policy'. *Industrial Relations Journal* 4:2, Summer, pp. 2–19.

Fryer, Robert H. (1980)'Redundancy and the restructuring of employment'. Paper presented to SSRC Research Workshop on Employment and Unemployment, January 1980.

Galbraith, J. K. (1958) *The Affluent Society* (Harmondsworth, Middx: Penguin Books).

Gans, Herbert J. (1968) 'Malemployment: the problem of underpaid and dirty work'. *New Generation* Winter.

Garraty, John A. (1978) *Unemployment in History* (New York: Harper and Row).

Gennard, J. (1979) *Job Security and Industrial Relations* (Paris: Organisation for Economic Co-operation and Development).

George, Henry (1879) *Progress and Poverty* (New York: Random House).

Gershuny, J. I. and Pahl, R. E. (1980a) 'Work outside employment: some preliminary speculations'. *New Universities Quarterly* 34:1, Winter 1979/80.

Gershuny, J. I. and Pahl, R. E. (1980b) 'Britain in the decade of the three economies'. *New Society* 3 January, pp. 7–9.

GHS (annual reports) Office of Population Censuses and surveys.

Gilbert, B. B. (1970) *British Social Policy 1914–39* (Batsford).

Ginsburg, Helen (1975) *Unemployment, Subemployment and Public Policy* (New York: Center for Studies in Income Maintenance Policy).

Ginzberg, Eli (1942) *Grass on the Slag Heaps: The Story of the Welsh Miners* (New York: Harper).

Golding, P. and Middleton, S. (1978) 'Making claims: news media and the welfare state'. *Media Culture and Society* 1.

Goodhart, C. and Bhansali, R. (1970) 'Political economy'. *Political Studies* 18.

Goodwin, Leonard (1972) *Do the Poor Want to Work?* (Washington, DC: The Brookings Institution).

Gordon, David M. (1972) *Theories of Poverty and Underemployment* (Lexington, Mass.: D. C. Heath).

Gould, Tony and Kenyon, Joe (1972) *Stories from the Dole Queue* (Temple Smith).

Gowing, M. (1972) 'The organisation of manpower in Britain during the Second World War'. *Journal of Contemporary History* 7.

Green, C. and Cousineau, J. M. (1976) *Unemployment in Canada: the Impact of Unemployment Insurance* (Ottawa: Economic Council of Canada).

Grubel, H. G., Maki, D. and Sax, S. (1975) 'Real and insurance-induced unemployment in Canada'. *Canadian Journal of Economics* May.

Gujarati, D. (1971) 'The behaviour of unemployment and unfilled vacancies: Great Britain 1968–71'. *Economic Journal* 81.

Haber, William, Ferman, Louis A. and Hudson, James R. (1963) *The Impact of Technological Change* (Kalamazoo, Michigan: W. E. Upjohn Insititute for Employment Research).

Hakim, Catherine (1978) 'Sexual division within the labour force: Occupational segregation'. *Department of Employment Gazette* November, pp. 1264–69.

Hakim, Catherine (1979) *Occupational Segregation* (Department of Employment, Research Paper no. 9).

Hall, P. *et al.* (1975) *Change, Choice and Conflict in Social Policy* (Heinemann).

Halsey, A. H. (ed.) (1972) *Educational Priority* 1, pp. 7–8.

Hamill, Lynne (1978) *Wives as Sole and Joint Breadwinners* (Government Economic Service Working Paper no. 13, Department of Health and Social Security).

Hannington, Wal (1936) *Unemployed Struggles 1919–36* (Lawrence and Wishart).

Harrington, Michael (1976) 'Full employment and social investment'. *Dissent* pp. 125–36.

Harris, Amelia I. and Clausen, Rosemary (1966) *Labour Mobility in Great Britain 1953–1963* (Government Social Survey SS 333).

Harris, Jose (1972) *Unemployment and Politics: A Study in English Social Policy 1886–1914* (Oxford: Oxford University Press).

Harris, J. F. (1977) *William Beveridge* (Oxford: Oxford University Press).

Harris, R. and Seldon, A. (1979) *Over-Ruled on Welfare* (Institute of Economic Affairs).

Harris, R. and Sewill, B. (1975) *British Economic Policy 1970–1974* (Institute of Economic Affairs).

Harris, R. *et al.* (1979) *Job 'Creation' — or Destruction* (Institute of Economic Affairs).

Harrison, Richard (1976) 'The demoralising experience of prolonged unemployment'. *Department of Employment Gazette* 84, April, pp. 330–49 (summary of his report *The Effects of Prolonged Unemployment* Department of Employment).

Hartley, Jean F. (1980a) 'The impact of unemployment upon the self-esteem of managers'. *Journal of Occupational Psychology*.

Hartley, Jean F. (1980b) Psychological approaches to unemployment'. *Bulletin of the British Psychological Society*.

Hartley, Jean F. (1980c) 'The personality of unemployed managers: myth and measurement'. *Personnel Review*.

Havermen, R. H. and Christiansen, G. B. (1978) *Public Employment and Wage Subsidies in Western Europe and the US* (Madison: University of Wisconsin, Institute for Research on Poverty).

Hawkins, Kevin (1979) *Unemployment* (Harmondsworth, Middx: Penguin Books).

Heimler, Eugene (1967) *Mental Illness and Social Work* (Harmondsworth, Middx: Penguin Books).

Henle, P. (1976) *Work Sharing as an Alternative to Layoffs* (Washington, DC: Congressional Research Service).

Henle, P. (1978) 'EEC — major initiative on work sharing'. *European Industrial Relations Review* March.

Hill, J. M. (1978) 'The psychological impact of unemployment'. *New Society* 19 January, pp. 118–20.

Hill, M. J. (1974) *Policies for the Unemployed: Help or Coercion?* (Child Poverty Action Group).

Hill, M. J. (1978) 'Unemployment: an isolated experience or a recurrent event in a disadvantaged life?' in RCDIW.

Hill, M. J., Harrison, R. M. Sargeant, A. V. and Talbot, V. (1973) *Men Out of Work* (Cambridge: Cambridge University Press).

Hirsch, F. (1977) *Social Limits to Growth* (Routledge and Kegan Paul/ Cambridge, Mass.: Harvard University Press).

Hirsch, Fred and Goldthorpe, John H. (eds) (1978) *The Political Economy of Inflation* (Martin Robertson).

Hobson, J. A. (1896) *The Problem of the Unemployed* (Methuen).

Holland, S. (1975) *The Socialist Challenge* (Quartet Books).

Holland, S. (1978) *Beyond Capitalist Planning* (Oxford: Blackwell).

House of Commons (1977) *Expenditure Committee, Seventh Report Session 1976–77.*

House of Commons (1978) *Committee of Public Accounts, Ninth Report Session 1976–77.*

Howson, S. and Winch D. (1977) *The Economic Advisory Council 1930–1939* (Cambridge University Press).

Hughes J. J. (1975) 'How should we measure unemployment?' *British Journal of Industrial Relations* 13.

Hunter, Laurence C. (1980) 'The end of full employment?' *British Journal of Industrial Relations* 18:1, March, pp. 44–56.

Hunter, Laurence C. and Reid, Graham L. (1968) *Urban Worker Mobility* (Paris: Organisation for Economic Co-operation and Development).

Hutchison, T. W. (1977) *Keynes v the Keynesians . . . ?* (Institute of Economic Affairs).

Hyman, Herbert H. (1979) 'The effects of unemployment: a neglected problem in modern social research' in Robert K. Merton, James S. Coleman and Peter H. Rossi (eds) *Qualitative and Quantitative Social Research: Papers in Honor of Paul F. Lazarsfeld* (New York: Free Press).

ILO (1954) *Employment and Unemployment Statistics* (Geneva: International Labour Office).

ILO (1977) *Labor Force Estimates 1950–70 and Projections 1975–2000* vols IV and V (Geneva: International Labor Office).

Jahoda, Marie (1979) 'The impact of unemployment in the 1930s and the 1970s'. *Bulletin of the British Psychological Society* 32, p. 309–14 (mainly reprinted in 'The psychological meanings of unemployment', *New Society* 6 September, pp. 492–5).

Jahoda, Marie, Lazarsfeld, Paul F. and Zeisel, Hans (1972) *Marienthal: The Sociography of an Unemployed Community* (Tavistock; first published in German, 1933).

Jay, P. (1976) *Employment: Inflation and Politics* (Insititute of Economic Affairs).

Jenkins, Clive and Sherman, Barrie (1979) *The Collapse of Work* (Eyre Methuen).

Jenkins, D. (1976) 'Job security measures growing throughout Europe'. *World of Work Report* July.

Johnson, H. G. (1971) 'The Keynesian revolution and the monetarist counter-revolution'. *American Economic Review: Papers and Proceedings* 61.

Jones, Trevor W. (ed.) (1980) *Microelectronics and Society* (Milton Keynes: Open University).

Jordan, David (1979) *A New Employment Programme for Disabled People* (Disability Alliance with Low Pay Unit).

Joseph, Sir Keith (1978) *Conditions for Fuller Employment* (Centre for Policy Studies).

Kahn, R. (1976) 'Unemployment as seen by Keynesians' in Worswick (ed.).

Kaldor, N. (1970) 'The new monetarism'. *LLoyds Bank Review* 97.

Kaufman, R. T. (1978) 'An international comparison of unemployment rates: the effects of job security and job continuity'. Massachusetts: Institute of Technology unpublished PhD dissertation.

Keegan, W. and Pennant-Rea, R. (1979) *Who Runs the Economy?* (Temple Smith).

Keil, Teresa E., Riddell, D. S. and Green, B. S. R. (1966) 'Youth and work: problems and perspectives'. *Sociological Review* 14, pp. 117–37.

Kerr, Clark (1954) 'The Balkanisation of labor markets' in E. W. Bakke (ed.) *Labor Mobility and Economic Opportunity* (New York: John Wiley).

Keynes, J. M. (1936) *The General Theory of Employment, Interest, and Money* (Macmillan).

Kranse, L. B. and Salant, W. S. (eds) (1977) *Worldwide Inflation* (Washington, DC: Brookings Institute).

Labour Party (1967) *Report of 65th Annual Conference.*

Labour Party (1976) *Report of 74th Annual Conference.*

Labour Party (1977) *Report of 75th Annual Conference.*

Land, Hilary (1979) *The Family Wage* (Leeds: Eleanor Rathbone Memorial Lecture, 12 November).

Leicester, C. V. (1978) 'Keeping the jobless in touch with work'. *The Times* 15 May.

Lekachman, R. (1976) *Economists at Bay* (New York: McGraw-Hill).

Levitan, S. A. and Belous, R. S. (1977) 'Work-sharing initiatives at home and abroad'. *Monthly Labor Review* September.

Lewis, J. (1978) *Local Labour Market Administration in England* (Policy Studies Institute).

Liebow, Elliot (1967) *Tally's Corner* (Boston: Little, Brown).

Liebow, Elliot (1970) 'No man can live with the terrible knowledge that he is not needed'. *New York Times Magazine* 5 April.

Lindley, R. M. *et al.* (1978) *Britain's medium-term employment prospects* (Coventry: University of Warwick Manpower Research Group).

Lister, Ruth and Field, Frank (1978) *Wasted Labour* (Child Poverty Action Group).

Lockwood, David (1958) *The Blackcoated Worker* (Allen and Unwin).

Lynd, Robert S. and Lynd, Helen Merrell (1937) *Middletown in Transition* (New York: Harcourt Brace).

Macarov, David (1970) *Incentives to Work* (San Francisco: Jossey-Bass).

Macintyre, Alasdair (1968) 'The strange death of social democratic England'. *The Listener* 4 July pp. 7–8.

Mackay, D. I. and Reid, G. L. (1972) 'Redundancy, unemployment and manpower policy'. *Economic Journal* 81.

Maddison, A. (1964) *Economic Growth in the West* (Allen and Unwin).

Maki, D. and Spindler, Z. A. (1975) 'The effect of unemployment compensation on the rate of unemployment in Great Britain'. *Oxford Economic Papers* 27, November.

Manley, Peter and Sawbridge, Derek (1980) 'Women at Work'. *Lloyds Bank Review* 135, January, pp. 29–40.

Marsden, Dennis and Duff, Euan (1975) *Workless — some unemployed men and their families* (Harmondsworth, Mddx: Penguin Books).

Marston, S. T. (1975) 'The impact of unemployment insurance on job search'. *Brookings Papers on Economic Activity* 1 (Wahington, DC: Brookings Institution).

Martin, Roderick and Fryer, R. H. (1972) *Redundancy and Paternalist Capitalism* (Allen and Unwin).

Marx, Karl (1930) *Capital* (Dent).

Mathews, R. C. O. (1968) 'Why has Britain had full employment since the war?' *Economic Journal*.

May, Edgar (1964) *The Wasted Americans* (New York: Signet).

McGregor, Alan (1979) 'Manpower services' in J. English and F. M. Martin (eds) *Social Services in Scotland* (Edinburgh: Scottish Academic Press).

McKay, D. H. and Cox, A. W. (1979) *The Politics of Urban Change* (Croom Helm).

Meacher, M. (1974) *Scrounging on the Welfare* (Arrow Books).

Mencher, Samuel (1968) *From Poor Law to Poverty Program* Pittsburgh: University of Pittsburgh Press).

Metcalf, David (1980) 'Unemployment: history, incidence and prospects'. *Policy and Politics* 8:1, pp. 21–37.

Metcalf, David and Nickell, Stephen (1978) 'The plain man's guide to the out-of-work: the nature and composition of unemployment in Britain' in RCDIW.

Meyers, Frederic (1964) *Ownership of Jobs: A Comparative Study* (Los Angeles: Institute of Industrial Relations, University of California).

Michon, François (1975) *Chômeurs et chômage* (Paris: Presses Universitaires de France).

Mills, C. Wright (1959a) *The Sociological Imagination* (New York: Oxford University Press).

Mills, C. Wright (1959b) *The Power Elite* (New York: Galaxy Books).

Ministry of Labour (1948) *Report for 1947* Cmd 7559.

Ministry of Reconstruction (1944) *Employment Policy* Cmd 6527.

Minkin, L. (1979) 'Left-wing trade unionism and the tensions of British labour politics' in B. Brown (ed.) *Eurocommunism and Eurosocialism* (New York: Cycro Press).

Moore, B. and Rhodes, J. (1976) 'The relative decline of the U.K. manufacturing sector'. *Economic Policy Review* 2.

Mosley, P. (1978) 'Images of the floating voter'. *Political Studies* 26:3.

MSC (1977a) *Review and Plan 1977* (Manpower Services Commission).

MSC (1977b) *The New Special Programmes for Unemployed People* (Manpower Services Commission).

MSC (1978a) *Job Centres: An Evaluation* (Manpower Services Commission).

MSC (1978b) *Developing Employment and Training Services for Disabled People* (Manpower Services Commission).

MSC (1979a) *The Employment Service in the 1980s* (Manpower Services Commission).

MSC (1979b) *The Quota Scheme for the Employment of Disabled People* (Manpower Services Commission).

Mukherjee, S. (1972) *Making Labour Markets Work* (Political and Economic Planning, Broadsheet 532).

Mukherjee, S. (1973) *Through No Fault of Their Own* (Political and Economic Planning).

Myers, R. J. and Chandler, J. (1962) 'Comparative levels of unemployment in industrial countries' in *Measuring Employment and Unemployment: Report of the President's Committee to Appraise Employment and Unemployment Statistics* (Washington, DC: US Government Printing Ofice; for shorter version see *Monthly Labor Review* August and September 1962).

NAB [National Assistance Board] (1957) *Report for 1956* Cmnd 181.

NAB (1959) *Report for 1958* Cmd 781.

NAB (1966) *Homeless Single Persons*.

NCEUS [National Commission on Employment and Unemployment Statistics] (1979) *Counting the Labor Force* (Washington, DC: US Government Printing Office).

NEDC and MSC (1977) *Engineering Craftsmen: Shortages and Related Probems* (NEDC).

Nelson, Daniel (1969) *Unemployment Insurance — the American Experience 1915–1935* (Madison: University of Wisconsin Press).

Newcastle upon Tyne City Council (1980) *Redundancy in Newcastle upon Tyne: a case study* (Newcastle: Policy Studies Department).

Nicholas, H. G. (1951) *The British General Election of 1950* (Macmillan).

Nickell, S. (1979) 'The effect of unemployment and related benefits on the duration of unemployment'. *Economic Journal* 89.

NIESR (1977) *National Institute Review* 79.

Norris, G. M. (1978) 'Unemployment, subemployment and personal characteristics'. *Sociological Review* 26, pp. 89–103, 327–47.

North Tyneside Community Development Project (1978) *In and Out of Work* (Home Office).

Norton, P. (1978) *Conservative Dissidents* (Temple Smith).

Nove, Alec (1980) 'The labour market in the Soviet Union'. *New Society* 10 April, pp. 58–9.

OCPU [Outer Circle Policy Unit] (1978) *Policing the Hidden Economy: the significance and control of fiddles* (Outer Circle Policy Unit).

OECD (1964) *Recommendations of the Council on Manpower Policy as a Means for the Promotion of Economic Growth* (Paris: Organisation for Economic Co-operation and Development).

OECD (1966) *The Public Employment Services and Management* Final Report and Supplement (Paris: Organisation for Economic Co-operation and Development).

OECD (1970) *Manpower Policy in the United Kingdom* (Paris: Organisation for Economic Co-operation and Development).

OECD (1973) *Economic Outlook* (Paris: Organisation for Economic Co-operation and Development).

OECD (1976) 'How women fared during the recession'. *OECD Observer* October.

OECD (1978a) *A Medium term strategy for Employment and Manpower Policies* (Paris: Organisation for Economic Co-operation and Development).

OECD (1978b) 'Unemployment compensation: a comparison'. *OECD Observer* November.

OECD (1978c) *Youth Unemployment: A Report on the High Level Conference* (Paris:

Organisation for Economic Co-operation and Development).

OECD (1979) *Meausring Employment and Unemployment* (Paris: Organisation for Economic Co-operation and Development).

Okun, A. (1962) 'Potential GNP: its measurement and significance'. *Proceedings of the Business and Economics Statistics Section of the American Statistical Association.*

Oxford University (1975) *All Their Future: a study of the problems of a group of school leavers in a disadvantaged area* (Oxford: Department of Social and Administrative Studies).

PAC [Public Accounts Committee[(1967/7) *Ninth Report* H. C. 532.

Paish, F. W. (1970) *How the Economy Works and other essays* (Macmillan).

Parker, S. R., Thomas, C. G., Ellis, N. D. and McCarthy, W. E. J. (1971) *Effects of the Redundancy Payments Act* (Office of Population Censuses and Surveys).

Parkin, M. (1975) 'The politics of inflation'. *Government and Opposition* 10.

Pavitt, Keith (ed.) (1980) *Technical Innovation and British Economic Performance* (Macmillan).

Perkin, Harold (1969) *Key Profession* (Routledge and Kegan Paul).

Phelps-Brown, E. H. (1977) *The Inequality of Pay* (Oxford: Oxford University Press).

Phillips, A. W. (1958) 'The relation between unemployment and the rate of change of money wage rates in the United Kingdom, 1861–1957'. *Economica* 25.

Phillips, D. (1973) 'Young and unemployed in a northern city' in D. Weir (ed.) *Men and Work in Modern Britain* (Fontana).

Pigou, A. C. (1913) *Unemployment* (Williams and Norgate).

Pigou, A. C. (1933) *The Theory of Unemployment* (Macmillan).

Pilgrim Trust (1938) *Men Without Work* (Cambridge: Cambridge University Press).

Piven, Frances Fox and Cloward, Richard (1972) *Regulating the Poor: The Functions of Public Welfare* (Tavistock).

Pond, Chris (1979) 'The high paid and the crisis of living standards' in Frank Field (ed.) *The Wealth Report* (Routledge and Kegan Paul).

Pond, Chris (1980) 'What is full employment?' *The Structure of Unemployment.* Paper presented to SSRC Research Workshop on Employment and Unemployment, March 1980.

Pringle, R. (1977) *The Growth Merchants* (Centre for Policy Studies).

PRO (1) W. P. (44) 23, CAB 66/45.

   (2) P. R. (43) 26, CAB 87/13.

   (3) Letter Woolton to W. S. C. PREM 4 96/6.

   (4) Report of Official Committee PIN 8/115.

   (5) Minutes CAB 87/63.

   (6) *Memo on Sir William Beveridge's Full Employment in a Free Society* PREM 4 96/8.

   (7) Conclusions of 9.9.47, 75 (47) CAB 128/10.

   (8) CAB 129/20, C. P. 248.

   (9) EM 5431/47, LAB 8/1362.

   (10) P. R. (43) 64, CAB 87/13.

RCDIW [Royal Commission on the Distribution of Income and Wealth] (1978) *Selected Evidence to the Royal Commission for Report no. 6: Lower Incomes.*

Reubens, Beatrice G. (1970) *The Hard-to-Employ: European Programs* (New York: Columbia University Press).

Reubens, Beatrice G. (1977) *Bridges to Work: International Comparisons of Transition Services* (New York: Universe Books).

Reynolds, Lloyd G. (1951) *The Structure of Labor Markets* (New York: Harper).

Robbins, L. (1934) *The Great Depression* (Macmillan).

Robbins, L. (1971) *Autobiography of an Economist* (Macmillan).

Roll, E. (1978) *The Uses and Abuses of Economics* (Faber and Faber).

Rothwell, Roy and Zegveld, Frances (1980) *Technical Change and Employment* (Frances Pinter).

Routh, Guy (1965) *Occupation and Pay in Great Britain 1906–60* (Cambridge: Cambridge University Press).

Routh, Guy (1975) *The Origin of Economic Ideas* (Macmillan).

Royal Commission on the Poor Laws and Relief of Distress (1909) *Report.*

Runciman, W. G. (1966) *Relative Deprivation and Social Justice* (Routledge and Kegan Paul).

Ryan, William (1973) *Blaming the Victim* (Orbach and Chambers).

SBC (1977) *Low Incomes* (Supplementary Benefits Administration Paper 6).

SBC (1978) *Annual Report for 1977* Cmd 7392.

SBC (1979) *Annual Report for 1978* Cmd 7725.

Scott, Maurice with Laslett, Robert A. (1978) *Can We Get Back to Full Employment?* (Macmillan).

Sennett, Richard and Cobb, Jonathan (1973) *The Hidden Injuries of Class* (New York: Vintage).

Sheppard, Harold L. (1965) 'Mobility, methods of job search, attitudes and motivation of displaced workers' in OECD *The Requirements of Automated Jobs* (Paris: Organisation for Economic Co-operation and Development).

Sheppard, Harold L. and Belitsky, Saul (1966) *The Job Hunt* (Baltimore: John Hopkins).

Sherman, H. J. (1976) *Stagflation: a radical theory of unemployment and inflation* (New York: Harper and Row).

Showler, Brian (1974) *Employment in Retirement* (Age Concern).

Showler, Brian (1976) *The Public Employment Service* (Longmans).

Showler, Brian (1977) 'Employment and the older worker'. *Age Concern Today* 21, Spring.

Showler, Brian (1980) 'Racial minority group unemployment: trends and characteristics'. *International Journal of Social Economics* 7:5, special issue.

Simmel, Georg (1965) 'The poor'. *Social Problems* 13:2, Fall, pp. 118–40, translated fron the German.

Simpson, Dennis (1975) *The Quota Scheme: A Policy of Non-Enforcement* (University of Essex, dissertation of MA for Social Service Planning).

Sinfield, Adrian (1968) *The Long-term Unemployed* (Paris: Organisation for Economic Co-operation and Development).

Sinfield, Adrian (1970) 'Poor and out of work in Shields' in Townsend (ed.).

Sinfield, Adrian (1976a) 'Unemployment and the Social Structure' in Worswick (ed.).

Sinfield, Adrian (1976b) 'Unemployment and inequality'. Paper presented to Social Administration Association conference, University of Exeter, July 1976.

Sinfield, Adrian (1977) 'The social meaning of unemployment' in Kathleen Jones *et al.* (eds) *The Year Book of Social Policy in Britain 1976* (Routledge and Kegan Paul.

Smee, Clive (1980) 'Unemployment and poverty: some comparisons with Canada and the Untied States'. Paper presented to the SSRC Research Workshop on Employment and Unemployment, June 1980.

Smith, S. and Lasko, R. (1978) 'After the Work Experience Programme'. *Department of Employment Gazette* August.

Sobel, Irvin and Wilcock, Richard C. (1966) *Placement Techniques* (Paris: Organisation for Economic Co-operation and Development).

Sorrentino, C. (1971) 'Comparing employment shifts in 10 industrialised countries'. *Monthly Labor Review* October.

Sorrentino, C. (1976) 'Unemployment compensation in eight nations'. *Monthly Labor Review* July.

Sorrentino, C. (1978) *International Comparisons of Unemployment* (Washington, DC: Bureau of Labor Statistics, US Department of Labor).

SRS [Social and Rehabilitation Service] (1979) *Aid to Families with Dependent Children* (Washington, DC: National Center for Social Statistics, US Department of Health, Education and Welfare, Report D–2).

Steiner, Gilbert Y. (1966) *Social Insecurity: The Politics of Welfare* (Chicago: Rand McNally).

Steiner, Gilbert Y. (1971) *The State of Welfare* (Washington DC: The Brookings Institution).

Stern, Jon (1979) 'Who bears the burden of unemployment?' in Beckerman (ed.).

Stewart, M. (1967) *Keynes and After* (Harmondsworth, Mddx: Penguin Books).

Swan, N., Macrae, P. and Steinberg, C. (1976) *Income Maintenance Programmes: Their Effect on Labour Supply and Aggregate Demand in the Maritimes* (Otttawa: Economic Council of Canada).

Taira, Koji, (1970) *Economic Development and the Labor Market in Japan* (New York: Columbia University Press).

Tarling, R. and Wilkinson, F. (1977) 'Inflation and money supply'. *Economic Policy Review* 3.

Tenbroek, Jacobus (1971) *Family Law and the Poor: Essays* (ed. Joel F. Handler; Westport: Greenwood).

Thompson, E. P. and Yeo, Eileen (1971) *The Unknown Mayhew* (Merlin Press).

Timbrell, M. (1980) 'Unemployment in the 1980s'. *Lloyds Bank Review* April.

Titmuss, Richard M. (1958) 'Industrialisation and the family'. *Essays on 'The Welfare State'* (Allen and Unwin).

Tobin, J. (1972) 'Inflation and unemployment'. *American Economic Review* 62.

Townsend, Peter (ed.) (1970) *The Concept of Poverty* (Heinemann).

Townsend, Peter (1973) *The Social Minority* (Allen Lane).

Townsend, Peter (1978) 'Ending the phoney war against unemployment'. *Community Care* 10 May, pp. 16–18.

Townsend, Peter (1979a) *Poverty in the United Kingdom* (Allen Lane).

Townsend, Peter (1979b) 'Return to the two nations'. *New Statesman* 20 April, pp. 546–7.

Trevithick, J. A. (1977) *Inflation: A Guide to the Crisis in Economics* (Harmondsworth, Mddx: Penguin Books).

TUC (1948) *79th Annual Report*.

Turvey, R. (1977) 'Structural change and structural unemployment'. *International Labour Review* September/October.

UAB [Unemployment Assistance Board] (1939) *Report for 1938* Cmd 6021.

UMS [Unit for Manpower Studies] (1977) *The Role of Immigrants in the Labour Market* (Department of Employment).

US Department of Labor (1967) *1967 Manpower Report of the President* (Washington, DC: US Government Printing Office).

US Department of Labor (1968) *1968 Manpower Report of the President* (Washington, DC: US Government Printing Office).

Vietorisz, T., Mier, R, and Giblin, J. (1975) 'Subemployment: exclusion and inadequacy indexes'. *Monthly Labor Review* May, pp. 3–12.

Wabe, Stuart (1977) *Manpower Changes in the Engineering Industry* (Watford: Enginering Industrial Training Board).

Wacker, Ali (1976) *Arbeitslosigkeit* (Frankfurt: Europaische Verlagsanstalt).

Wacker, Ali (ed.) (1978) *Vom Schock zum Fatalismus?* (Frankfurt: Campus).

Walker, Alan (1980) 'The social creation of poverty and dependency in old age'. *Journal of Social Policy* 9:1, January, pp. 49–75.

Walker, Alan and Lewis, Patricia (1977) 'Careers advice and employment experience of a small group of handicapped school leavers'. *Careers Quarterly* 29:1, pp. 5–14.

Walker, Alan, Ormerod, Paul and Whitty, Larry (1979) *Abandoning Social Priorities* (Child Poverty Action Group).

Wedderburn, D. (1973) 'Working and no working' in D. Weir (ed.) *Men and Work in Modern Britain* (Fontana).

West, John and Martin, Peter (1979) 'Employment and unemployment in the English inner cities'. *Department fo Employment Gazette* August, pp. 746–9, 752.

Whybrew, E. G. (1964) 'Overtime and the reduciton of the working week: a comparison of British and Dutch experinece'. *British Journal of Industrial Relations* 2, pp. 149–64.

Wilensky, Harold L. (1961) 'Orderly careers and social Participation: the impact of work history on social interpretation in the middle mass'. *American Sociological Review* pp. 521–39.

Wilkinson, Ellen (1939) *The Town that was Murdered* (Left Book Club).

Williams, Gertrude (1967) *Counselling for Special Groups* (Paris: Organisation for Economic Co-operation and Development).

Williams, Raymond (1976) *Keywords* (Fontana).

Willis, Paul (1977) *Learning to Labour: How working class kids get working class jobs* (Westmead: Saxon House).

Winch, D. (1972) *Economics and Policy: A Historical Survey* (Hodder and Stoughton/Bungay: Fontana).

Wood, J. B. (1972) *How Much Unemployment?* (Institute of Economic Affairs).

Wood, J. B. (1975) *How Little Unemployment?* (Institute of Economic Affairs).

Wood, Stephen, (1977) 'A consideration of the study of redundancy'. *Scottish Journal of Sociology* 2;1, November, pp. 51–70.

Worswick, G. D. N. (ed.) (1976) *The Concept and Measurement of Involuntary Unemployment* (Allen and Unwin).

Wright, R. P. (1969) *For Men Must Work* (Harrap).

Yemin, E. (1976) 'Job security: influence of ILO standards and recent trends'. *International Labour Review* January/February.

Young, Michael and Prager, Theodor (1945) *There's Work For All* (Nicholson and Watson).

Index